# POLITICS OF ETHNIC DISCRIMINATION IN SUDAN

*A Justification For The Secession Of South Sudan*

2ND EDITION

*Dhieu Mathok Diing Wol Ph.D.*

*The publisher wishes to acknowledge and thank Dr. Douglas H. Johnson for his invaluable help and support for Africa World Books and its mission of preserving and promoting African cultural and literary traditions and history. Dr. Johnson and fellow historians have been instrumental in ensuring that African people remain connected to their past and their identity. Africa World Books is proud to carry on this mission.*

*Paperback ISBN: 978-0-6455832-6-7*
*Hardback ISBN: 978-0-6455832-3-6*

*Cover design, typesetting and layout: Africa World Books*
*Unit 3, 57 Frobisher St, Osborne Park, WA 6017*
*P.O. Box 1106 Osbourne Park, WA 6916*

Africa World Books Pty Ltd

*"I and those who joined me in the bush and fought for more than twenty years have brought to you a CPA on a golden plate. Our mission is accomplished. It is now your turn, especially those who did not have a chance to experience the bush life.*

*When time comes to vote at referendum, it is your golden choice to determine your fate. Would you like to vote to be a second-class citizens in your own country? It is absolutely your choice."*

**Dr. John Garang de Mabior**

# DEDICATION

*To the souls of the late Professor Angelo Lobale
Lioria, and the late Professor Samson S. Wassara.*

# CONTENTS

## *List of Tables*

## *List of Figures*

# LIST OF ABBREVIATIONS

**AASG:** American Anti-Slavery Group
**ABC:** Abyei Boundary Commission
**ADC:** Assistant District Commissioner
**ARSISS:** Agreement on the Resolution of the Conflict in South Sudan
**ASI:** Anti-Slavery International
**AU:** African Union
**AUCISS:** African Union Peace Commission of Inquiry on South Sudan
**AUHPI:** African Union High Implementation Panel
**AUPSC:** African Union Peace and Security Commission
**BBC:** British Broadcasting Corporation
**BGAA:** Bahr El Ghazal Administrative Area
**BGP:** Bahr El Ghazal Province
**BNP:** Blue Nile Province
**Brig:** Brigadier
**CDR:** Commander
**CEAWC:** Committee for Eradication of Abduction of Women and Children
**CIC:** Commander-in-Chief
**CIS:** Christian International Solidarity
**CNN:** Cable News Network (U.S.A.)
**Col:** Colonel
**CPA:** Comprehensive Peace Agreement
**CSI:** Christian Solidarity International

**CSO:** Civil Society Organizations
**CSW:** Christian Solidarity Worldwide
**DC:** District Commissioner
**DCC:** Dinka Chief Committee
**DDR:** Demilitarization Demobilization and Reintegration
**DP:** Darfur Province
**DMR:** Dinka Misseriya Riziegat
**DTC:** Dinka Tribal Committee
**DUP:** Democratic Unionist Party
**Ed:** Editor or Edited
**ESRC:** European Sudanese Relations Council
**EU:** European Union
**FPD:** Former Political Detainees
**FLF:** Front Line Fellowship
**GOS:** Government of Sudan
**GOSS:** Government of Southern Sudan
**H.E.:** His Excellency
**HPL:** High Political Level
**HQ:** Headquarters
**HRD:** Human Right Department
**ICESCR:** International Commission for Economic, Social and Cultural Rights
**IEPG:** International Eminent Person Group
**IGAD:** Inter-Governmental Authority on Development
**INGOs:** International Non-Governmental Organizations
**IPF:** IGAD Partner Forum
**JTCs:** Joint Tribal Committees
**KICHR:** Khartoum International Center for Human Rights
**KP:** Kordofan Province
**LCM:** Lutherum Church Missionary
**Liet.Col:** Lieutenant Colonel
**MA:** Master of Arts
**NA:** National Assembly
**NAE:** National Association of Evangelicals

**NBL:** National Black Leadership
**NCP:** National Congress Party
**NGOs:** Non-Governmental Organizations
**NMP:** Nuba Mountains Province
**NSR:** National Salvation Revolution
**PBPSM:** President Bashir - President Salva Mechanism
**PCA:** Permanent Court of Arbitration
**PDF:** Popular Defense Forces
**POW:** Prisoners of War
**R-ARCISS:** Revitalized Agreement on the Resolution of the Conflict in South Sudan
**SANU:** Sudanese African National Union
**SBC:** Southern Baptist Church
**SCUK:** Save the Children United Kingdom
**SGG:** Sudan Government Gazette
**SIR:** Sudan Intelligence Report
**SMIR:** Sudan Monthly Intelligence Report
**SPLA/M:** Sudan People's Liberation Army/Movement
**SPLA/M-IO:** Sudan People's Liberation Army/Movement In Opposition
**SPLM-FDs:** Sudan Peoples' Liberation Movement-Former Detainees
**SPLM-R:** Sudan Peoples' Liberation Movement-Real
**SRRA:** Sudan Relief and Rehabilitation Association
**SSU:** Sudan Socialist Union
**TMC:** Transitional Military Council
**TV:** Television
**UK:** United Kingdom
**UN:** United Nations
**UNICEF:** United National International Child Emergency Fund
**UNMISS:** United National Mission in South Sudan
**UNP:** Upper Nile Province
**UNSC:** United Nations Security Council
**USA:** United States of America
**WHTT:** We Hold These Truths
**WNP:** White Nile Province

# ACKNOWLEDGMENT

My sincere gratitude goes to Professor Samson S. Wassara (RIP) who directed and guided this work with high professionalism. Without his comments, criticism, advice and guidance this research would not have taken this form.

The Examination Board was formed with Dr. Wassara and two professors to whom I am indebted to. These were Associate Professor Dr. Ibrahim Margani Mohamed Ali, the Dean of the Faculty of Political Science and Strategic Studies at the University of al Ziem al Azhari, who was the external examiner, and Professor Ibrahim Ahmed Hamra of the Center for Peace and Development Studies, at the University of Juba, as the internal examiner.

My deep gratitude goes to Professor Angelo Lobale Lioria (RIP) who started the supervision of this work. Many thanks go to everybody that assisted me in this work, including; Rachel Mania and Abdel Mageed al Shingetti for their role in typing the thesis and Mawien Abouk Mathet who revised the Dinka terminologies used in this text.

I would like to thank the former Director of the Peace and Development Studies Center, Associate Professor Simon Manoja, and his former Deputy Dr. Mohamed Mukhatar for taking special interest in this study. Many thanks go to the entire staff of the Center for Peace and Development Studies, at the University of Juba, (Currently the Institute of Peace, Development, Strategic and Security Studies) for the cooperation they showed during my time there. Sincere thanks and appreciation go to members of my family, friends, and colleagues who encouraged me to pursue this work.

As we publish the Second Edition of this book, I would like to acknowledge Peter Lual Reech Deng, Dr Sara Maher whose dedication to editing this book deserves special mention, as well as Daniel Barwick for the design and typesetting.

Last but not least, thanks to Almighty God for this work.

*- Dhieu Mathok Diing Wol (Ph.D.)*

# FOREWORD

### The Book and the People

*Politics of Ethnic Discrimination in Sudan: A Justification for the Secession of South* Sudan by Dr. Dhieu Mathok Diing Wol, is unique in that the author writes from the vantage point of an exceptional combination of qualifications for performing the task he has set for himself. Apart from the academic credentials that qualify the manuscript for the Ph.D. degree, it has the added advantage of a participant-observer with the insight from his background as a member of Malual Dinka in which his father was Paramount Chief. Dr. Dhieu Mathok is also a politician and statesman, having been a minister in the Government of Sudan, when it was one country, and is now a cabinet minister in the government of National Unity of South Sudan.

With these credentials, the reader is privileged to get into the complex and intricate world of inter-tribal relations in the wider national context of racial, ethnic, religious, and cultural diversity. The book covers a wide range of issues with remarkable depth and insight. Although it primarily focuses on Malual-Rezeigat relations, it links them to the national levels of North-South Sudanese politics and inter-communal politics of South Sudan. Commensurately, this Foreword addresses those aspects of the study that relate to the politics of identity and diversity in the context of Malual-Rezeigat relations, the extent to which they link local and national levels through the penetration of central authorities, and their extension to the international level, largely through a concern with humanitarian and human rights issues in the country.

The book was first published in December 2010. The author explains that he made three predictions that came to be and which motivated him to revise the book for issuing this second edition. These predictions include the overwhelming choice of the people of South Sudan for independence; the outbreak of border conflict between South Sudan and Sudan in 2012; and the eruption of civil war in South Sudan in 2013. The author thoroughly examines the dynamics of locally generated conflicts that grow to become nationwide and extend further to involve international actors. This was the case with both Dinka Makual-Rezeigat Arab and Dinka Ngok-Misseriya Arab situations.

Dinka Malual, like all their fellow Dinka groups, are known to be very proud and ethnocentric. Central to their cultural value system is a concept of immortality through progeny, the continuation of the identity and influence of the dead among the living, and inter-generational linkages in change and continuity. Although this is an agnatic system that favors the male line, women are very powerful and influential as mothers of the line. It is precisely because of their influence that the role of the father must be emphasized as a function of the mind, while the closer attachment to the mother is acknowledged as a function of the heart. In both cases, ancestral values require solidarity, unity, and harmony within the family, the kin-group, and the wider community. Being remembered and revered also demands adhering to the principles of individual and communal dignity and integrity. The place of the individual in society is determined by conformity to these fundamental values.

It is not an exaggeration to say that in their traditionally isolated world, the Dinka saw themselves and their culture as the ideal model of God's creation. But they are not unique in their self-esteem. Exalting one's identity is the essence of being human and it is universal. Identity is inherent in every individual as a member of the family, kinship and the wider community. Also inherent in identity is a sense of pride and dignity as a human being in a given social and cultural context. Subjectively, and especially viewed in isolation, every social and cultural group idealizes itself as a model of human dignity. It is only when the group gets in contact with other groups and issues of diversity arise that the subjective sense of superiority comes into question. Diversity almost inevitably raises the challenge of inter-group interaction, mutual influence, stratification, and potential inequality.

Melville J. Herskovits, the founding father of Africanist studies in the Western world, observed, "Whenever people having different customs come together, they modify their ways by taking something from those with whom they newly meet. They may take over much or little, according to the nature or intensity of their contact, or the degree to which the two cultures have elements in common, or differ in basic orientation. But they never take over or ignore all; some change is inevitable." (Herskovits, *The Human Factor in Changing Africa*, 6, 1962)

### Malual-Rezeigat and Ngok-Misseriya Contexts

The author of this confirms that the relations between Malual and Rezeigat in the context of North and South Sudan, (now two different countries of Sudan and South Sudan), are far more complex than is normally reflected in popular discourse. This complexity is most pronounced between the ethnic groups at the borders of Upper Nile and Bahr el Ghazal, whose interaction with their Northern Sudanese neighbors are for the most part permeated by ambiguities and ambivalences. This may involve a contradictory combination of both embracing and resisting interracial cross-cultural influences and assimilation. But as Herskovits observed, they give and take in varying forms and degrees, but some mutual influence is unavoidable. Ironically, this often entails a degree of discrepancy between what is perceived and what is real. Animosity between ethnic groups sometimes leads to not seeing anything positive in the other group and not recognizing or acknowledging any shared characteristics of mutual influences. Evidence of inter-racial and cross-cultural influences between the neighboring groups across the North-South borders are often visible, but tend to be ignored or dismissed, because of hostility and animosity.

The anomalies of inter-communal relations between North and South Sudan are often associated with Abyei, probably because the Ngok Dinka represent a people who are for all intents and purposes South Sudanese, but are administered in the North in the same province of Abyei, with their Misseriya Arab neighbors. Dr. Dhieu Mathok in fact devotes a section of his book to the case of Abyei. But as this book reveals, the relationship between Malual and Rezeigat has many similarities as well as differences with the Ngok Dinka Misseriya situation. The differences in their situation relate largely to their separate administrative affiliation to the North and South Sudan. The author presents the relationship between the Malual Dinka and the Rezeigat as involving a dynamic interaction that alternates between peaceful coexistence and cooperation through trade and violent confrontation over resources. While this is also true of the Ngok-Misseriya relations, reports of the British administrators indicate that the Malual-Misseriya relations have generally been more conflictual, perhaps because the Ngok and the Misseriya were administered in the same province and district.

For the same reason, historical memories of conflicts between the Ngok and the Misseriya tend to be more intense. It is a well-known sociological fact that conflicts within close relationships tend to be more embittering than conflicts with more distant adversaries. At moments when relations are peaceful and cooperative, people tend to see the positive as peers in their interaction, including historical memories. When conflict becomes violent, much of what people see and remember is animosity and nothing peaceful. A personal experience revealed to me the alternating views on history and the influence of peace and conflicts in their perception. I conducted two sets of interviews with Ngok Dinka chiefs and elders in mid-1970s. I had already interviewed prominent Dinka chiefs from different tribes of South Sudan. The specific questions posed concerned the history of contact and relationship with the Arabs of Northern Sudan and the future prospects for unity and integration.

I conducted the first interview shortly after the Misseriya had attacked lorries carrying Dinka passengers going back to their home areas and massacred about a hundred people, including women and children. The perspective of those interviewed was totally negative. They said, "God created us different from the Arabs. We were created black and the Arabs were created brown. And our ways have been totally different since creation." Arab character and moral values were presented in a very negative light, while Dinka character and culture were perceived as embodying moral ideals. According to the Dinka, there was no basis for unity, far less integration; the two people must remain separate into the distant future.

I conducted the second set of interviews after a successful Ngok Dinka-Misseriya Arab peace and reconciliation conference in which I assisted Abdel Rahman Abdalla, the Minister of Public Service, who chaired the negotiations. The perspective of those interviewed was radically different from those of my first interviewees: "God created us with the Arabs as twins" they asserted. Some added the white race to make for triplets. They also acknowledged that people had mixed racially and culturally, and that there were many well-known families in Ngok Dinka society with Arab blood. They even predicted that mixing would continue and that people in the end would all become one.

The materials from those interviews produced two books, *Africans of Two Worlds: The Dinka in Afro-Arab Sudan* (Yale Press, 1978), and *Dinka Cosmology* (Ithaca Press, 1980), which Africa World Books reissued respectively under the titles: *The Changing World of the Dinka* and *Dinka Worldview: The Wisdom of the Elders,* both published in 2022.

A balanced view of the situation is that the Dinka have been more resistant than receptive to intermarriage and cultural assimilation with the Arabs. In the exceptions, cases where intermarriage takes place, both the Arabs and the Dinka prefer that their men rather than women marry across the divide. This is because their patriarchal system favors integrating the progeny of mixed marriages into the kinship. Ironically, because of their proximity to the North, both the Malual and the Ngok Dinka have been defensively impervious to Arab influence. The Ngok Dinka, though administered in the North, has paradoxically been even more resistant to Arab-Islamic influence. There is probably less interracial marriage between the Arabs of Sudan and the Ngok Dinka than there is between the North and other Southern Sudanese in other border areas in Upper Nile and Bahr el Ghazal. This is however a complex situation where what is admitted may be different from what is in fact the case. People who display hostility to all that is Arab may well be among the most influenced by Arab culture.

### Connection to Other Regional and National Actors

There is reason to believe that while interaction between Malual Dinka and their Rezeigat neighbors have been broadly inter-communal, the relationship between the Ngok Dinka and the Misseriya Arabs was traditionally personal at the level of their respective leaders, going back several generations, although education has now broadened the bases of contact. Anthropologists and British administrators who served in the area have observed that the Ngok Dinka are more centralized under one leadership than the other Dinka tribes and that their political system has been significantly influenced by the association of their leaders with their Arab counterparts. It is also argued that the geographical isolation of the Ngok Dinka from the control of the central government has also strengthened their autonomous indigenous system of administration. This indicates the extent to which linkage to external sources of control and authority impacts the local power dynamics.

In contrast to the case of the Ngok-Misseriya elite-led inter-relationship, the Malual-Rezeigat contacts and conflicts appear more inter-communal. Dr. Dhieu Mathok indeed explains that the conflicts between the communities revolved around competition over natural resources like grazing land, water, and fishing prospects, but an aggravating factor was the involvement of the central government which exploited the tribes and turned them into agents of the government in its power struggle, especially in North-South civil wars. According to the author, "Arab tribes, like Riziegat of Southern Darfur and Misseriya of Southern Kordofan, were used in order to fight their neighbors in Northern Bahr el Ghazal and Northern Upper Nile, resulting in soured tribal relations at the South–North border, and undermining the fact that there are common interests between these tribes." The situation also gave the Malual the support of the armed rebel groups in the South which created a relative balance of power that contributed to inter-communal peace and reconciliation.

Dr. Dhieu Mathok observes that when the SPLA/M leadership and the local authorities of Riziegat, Misseriya, and Dinka Malual people real-ized that the war had cost the people dearly and those suffering the most were innocent people living on the border, they formed Peace Markets with Riziegat and Misseriya. "This motivated them to devise means of making people- to-people grass-roots peace. They made local peace agree-ments without the consent of the government or the SPLA/M leadership. They maintained their contacts in the peace markets, setting up adminis-tration units of the markets between the tribes. The markets became an effective unifier for the Dinka Malual, Misseriya, and Riziegat people. The exchange of goods and materials went on smoothly. Sometimes the traders came from Khartoum and other big towns to purchase from the peace markets." The protection the Malual had received from the rebel forces in the South has now been strengthened by the even more effective protection of the government of South Sudan.

The use of markets as peace-building institutions has also been experi-enced in Ngok Dinka- Misseriya Arabs relations. Despite the intensified conflicts with the Misseriya since the independence of South Sudan with which the Ngok Dinka have had internationally unrecognized de-facto affiliation as citizens, which is deep in Ngok Dinka territory, Aneet market has been playing the role of an important trade link with South Sudan. The peace committees and community police established by the two communities have been instrumental in fostering peace and recon-ciliation at the grassroots, albeit with obvious limitations. The market has also been an agent for promoting a broader-based trade with various areas in South Sudan, including major urban centers. Aneet market, at the border with the Twic Dinka, has also played a similar role, although it recently experienced violent border conflict between the Ngok and Twic.

The main difference between the Malual-Rezeigat situation and that of the Ngok Dinka and the Misseriya has been the support Malual have received from South Sudanese armed groups and since independence from the government of South Sudan. Prior to the involvement of external forces, there was a degree of parity in the military capacity of both sides of the North-South border. The Dinka had the advantage of using light spears that could be darted from a distance, as opposed to the heavy spears that the Arabs used and which required close proximity for stabbing the enemy. But the Arabs used horses that gave them a comparative advantage. These relative advantages on both sides resulted in a degree of parity in their fighting capacities that fostered peaceful coexistence. The author quotes the Assistant District Commissioner of Baggara (Misseriya) as reporting: "These Dinkas have never been subdued by the Arabs when it comes to fighting, they gave as good as they got." The author also observed, "The balance of power between Riziegat, Misseriya, and Dinka Malual was more or less the same and no tribe could overweigh the other." Later, however, the fact that the Arabs were the first to acquire modern weapons gave them a decisive advantage over the Dinka. Under British colonial rule, the even-handedness of the central government administration ensured a degree of parity that maintained peaceful coexistence.

After independence, during the two North-South wars, Abyei was under the administration of the North and therefore in the lion's den, so to speak. The independence of South Sudan has offered the Ngok Dinka significant support, but Abyei is still contested and remains in a relative vacuum of state responsibility between the two Sudans. As a result, the Ngok Dinka have not had the kind of protection the Malual have received from (the Southern-based armed rebel groups and) the government of independent South Sudan.

Since most South Sudanese ethnic groups at the borders with the North have enjoyed the relative protection of their Southern security forces, they are ironically more secure and less antagonistic toward the Arabs than the Ngok Dinka. When people are not oppressed and have the freedom of choice, they tend to be more receptive to influence from the people with whom they interact than when they feel coerced or threatened into assimilation. That was indeed the experience of South Sudanese before and after the two agreements with the North, the 1972 Addis Ababa Agreement and the 2005 Comprehensive Peace Agreement (CPA). Although South Sudan Liberation Movement, and its military wing, Anya-Nya, fought a separatist war, once the peace agreement was concluded, Southern Sudanese became more unionist than Northern Sudanese.

And after the CPA, Muslim calls for prayers in Juba today are now being heard in a way that indicates that resistance to Arab cultural and Islamic influence is being replaced by greater receptivity to both. South Sudanese have become very much at home with the Arabic culture, much of which they had already absorbed without openly acknowledging it. Today, weddings, funerals, and cuisines in South Sudan are unmistakably Northern Sudanese in origin. One can validly say that while the Northern Sudanese political agenda in the South failed, their cultural program has been a success.

I recall occasions when I gave lectures or talks around Juba, including in the universities, and although I had assumed that I should talk English as the widely known language, I received notes requesting me to speak Arabic. Although English is the official language, and some prejudice against the Arabic language may be lingering, this also indicates a significant moderation of the previous prejudice against Arabic as a language of oppression. This prejudice came across most vividly in my interview with Chief Makuei Bilkuei of Paanaruw, who said, "I don't speak Arabic. God has refused my speaking Arabic. I asked God, 'Why don't I speak Arabic?' And he said, 'If you now speak Arabic, you will turn into a bad man.' And I said, 'There is something good in Arabic?' And he said, 'No, there is nothing good in it.' So your father would go and talk with Babo and I would remain with the others" (*Dinka Cosmology (1980)/Dinka Worldview: Wisdom of the Elders* (2022). I have had many highly educated Ngok tell me that they resisted learning Arabic or are not good at it because of their resistance to the language.

## *The Involvement of International Actors*

One of the issues that the book discusses in depth is slavery which attracted the involvement of the international community in response to the alleged violation of human rights and humanitarian principles. The issue apparently raised some controversy, with the Sudanese government arguing that what was involved was abduction, not slavery. Whatever the label, the abduction or enslavement of women and children became one of those areas which drew the attention of international human rights and humanitarian organizations, and activists. External involvement supported a program of slave redemption that allegedly became a source of large-scale corruption. Many South Sudanese and international observers found it unfathomable to pay the abductors for their crime, instead of being held criminally accountable. Worse, the practice is reported to have entailed a practice by which South Sudanese, posing as Arab abductors, presented Dinka children from the surrounding areas to play the role of abducted children.

Dr. Dhieu Mathok writes: "Local villagers are rounded up to pose as slaves when Christian groups arrive with briefcases full of money. The 'slave traders' are sometimes disguised as (sic) rebel soldiers from the SPLM." The author gives a graphic description of the process: "The slave redemption made for powerful human drama. A line of children emerged from the African bush. A slave trader in front wrapped in the white robes of an Arab. Furthermore, before them, waiting with a bag of money at his feet, was a white, Christian man. The procession halted under the shade of a tree. There was discussion, then money changed hands. Suddenly, the trader gave a nod, the slaves walked free and there were cries of joy as families were reunited in freedom at last. Many newspapers focused their attention on this issue." The practice was eventually brought to an end by the Sudan People's Liberation Movement/Army (SPLM/A). The pressure of the international community forced the Government of Sudan to cooperate in the creation of the Committee for the Eradication of Abducted Women and Children (CEAWC). This was a government mechanism in which Arab and Dinka tribal leaders cooperated. Nevertheless, only a relatively small number of women and children were redeemed.

What I found particularly intriguing in the book with respect to the issue of slavery was the confirmation of the differences in the practice in African and Arab societies compared to that of the Western world. In the case of Sudan, abductees/slaves were adopted and assimilated into the family and community and indeed into the wider society. A child of an Arab slave master and his slave woman was considered free and equal to the children of free mothers. In the West, to the contrary, a child of a slave master with his slave woman is the slave of his own father, who treats him/her as such and would even sell him/her to another slave owner. It is well known that many proud so-called Arabs of Northern Sudan are descendants of slave women from the South and the West. It is indeed ironic that these individuals of partial slave background insult Southerners whose ancestors had successfully resisted or escaped slavery as slaves.

Dr. Dhieu Mathok wrote, "When a captive left the battle area and reached the enemy territory, he/she felt quite secure. For Dinkas, ladies were treated as daughters and sisters. It was prohibited to marry a girl or woman captured by your immediate family or clan. Men automatically became members of that community. They got married and were treated as part of the family. At Dar Riziegat, war victims and those captured reaching their area were considered as family members; nobody was allowed to assault them or even point them out, otherwise, he/ she faced legal measures from the tribal leadership." One of the reported ironies in the work of CEAWC was that many abductees got quickly assimilated and did not want to return to their Dinka parents or community. Some of them would even deny being Dinka and become contemptuous of their own Dinka ethnicity and culture.

Dr. Dhieu Mathok, quoting from a British Assistant District Commissioner, observed: "It might be true that cases of Dinka slaves in Arab hands and vice versa would be the most difficult to deal with. In reality, they are the easiest of all because both tribes realize that it is useless to claim the return of a relative long in Arab hands as the slave will not agree to return to his own people. It is the same with Arabs in Dinka hands. They become Arabicized and Dinkaized after a few years."

Despite these divisive practices, relations between the ordinary Dinka Malual and Rezeigat were generally cooperative and conciliatory. The author wisely observes that while governments at the center come and go, neighbors remain: "The neighborhood between the Dinka tribe in the South and Baggara tribes in the North will not change because of separation or unity between South and North Sudan. So, it is important for these tribes to bear in mind that political institutions do change but neighborhoods do not unless someone decides to move to another place. Something that is not possible for tribes like the Dinka Malual or Riziegat." National authorities must also realize that conflicts between their proxies at the local level can escalate and eventually affect their relations. They might even provoke civil wars.

This has indeed been the result of using tribal militias in North-South wars in Sudan. I addressed this issue in my two books, *Sudan at the Brink: Self-Determination and National Unity* (Fordham University Press, 2010), and *Bound by Conflict: Dilemmas of the Two Sudans* (Fordham University Press, 2016). *Sudan at the Brink* was published as the referendum was approaching and predicted to overwhelmingly favor secession. In the book, I argued that unity and separation were degrees of an ongoing relationship, which could be strengthened or weakened, depending on the will of the people and their leaders. The central argument of *Bound by Conflict,* which was published after the secession of the South, was that despite the partition of the country into two different states, they remained negatively bound together by conflicts. The two countries were each recruiting, arming, and deploying tribal militias to fight their conflicts by proxy. The policy implication was that if they were to achieve national unity and improve their bilateral relations, they had to turn being bound by conflict to being bonded by solutions. This would require that they cooperate and help one another to resolve each other's internal wars. The first concrete step in that direction was the role Sudan played in brokering the Revitalized Peace Agreement in South Sudan.

South Sudan then reciprocated by mediating the resolution of Sudan's internal conflicts, a process that is still ongoing.

## *Diversity and the Crisis of National Identity*

Sudan and South Sudan are both experiencing a crisis of identity which may differ in form and degree, but the essence of which calls for ensuring unity in the context of competing identities. It should be stressed that the source of conflict is not the mere differences of identity, but how diversity is managed. In pluralistic states, identity conflicts often entail discrimination, marginalization, and exclusion. The population is often dichotomized into those who are viewed as first-class citizens and enjoy all the rights and duties of citizenship, and those who are denigrated into the status of second-class citizens and denied the full rights of citizenship. In most cases, this results in conflicts that could be violent and might escalate to genocidal levels.

The challenge then is to adopt a strategy for constructively managing diversity toward inclusivity and equality. As the author observes, "Diversity of nations has not been a problem, but if people are denied their rights and live in a situation of political exclusion then, it will turn into a problem. This may result sometimes in a rebellion or a military coup in some countries. For this reason, Sudan has been witnessing a long political struggle between the South, whose largest population is Christian and of African ethnic origin, and the North whose origins are Arab and Muslims by religion."

Successive governments "failed to evolve a Sudanese identity, a Sudanese commonality, a Sudanese commonwealth that includes all Sudanese and to which all Sudanese pledge a united loyalty irrespective of their religion, race, or tribe." This dichotomy proved difficult to bridge to the degree that justified the secession of the South into the independent state of South Sudan. Viewed in a wider global context, identity factors are generic and dynamic. Differences can go down to divide members of a community and even a family.

Three options seem obvious to resolve the crisis of national identity.

The ideal is to create an identity framework of inclusivity and full equality as citizens. That was the vision of New Sudan which the Sudan People's Liberation Movement and its Army, (SPLM/A), stipulated and fought for, but could not achieve militarily. The second option is one of unity in diversity, which entails respect for the differences within a unified national framework. Sudan experimented with this option through the regional autonomy for Southern Sudan under the 1972 Addis Ababa Agreement. It was also practiced under the 'One Country Two Systems' formula for the interim period under the 2005 Comprehensive Peace Agreement.

Dr. Dhieu Mathok writes that the ruling National Congress Party and Sudan Government "required that the Sharia be the center of any agreement that must be concluded with the South ... until the concept of "one country, two systems" was introduced in Naivasha as a temporary arrangement for the six-year and half interim period, 2005 – 2011. This led the SPLM to opt for self-determination as a fall-back position." The formula of "one country, two systems," was in fact developed by the Task Force on U.S. Sudan Policy, which I was honored to co-chair with Steve Morrison. The Task Force was established by the Washington-based Center for Strategic and International Studies (CSIS) to develop a coherent policy for the role of the United States in mediating the Sudan peace process.

Our objective in developing and proposing that formula was to salvage the unity of the country through a system of "unity in diversity" during the interim period that would enhance the prospects for making unity an attractive option. As I argued to the Task Force, since preserving the unity of Sudan was the preferred option of the international community, we should strive to make the impossible possible and reconcile the irreconcilable. One country, two systems was our proposed solution to the riddle (*U.S. Policy to End Sudan's War, Report of CSIS Task Force on U.S. Sudan's Policy,* co-chaired by Francis M. Deng and Stephan J. Morrison, 2001). While the formula was effectively applied by the mediation team led by Senator John Danforth that facilitated the negotiation of the CPA, it turned out to be a step toward the unavoidable secession of South Sudan.

Burundi and Rwanda, which have identical ethnic compositions and divisions involving three groups; Hutu by far the majority, Tutsi a third, but the most powerful group, and Twa, a small minority. Following the 1994 genocide, Rwanda decreed a policy that requires the national identification of all the citizens as Rwandese and outlaws any references to ethnicity as a divisive colonial construct. This strategy, though representing the preferred model, appears to ambiguously present what ought to be - as what in fact is. It also puts the cart before the horse in that recognizing the reality of diversity should precede evolving an integrated national identity.

In a way, this is the policy that Burundi seems to have adopted by acknowledging the diversity of the country into the three ethnic groups and developing a strategy for accommodating them equitably. Although no strategy for evolving an integrated national identity is declared, this should be understood to be an implicit aspect of nation-building.

Most African countries follow the dual strategy of accommodating diversity while aspiring toward an integrated national identity. This was reflected by an African head of state, President Yuweri Museveni of Uganda, in his comment on my keynote presentation at a high-level African symposium in which I advocated constructive management of diversity for addressing the national identity crisis in Africa. He argued that while managing diversity is an applaudable strategy, the goal of nation-building in Africa must be integration.

### A Vision for the Way Forward

Although Dr. Dhieu Mathok's book focuses on the relationship between Malual Dinka and the Rezeigat, it applies with equal poignancy to other South Sudanese bordering Sudan generally and the Ngok Dinka in particular. In the end, it is very much about the two Sudans who, despite the secession of South Sudan, remain connected by internal conflicts that spill over their borders. South Sudanese fought long wars against successive governments in Khartoum, with resistance as their uniting identity framework. It was largely a negative self-identification by which Southerners largely defined themselves as non-Arab and non-Muslim.

The vision of New Sudan called for inclusively and equality within a national framework of Sudanism. But that vision was mostly perceived as the invention of John Garang which South Sudanese accepted only as a tactical or strategic ploy for neutralizing opposition against secession, which remained the hidden objective of the overwhelming majority of South Sudanese struggle. When that goal was achieved, the prediction that South Sudan would fall apart once the uniting factor of resistance to Northern domination was gone proved to be true. In a way, that was a self-fulfilling Northern Sudanese prophecy that they endeavored to bring about.

So, where does South Sudan go from here? It seems to be that the vision of New Sudan of inclusivity and full equality without discrimination on any ground still holds. After all, identity is a relative term and cannot be focused only on the Arab-Islamic North and the African-Secular South of the Old Sudan. As the case of Somalia demonstrates, identity differences can go down to the level of clans and even pit families and ambitious individuals against one another. South Sudanese identity groups that are now in conflict need to reverse their negative self-definition as non-Arab and non-Muslim, or negatively distinguish themselves from each other. We need to develop a positive perspective on our national identity and related cultural values. We need to understand the cultural values of each of our multiple ethnic groups, individually and comparatively, to discern their commonalities and differences, and explore the prospects for their complementarity. We need to construct a uniting national identity framework based on the potential enrichment from our pluralistic sources, one in which all South Sudanese can share a common sense of belonging with pride and dignity.

*Francis Mading Deng*
*Woodstock, New York, USA,*
*August 2022*

# PREFACE

As people of Southern Sudan fought for justice, equality, prosperity and basic human rights, including the right to choose between staying united with rest of Sudan or becoming an independent country – which was exercised through a referendum in 2011.

The need for studies of this kind became important to assess how the people in the South would relate in the future with their neighbours in the North.

Many political analysts predicted that if a referendum were carried out fairly, Southerners would opt for secession. This was evident in the growing schisms in the country and ongoing border tensions.

It was against this background that the author, using the Dinka Malual tribe from Northern Bahr el Ghazal and the Riziegat of Southern Dafur, carried out this study to bring to light the issues of the border relations and the prospects of cooperation.

While there were many assumptions informing the study, the working hypotheses were:

The ethnic politics used by Sudanese elites made unity unrealistic and this played a central role in the separation of South Sudan from Sudan.

What appeared to be an ethnic competition between the Dinka Malual and Riziegat Arabs over natural resources (water and grazing land) was escalated by wider political motives in the North-South political divide.

It was possible for the two communities of Dinka Malual and Riziegat to live together at the South Sudan-Sudan border peacefully, like other bordering communities did.

In undertaking this study, the following objectives were to be served:

- Investigate the impact of ethnic politics on South Sudan-Sudan relations.
- Identify causes and factors contributing to the worsening and possible improvement of South-North future relations.
- Examine the factors of conflict and interests of both tribes and relate them to the issue of unity or secession in Sudan.
- Explore the possibilities of mobilizing the communities in both Dinka Malual and Riziegat tribes to play a positive role in promoting peace and reconciliation in the area.
- Assess and analyze the effects of unity or secession in the area.
- Suggest possible approaches to strengthening positive relations between the two tribes in the future.

In order to fulfill this important task, the following methods and techniques were deployed;

- Secondary data was collected from existing literature on the topic.
- Historical and descriptive approaches to analyzing past relations between the South and the North and other parties involved.
- Surveys comprised of interviews and observations of the communities chosen as the case study.
- Structured interviews, which covered all areas of the study, with key actors such as; politicians, chiefs, youths, armed forces, workers, and women among others.

Participants from both tribes were selected to give their opinions in Khartoum, Southern Darfur and Northern Bahr el Ghazal.

In addressing the issue extensively, three distinct scopes were adopted. First, the periodical scope from 1821-2005 with predictions of the future during the country's referendum in 2011. This was done through a designed questionnaire. The second scope was the ethnic line of the two communities of Dinka Malual and Riziegat, and the third was the geographical scope of the two communities including those community members living in Northern Bahr el Ghazal, South Darfur, and Khartoum.

As a Ph.D. thesis the author encountered many challenges and obstacles which included but were not limited to:

The project's first supervisor, assigned by the College of Graduates Studies at the University of Juba, was Professor Angelo Lobale Loiria (RIP) from the Political Science Department. Upon taking up his role as the supervisor in February 2004, Prof Loiria was appointed as Political Adviser in the State Government of Eastern Equatoria (Status of Minister in the State Government) in 2006, as such he left the supervision and took up the new job in Torit, Southern Sudan.

The author spent more than one and half years between January 2006 and July 2007 without a supervisor. The project stalled as a result. The absence of Professor Loiria had its advantages as well as disadvantages. The disadvantage was that the work could not proceed for the said period and the project would not have been finished in the specified time. The advantage was that Professor Angelo, as our most senior lecturer, not only in the University of Juba but in Southern Sudan as a whole, was given that opportunity as a reward for his diligent work towards the welfare of generations. He deserved a ministerial position at that time in his life. Many congratulations to him and, for those who made that appointment possible.

Luckily his successor was Dr. Samson S. Wassara (RIP), Associate Professor of Political Science and the Dean of College of Social and economic Studies in the University of Juba, the very college which had awarded the researcher's first degree in 1992. The author met with Dr. Wassara as a lecturer in the College before he was sent to France to pursue his Ph.D. He later returned and found the author was about to graduate. The author took up some of his courses, and therefore Dr Wassara was not a stranger to the author. He was among a few young lecturers whose lectures and instructions were enjoyable and as such contributed a lot to the author's education.

Coming back to the point, when Dr. Wassara was assigned to supervise the author, he suggested a number of changes, which also caused challenges and the author had to return to the drawing board to inculcate these new suggestions. The upside was that the revisions suggested by Dr. Wassara resulted in this book.

Another event which is no less important as regards to this work was the author's migration from Khartoum to South Sudan, leaving behind the supervisor and all facilities for the study. This therefore meant that the author had to spend time away from family in South Sudan to be in Khartoum working.

The readers will find that a good number of references are from Arabic sources. This means there was a great effort exerted in order to translate the contents of some quotations from Arabic to English. These translations in the text are not literally authentic.

# ABSTRACT

The conflict between Dinka Malual of Northern Bahr el Ghazal and Riziegat of South Darfur is deep-rooted and multifaceted. Initially, the conflict was fuelled by rivalry over grazing lands and sources of water around the River Kiir; known as the Bahr Arab to the Riziegat. But after independence in 1956, the conflict evolved into a political issue where the government in Khartoum exploited ethnic differences between the Dinka Malual and Riziegat to strengthen their own dominance. The conflict escalated into war leading to slavery, abduction, human rights violations, looting of resources and destruction of infrastructure.

These human rights violations resulted in interventions by the International Community. However, these third parties instead worsened the situation by causing further disunity in an already divided nation. Finally, the North and the South signed a Peace Agreement 2005 which grant self-determination and autonomy to the people of Southern Sudan.

In 2011, a referendum was held that allowed the South to secede from the North. However, there was no formal division of natural resources such as the oil wells which have become a battleground as each party clamors for ownership.

Prior to the referendum, the First Edition of this book was published making predictions that South Sudanese would vote by 94% in favor of secession. In that edition the author also predicted post-independence conflict – which has also occurred. This Second Edition includes a chapter describing events as witnessed first-hand by the author since independence involving the current government – which the author is part of.

## مستخلص البحث

أن النزاع الدائر بين قبيلتى الدينكا ملوال فى شمال بحر الغزال والرزيقات
جنوب دار فور يرجع لسنوات عديدة ، بدأ  هذا النزاع منذ قدوم القبائل العربية إلى
المنطقة ولكن لم يسجل التاريخ هذا النزاع إلا فى العهد التركى المصرى فى القرن
التاسع عشر الميلادى. أن سبب هذا النزاع الممتد هو الصراع حول موارد الرعى
ومصادر المياه فى منطقة بحر العرب ( كير) .  وبعد  الإستقلال تبنت الحكومة
الوطنية هذا النزاع وتم إستغلاله لصالح الأجندة السياسية فى البلاد .

ومع تراكمات سلبيات الحروبات الأهلية مثل إنتهاك حقوق الإنسان وال
وإختطاف الأطفال والنساء خرج من إطاره المحلى الى الإطار الدولى وأصبح
عنصرا  هاما فى تدخل المجتمع الدولى فى قضايا السودان الداخلية وإستخدام ه
القضايا لإستهداف النظام الإسلامى الذى إستولى على السلطة فى السودان فى الد
1989م.

الكثيرون يرون أن الحرب أخذت طابعا خطيرا بإستخدام عنصري الدر
والذين فى تحقيق الأغراض السياسية فى البلاد وامتد الأمر إلى الإستيلاء عل
الأراضى الواقعة فى الحدود الجنوبية بغرض إتباعها للشمال وخاصة بعد ثبوت
وجود الموارد الطبيعية فى هذه المناطق مما زاد من حدة النزاع بين الشما
والجنوب حول هذه الأراضى بعد توقيع إتفاقية السلام الشامل عام 2005م ومذ
شعب جنوب السودان حق تقرير المصير عبر الإستفتاء الشعبى الذى سوف يجر
عام 2011م.  هذا الأمر يقودنا للتساؤل حول مستقبل العلاقة بين الجنوبوالشما
فى ظل تداعيات هذه الحروبات وقد أكدت الدراسات على أن جنوب السودا
سينفصل عن الشمال فى هذا الإستفتاء نسبة لما يرونه من المضايقات حسب
تقديراتهم.

# GENERAL INTRODUCTION

Issues of ethnicity and politics continue to play a central role in the acquisition of political power in Africa and other Third World countries. It is imminent that elites continue to use ethnic differences to pursue political power in their countries.

An ethnic group is defined as a group of people that share a common cultural background or descent. It has become common practice for a particular tribe to use their commonalities to stage *coup d'etats*. This obviously leads to sectarianism and consequently political unrest as the various tribes and ethnicities try to wrest power from each other.

The long struggle between South and North Sudan is an example of ethnic differences that existed between two parts of a single country. South Sudanese believed, and still do, that the oppression that came from the North was an ethnic based marginalization. This could be clearly seen through an absence of prerequisites for unity like common history, common language, and common religion. Even the ecology is different in the two parts of the country.

The conflict over political power and social recognition which has been ongoing in Sudanese politics since before independence in 1956, trickled down to local communities, especially those communities living at the North-South border. As an attempt to address the issue from its roots, this study traces the conflict as far back as the era of colonization when the Condominium rule, in an attempt to control the communities, instituted laws in 1922 to organize the native administration.

After independence, the newly established national government used the same system of exploiting tribal allegiance to gain political power. The system put sectarian political parties into power, but this had a negative effect on communal relations. Some tribes especially, those on the South-North border where there had been a political rivalry between North and South became disenfranchised. The fate of Riziegat of Southern Darfur and Dinka Malual of Northern Bahr el Ghazal are examples of the system's lasting effects.

The South-North border is known in Sudanese politics as a Contact Area inhabited by nomadic shepherds from rival tribes. Both tribes face similar challenges of scarce pasture and water for their animals. During the dry season, the only source of water is the small river called Kiir in Dinka but known to Riziegat as Bahr Arab. Although Kiir separates the territories of the two tribes, there are disputes over ownership of the land beyond the river. The politicians in Khartoum continue to prey on this dispute to divide and conquer which helps to entrench their political power.

The struggle for power between the North and the South started four months before independence, Southerners, feeling marginalized by their counterparts in the North, mutinied at Torit garrison in August 1955.

The administrative measures taken by the British colonial administration in 1930 had adversely affected chances of education for Southerners as the Sudanization of positions in the government was later based on educational qualifications and work experience; Southerners eligible to compete with Northerners were very few.

In 1954, out of 800 senior posts in the civil service careers, only six were given to Southerners. This imbalance caused bitter reactions from Southerners who viewed independence as just a replacement of old colonizers by new ones. Southern representatives tried through the legislative body (House of Representatives) to correct the situation, but the intransigence of Northern political parties over the matter, made Southerners seek an alternative approach as a means of addressing the situation in Sudan. When violence erupted in the South, Arab soldiers and traders were murdered at Torit and Anzara in 1955.

Ethnic oppression underscored the conflict. Dinka Malual, Dinka Ngok, and other tribes along the border were among the first victims because of their geographical locations. Mass killing of Dinka citizens was planned and executed by the government at Babanousa railway station in 1964. Other murders took place at a wedding party in Wau in 1965 where many intellectuals from Bahr el Ghazal perished. All evidence in these mass killings pointed at the government in Khartoum, and no evidence pointed at tribal involvement.

Major General Albino Akol, an ex-Anya Nya officer, believes that Anya Nya One fighter relations with the Baggara during that time were cordial. After having signed the agreement, Nimeiry went on with the policy of "ethnic confrontation" at the border. The mass killings of Ngok Dinka people in 1972 and Dinka Malual people in 1974 at Rumaker were indications of the continuation of conflict between Arabs and Africans in Sudan. Dinka Malual carried out a bloody revenge at Ashana in 1976.

The situation worsened when innocent traders were killed by some Dinka Ngok rebels, as a revenge, at Araith town in 1982. There were many counter attacks between Riziegat militia and guards of Dinka chiefs (Baszingers), who declared themselves as Anya Nya Two in 1982. In 1987 the Riziegat tribe carried out the most known genocide, in the history of human rights abuses, in Sudan, at Daein town.

Sudan People's Liberation Movement/Army (SPLM/A) took advantage of that flammable situation to recruit as many as possible from Northern Bahr el Ghazal, the most populated area in South Sudan. Large numbers of students, traders, farmers, and cattle herders decided to join the Movement to protect their children and properties from continuous raiding exercised by the Baggara.

Unfortunately, many fighters were sent to different missions in other war zones. The area occupied by the Dinka Malual continued to suffer until 1992, when small forces composed of Aweil fighters in SPLA/M escaped and settled at Aweil East (Pariak), near the border with the Misseriya tribe.

The situation was controlled at Aweil East, but Aweil North and West continued to experience organized raids from Riziegat and Misseriya militias until 2001, when Senator John Danforth, the special envoy of U.S. President George W. Bush, brokered the agreement on slavery/abduction eradication and civil population protection. More than 14,000 children and women were reported missing, having been taken as slaves/abductees by Riziegat and Misseriya tribes.

Another result of the political struggle in the North between various political parties was the acceptance of the Native Administration. Due to a conflict of interest between the Native Administration and some political groups, the former was considered a colonial stooge formed to suppress the masses and not to solve their problems.

The Native Administration being an administrative organ that functioned at the grass-roots level had an important role to play in conflict resolution. However, this was undermined by the subjection of Native Administration to political rivalry in the North. While in the South, the role of the Native Administration was weakened by instability in most areas.

At the time, there was urgent need to address competition over political power in Sudan which was the cause of instability in the area occupied by the Dinka Malual and Riziegat tribes. The Central Government, in waging war against the Liberation Movement in the South, tried to use the Riziegat and other tribes on the border to fight the war by proxy. The SPLA/M also did the same when it recruited thousands of Dinka Malual youths in its ranks. This all fuelled instability in the area.

More so, human rights violations in Sudan, especially those atrocities committed by Riziegat and Misseriya tribes against Dinka Malual people on the border, also contributed to the deterioration of the South-North relations.

Many observers on human rights believed that the issue of human rights violations in Sudan with special emphasis on slavery/ abduction, became an international concern at the beginning of the 1980s when Bona Malual, the former Minister in Nimeiry's Administration, began to publish articles on slavery in a Sudanese newspaper, the *Sudan Times* where he was the chief editor.

This situation gained further prominence from publications by two lecturers from the University of Khartoum which exposed the practice of slavery and mass genocide in Western Sudan. In 1987 more than 1,000 displaced Dinka people had been killed at Daien town by members of Rezeigat tribe under supervision of Sudan Government.

In the 1990s, reports reached some human rights activists, that there was government-instigated racial and religious discrimination in Sudan. Gaspar Biro, a human rights activists, decided to break international silence about the situation in Sudan. He paid visits to the country to investigate the rumors and submitted reports to the United Nations in his capacity as an expert in 1992. The UN subsequently appointed him as special rapporteur on the human rights situation in Sudan. He was replaced by Leonardo Franco, in 1999, who served until 2001, when he was replaced by Mr. Gerhart Baum whose report to the UN indicated, for the first time since 1992, that considerable steps had been taken to improve the human rights situation in Sudan.

During all these times of international inquiry about the situation of human rights in Sudan, US President Bill Clinton and his administration issued resolutions proclaiming the Government of Sudan (GOS) as uncooperative on human rights in the international arena. Meanwhile, other relevant matters of U.S. foreign policy had come to involve international organizations against the Sudanese Government by the Clinton Administration, including the issue of its relations with international Islamic terrorism.

Clinton's successor George W. Bush and his Administration, in the formulation of a new foreign policy on Sudan, concentrated on four points as issues of concern that the Government of Sudan had to resolve. These included cooperation in the war against terrorism, improvement of human rights conditions, commitment to peaceful settlement of conflicts in the South, and restoration of democracy in Sudan.

President Bush appointed his special envoy for peace in Sudan, Senator John Danforth in September 2001, who then visited Sudan in November 2001 and imposed on the government what he called "Test Points." These points were the issue of a ceasefire in the Nuba Mountains, civil population protection, zones of tranquility for humanitarian purposes, and the issue of slavery/abduction in South Sudan.

The Sudan government showed full cooperation on the above issues and there have not been any new cases registered in slavery and abduction since the time of the Danforth agreements.

Other international groups which played a role in the field of human rights in Sudan were USA-based Christian International Solidarity (CIS) and the first world's human rights organisation in the field of slavery, London-based, Anti-Slavery International (ASI), which exerted efforts on slave redemption in the areas held by SPLA/M in the South, through buying back slaves for cash. Their work was criticized by some international organizations, especially UNICEF. They were accused of adding more fuel to the existing situation.

UNICEF believed that the money used for redemption of slaves was further used by slave masters as revolving funds in the slave markets. Some SPLA/M commanders asked Christian groups to finance developmental projects in their controlled areas rather than the redemption of slaves. One of the executive managers from CIS confessed that the practice of paying for redemptions was a scam, a hoax, and scandalous.

At government level, considerable work has been done by the committee for Eradication of Abduction of Women and Children

(CEAWC) and Joint Tribal Committees (JTCs) under the facilitation of UNICEF and Save the Children United Kingdom (SCUK). However CEAWC and JTC needed more support to complete documentation, reinstatement, and reunification of abducted children and women with their families.

There were tremendous improvements of the situation of new abductees compared to any other period. However, no progress has been made in as far as reinstatement and reunification. Out of 14,000 missing children and women, only 5,000 were reported as being traced and only 50 percent were actually reunited with their families and relatives.

Reasons for failure to trace the missing abductees/slaves was the result of a lack of information and lack of financial support from the government and the international organizations working in this field. Sometimes abductees were reluctant to go back to their relatives because of insecurity and poverty.

There was a need for CEAWC to address its organizational structures at the lower level, especially at the grass-roots. Moreso, there was need for participation of people at grass-root level in the process of tracing of the missing children and women. The people-to-people approach to solve problems proved to be effective as evidenced by the Dinka-Nuer at Wunlit in 1999, Mundari-Bari in Juba, and Dinka-Fertit in Wau in 1992.

The low response of the International Community to finance CEAWC activities was related to the conceptual differences about the reality of slavery/abduction. The Government of Sudan and some international groups considered events in Sudan as an obvious by-product of civil war and abduction, a natural phenomenon among the tribes in Sudan not only between Arab-African but African-African tribes in the South as well. While other groups led by the USA, believe the phenomenon to be slavery, and have called for associated international measures to be taken. But, regardless of the interpretation of the phenomenon, there is need for serious attention from all parties.

International Eminent Persons Group (IEPG) in its report about the slavery/abduction in Sudan in 2002, considered abduction to be the earliest stage of slavery. It is believed that the legal status between the two jargons in the international laws is different. As one Dinka interviewee noted, it is better to agree on its eradication. The intervention of the international human rights groups in Sudan, through the agenda of the violation of human rights as (slavery/ abduction) practiced in the area of Dinka Malual and Riziegat tribes needs to be addressed.

The third issue related to the conflict between the Dinka Malual and Riziegat tribes' is the competition over natural resources, which has always been a genuine local agenda.

The British colonial administration tried to solve this problem, but the solutions were problematic and fueled the conflict instead.

The organization of pastoral movements in the area was not effective in bringing the disputes between the two tribes to an end, because through their interaction, other confusing matters like illegal marriages arose. The boundaries made by the British Administration in 1918 and 1924 respectively were not recognised by Dinka tribal leaderships and becomes a source of violence in the area. It was said that the British were biased against the Dinka Malual in demarcating those boundaries due to continuous resistance that Dinka leaders had put up against British rule in Northern Bahr el Ghazal.

The rebellion led by Araith Mákuei (Bol Yel) in Northern Bahr el Ghazal was said to be the main cause of these differences. The contents of the 1924 Agreement were not disclosed to Dinka Malual leadership until 1935 at the Safaha Conference. Meetings were convened regularly, and deliberations were made but the resolutions and recommendations were separately formulated by the British administrators. The gathering of tribal leadership was successful in terms of public relations with chiefs, Nazirs and Omdas, but with no real contribution in solving matters.

National political forces, after taking responsibility of the Government of Sudan, spent most of their time in political conspiracy and forgot national interests. The issue of allocation of grazing land would have been solved if serious attention had been paid to it. There was need to empower the Native Administration to deal with these matters in the borders, in addition to the creation of some developmental projects in the area.

However, many political figures were more focused on how to liquidate the Native Administration, an institution which was regarded as a colonial stooge created to suppress the masses.

In addition to all these, the Central Government's leadership in Khartoum relied on the grazing boundaries between the Dinka Malual and the Riziegat tribe created by colonial rulers in 1924 as real borders between the North and the South, yet there was no need for boundaries in one country. The central government should not have insisted that the grazing boundaries be recognized as real administrative boundaries between the north and the south.

In this book, besides the Preface and General Introduction that focuses on the necessities of the research, the author also focused attention on the Dinka Malual and Riziegat people and their land in Chapter One. This is significant to understand the type of people and land considered in the study.

The evolution of tribal relations in all fields of human life, including social economic, and political relations between Dinka Malual and Riziegat tribes are extensively addressed in Chapter Two.

Chapter Three of the book illustrates the role of successive Sudan Governments in the Dinka Malual and Riziegat tribal relations. It is very significant to examine and assess how far the external influences played a role in communal relations.

Liberation Movements in Southern Sudan played their own role in the Dinka Malual and Riziegat tribal relations as addressed in Chapter Four. It is important to examine this role because the Riziegat tribe convincingly believed that Dinka Malual usually fell victim to the influence of the rebellions in Southern Sudan.

In Chapter Five, is an attempt to evaluate the role of the International Community in the management of the Dinka Malual and Riziegat tribal grievances. The roles of Western Countries, the UN, the International Non- Governmental Organizations (INGOs), the International media and press are examined too.

Chapter Six pays attention to those elements being considered as obstacles to the unity of Sudan. These include; competition over identity and territorial claims, the instrumentalization of ethnicity in the pursuit of power, the exploitation of religion for political ends, and recurring border conflicts.

Important work was done as regards to the field study and giving the targeted communities of Dinka Malual and Riziegat an opportunity to give their opinions on certain important aspects of the topic. The conclusion of the study is considered in Chapter Seven, which summarizes all the findings.

This Second Edition has examined the predictions made by the participants of the research on a number of issues which became realities. Chapter Eight looks at these issues by narrating how these predictions became realities after the independence of South Sudan.

The overall conclusions of the study suggest some ways forward for the country.

# PROLOGUE

The *Politics of Ethnic Discrimination in Sudan: A Justification for the Secession of South Sudan*, is a comprehensive study of a conflicts that started as a dispute between the two communities of the Dinka Malual and Riziegat and quickly shifted to national and international levels. The ability of these types of conflicts to grow depends on the dynamic of the issues and actors.

Relating this issue to a wider context, African peace and conflict studies usually begins with an anthropological outlook of the people, then accounts for historical events of the conflict escalation. Such is the case in understanding the relationship between Dinka Malual and Riziegat communities that were selected for the purpose of this study which examines how these two tribes lived, their cultures and social relations. It then further examines what new elements reinforced them.

Furthermore, we examine the economic security and political relationships between the two tribes since the time of the first colonial Condominiu rule in Sudan up to the time of independence in 1956, with the purpose of comparing their relationship under colonization and after. This helped in the analysis of South-North Sudan relations, and how this was a determinant as people decided whether to separate or remain one country in the January 2011 referendum.

Another important aspect of this study is linked with human rights and peace studies. It is no secret that African societies are constantly in conflict because of their tribal and ethnic composition. These conflicts are caused by competition over resources, rivalry for political power, the use of religion for political ends, instrumentalisation of ethnicity in the pursuit of power, interference with ethnic identity and recurring border conflicts among others.

Rwanda, Burundi, Congo, Uganda, Somalia, Liberia, Kenya, Sudan and many other African countries are case studies in examining how fighting over power, wealth, and identity turned into human rights disasters. Relatedly, in Southern Sudan, more than two million people were reported to have lost their lives and another four million were forced to leave their homeland either to the North or to take refuge during the 21-year protracted war before the signing of the CPA in 2005. A similar number of people were reported in Darfur as Internally Displaced Persons (IDPs) and refugees.

The Dinka Malual people were victims in the South-North conflict due to their proximity to the North which was fighting the South. Their wealth and children were reportedly taken to the North and many reports by human rights' groups state that these children were still working as cheap labourers or in bondage in Northern Sudan by the time this study was conducted. This situation still prevails in Northern Bahr el Ghazal and other areas bordering the North like Abyei, Twic, and Bentiu in Western Upper Nile.

The author was inspired, as a descendant of this area, to undertake the study and the information used in this book was either witnessed first-hand or narrated by relatives who have been victims of the wars since the 16th century to date.

The author's great grandfather, Wol Reec Lual (Wol Arumjok), who lived from approximately 1802-1872, was forced by the situation to take up arms and became a warlord against Riziegat and Misseriya tribes. His mother was later abducted with twin daughters in their home area at Matuoc village in Northern Bahr el Ghazal. It is believed that similar atrocities were committed against the Riziegat people of Darfur and to date generations from the two tribes face similar challenges. The war should not continue forever. It must stop so that the two communities can enjoy peace and stability in the area.

Another factor that motivated the author to undertake this research was his career as a peacemaker and conflict resolution activist in the Peace Advisory, at the Presidential Palace in Sudan. He has the conviction that as a peacemaker, he should start from home using available data to propose means of solving local conflicts.

His research findings assume that instability in the borders or "contact/transition areas" (as the areas are known) will create disunity in Sudan. The unifying factor in this country is tranquility in the contact areas, not only between Dinka Malual and Riziegat but also through what is known to be the 1/1/1956 geographic boundaries of Sudan which separate the South from the North.

The study has benefited from many writers of anthropology, history, human rights, peace studies and conflict resolution, but the most viable contribution comes from Dr Francis Deng, a Sudanese scholar and legal anthropologist, then working with the UN in the field of IDPs. Dr Deng is an authority in the field of Dinka customs and identity. He also wrote about the Baggara and the Misseriya, particularly its leader Babo Nimir. His work contributed in the exposition of the Baggara's social thinking and behaviour.

Another wonderful piece of work in this field was done by Ahmed Abdalla Adam, who wrote a lot about all the tribes in Sudan including Dinka and Riziegat. Great work has also been done by John Wol (RIP) of the Sudanese Higher Appeal Court who later served as Chief Justice in the Government of Southern Sudan in Juba. Mr. Wol managed to integrate and explain different aspects of Dinka life in his book "*Dinka Customary Law.*" This work is not just a collection and analysis of materials as such, but goes further to provide a comprehensive comparison and contrast between Dinka laws and those of western societies (Europe and USA) on one hand, and the Islamic laws on the other. This is where his work becomes relevant to the study. This book facilitates the understanding of Dinka society and how they deal with life. By reading the book you discover that the matters of life in the Dinka society are systematic from birth to death.

Many writers have widely contributed to this field and these include; Captain J.M. Stubb, *Notes on Malual Section Khartoum Central Records Office, 1930.* Captain J.M Stubb was a District Administrator at Aweil town in the 1930s.

Abdalla Mohamed Adam's book; *"Political Organisation and Ideological Dimensions of SPLA/M,"* was a thesis for a Ph.D. in the Africa International University, Sudan. The book attempts to expose the SPLA/M ideologies, thinking, and organization.

In the field of history and conflict resolution, there are a lot of works in the area of Dinka Malual and Riziegat tribes. The most essential contributions are the work of Douglas Johnson, who contributes on peace issues in Sudan. In his book, *"The Root Causes of Sudan Civil War,"* he gives elaborate accounts on the historical background of the conflict from the time of the first civil war to the current conflict. Johnson was among those experts who wrote the Abyei Boundary Commission report (ABC) and he was asked by the Government of Southern Sudan (GOSS) to advise the South on the issues of the 1/1/1956 South-North boundary demarcation and he published his findings.

Late Professor Mohamed Omer Bashir wrote about the history of the first conflict in Sudan in his capacity as the Secretary of the 12-man committee Round Table Conference. His books, *"The Southern Sudan: Background to Conflict,"* *"The Southern Sudan from Conflict to Peace,"* and *"Southern Sudan: Regionalism and Religion,"* greatly contributed in explaining the historical background of the conflict between the North and the South. He provided all the attempts the central governments made to solve the conflict in Southern Sudan.

Jok Madut Jok wrote about the war and slavery in Sudan. His book; *"War and Slavery in Sudan"* was a result of extensive interviews with victims of slavery/abduction in Northern Bahr el Ghazal previously (before signing the CPA in 2005) SPLA/M held areas.

The only shortfall in his work was that it represents one view and neglects the other opinions. Nonetheless, there are issues which arose that deserve special consideration.

There were great contributions from many peace researchers,

especially those who wrote about human rights, ethnicity, tribalism, and democracy in Africa. These include; Alexis Rawlinson, Micheal Klare, and Marina Ottaway.

There were considerable contributions from some Islamic ideology writers like Ali Issa Abdulrahman, the author of a book titled "*Sudanese Islamic Movement: From the Organisation to the State 1949-2000*," al-Nazier Salah; "*The Constitutional Rights for Religious Minorities in the Islamic State: With Concentration on Sudan*," Hassan Ali al Sahuori "*Fundamentals of the Political Participation*," and many others.

Work done by two Sudanese scholars and human rights activists, Suliman Ali Baldo and Ushari Ahmed Mahmoud, "*Human Rights Violation in the Sudan 1987: The Daien Massacre: Slavery in the Sudan*" remains as the birth of modern human rights abuses ex- position in the history of modern Sudan. Similar work was done by Bona Malual when he was a chief editor of the *Sudan Times*, the only Sudanese English newspaper in the 1980s.

The study benefited from the work of CEAWC in gathering the information, documentation and reunification of abducted persons done by the Chairman of CEAWC, Ahmed al Mufti.

The reports presented by various rapporteurs on human rights in Sudan explained in detail the situation of human rights in the country with special attention to the periods from 1990 to 2005. The work of David Hoile, the Chairperson of the European-Sudanese Public Relations Council stood as another opinion in the case of slavery/abduction in Sudan defending the Government of Sudan against world media and press attacks on the issue of slavery.

Mr. Hoile was misunderstood and considered to be working with the Sudan government and his publications in this regard were assumed to be financed by Khartoum.

Good work has been done by many writers in the field of native administration in Sudan as an institution that faced problems for people at grass-root levels, including the work of Gaafar Mohamed Ali Bakheit "*Native Administration in the Sudan and its Significance to Africa in: Yousif Fadul Hassan, (ed.), Sudan in Africa 1985*."

This study is strongly based on the dominant attention that human rights abuse in Sudan acquired through international press since the 1990s. *The New Yorker, The Los Angeles Times, The Washington Post, The Irish Times, The Washington Times,* and *The Independent on Sunday;* to mention but a few, played leading roles in highlighting human rights abuse in Sudan.

It is also important at this stage to mention the contribution of the SPLM's Manifesto of 1983 (amended in 2008 and 2017) in analyzing the future of the country and the South-North relations.

The study mostly depends on opinions, and views of experts in the area. Among those interviewed were Major General Albino Akol Akol; former Anya Nya One officer, ex-governor of Bahr el Ghazal and later Minister in the Government of Southern Sudan (GOSS): Philip Geng Nyuol; former Minister in Northern Bahr el Ghazal State: James Aguer Alec; Chairperson of the Dinka Committee working with CEAWC in the field of slavery/abduction and member of the National Assembly: Chief Abdel Bagi Akol Agany from Northern Bahr el Gahzal, Ustaz Mohamed Issa; the former Chairperson of the Consultative Council of Riziegat tribe in Khartoum: Dr. Ahmed al Mufti; the former Chairperson of CEAWC and Director General of Khartoum Center For Human Rights: Adam Mohamed Hamid of Riziegat Consultative Council and many other people including students, youths, women and intellectuals in the area.

The study also benefited from the papers presented in the conflict resolution conferences, seminars, the work of the International Eminent Person Group (IEPG) in Sudan plus the ideas presented by the team led by Senator John Danforth the former U.S. President Special Envoy on Peace to Sudan, together with the International Crisis Group (ICG) on Sudan in 2000 in a booklet titled *"God, Oil and the Government."*

The study also conducted thorough investigations on the topic through a questionnaire presented to the two communities of Dinka Malual of Northern Bahr el Ghazal and Riziegat of Southern Darfur. This questionnaire was very instrumental in exposing opinions of the two communities on the issues raised in the study.

The study used the two words slavery and abduction simultaneously because the concerned parties and different organisations working in the field of human rights and international law have failed to agree on what was taking place in Sudan; was it slavery or abduction? The two terminologies are therefore used concurrently. However, the important thing is not the name of the phenomenon but the situation under which the victim lives.

Whatever the jargon, the situation needs careful treatment from all despite our awareness of the legal differences between the two terminologies (slavery/abduction) in international law. More research on this field remains viable.

# CHAPTER 1

## 1.1 Dinka Malual And Riziegat: The People And The Land

The setup of the two tribes and their administration are important contributors to the issues of tribal relations between Dinka Malual and Riziegat.

It is widely believed that the geographical setup of the land occupied by the Dinka Malual and Riziegat tribes has been and still remains the main source of conflict between the two tribes. The people in this area compete over the scarce resources of grazing, water and fishing grounds.

## 1.1.1 Dinka Malual: Geology, Topography and Soils

Dinka land is generally characterised by a variety of soils. The soil in the Northern parts bordering with the Riziegat land is clay, with under soils existing in most cases. It is rare to find thick trees, which guarantees movement towards the River Kiir with cattle, without fear of wild animals. At the river Dinka meet with Riziegat during the summer from February to April every year. When they reach the river, they find the Riziegat people, with their cattle, have been on the ground there since the month of January. The Dinka begin to leave the area in early April to go to their houses for cultivation. Meanwhile, the Riziegat remain in the area and sometimes move southwards until June when the rains intensify.

In the south, the land is characterised by top soils which make it possible to cultivate during the rainy season. In the west, there are small hills. However, the east of the Malual Dinka tribal area is occupied by many Toucs.[1] These make some members of the tribe move into that part during the summer for pasture instead of going into the north. However, they usually fear wild animals that especially roam in the southern part of the area. Dinka Malual are located at latitude 10° - 85° north and longitude 26.5° - 28° east in Sudan.

The word Dinka is not in their language. What they say is Monyjang which means "Master of Nations." The word Dinka is very recent in their history; it dates back to the time of the Turko-Egyptian era in Sudan. It was said that the colonial administrators found a Monyjang man around the White Nile, whose name was Deng Kak and mispronounced his name as Dinka. This mispronounced name was later applied to every "Monyjang" or "Jeing." However, there is still considerable debate, whether the story is true or not.

The word Jeing or Mongjang should have been used instead, but for the purpose of this study the word Dinka is conventionally applicable. Dinka is generally divided into two groups, Kuey (Black Eagle) and Lueth (White Eagle).

The Kuey occupy territories of Tonj, Gogrial, and Aweil. The people of this group are collectively known as Riak. Lueth on the other hand are found in Rumbek, Yirol, Sowbat, Bor, Panarang, Maluoth, Renk, and Abyei. Though the Lueth are widely spread in Bahr el Ghazal and Upper Nile, they represent only 40 percent of the entire Dinka population in the country.

As earlier mentioned, this study focuses more on the Riak who migrated from Gogrial to Aweil, though the exact time of this migration is not known. Some say, it was during the 13th century and some say during the 14th century. The Dinka Malual inhabited territories which belonged to Chad and Furgi tribes. Dinka Malual called them Jur Luel, (red strangers). This terminology indicates that there were many strangers, but with different colours. One of these strangers according

---

1       Touc, means wetland where cattle are grazed according to Dinka language.

to Dinka Malual are the Jur Chol, (Black strangers) who inhabit the western part of Northern Bahr el Ghazal.

Resettlement wars waged between Chad and Furgi tribes on one side and Dinka Malual on the other side resulted in confiscation of lands and cattle. The Chad and Furgi tribes were forced to move westwards until some entered Chad and others settled at Raja and the areas around it. At Raja, because of ecological factors, these tribes abandoned the cattle and became agrarian.

In the new settlement, the Dinka Malual organized themselves around the two rivers; Alok River in the South, and Kiir River in the north where River Lol divided the area into two parts the western bank and eastern bank indicating Pajok and Paliupiny respectively. During ceremonial processions at the new settlement, a big red bull (Malual) was killed as thanksgiving to the God, Laaj Nhalic. They asked their God of Garang Abuk to save them, their families and their animals in the newly discovered land. Some of them, who were settled on the west bank of the Lol River, were renamed after their spiritual leader Akot Tong and they became Malual Akot Tong. Those on the other side of the river were renamed after their spiritual leader Aturjong Giernyaag, to become Malual Giernyaag.[2] However, the name Pajok brings these two sections together.

After a while, further divisions took place, and those on the west bank of the Lol River were divided into Paliuping and Paliet, while those on the east bank divided into Malual Giernyaag and Abiem and became separate sections, though maintaining the same relations and contacts.

During Anglo-Egyptian Condominium rule, the Dinka Malual communities were further divided into native administrative units as follows:

Gomjuer chieftainship of Chief Akot Autiak was at Nyamlel. Chamil chieftainship of Chief Kuac Kuac was at Wodum. Ajwet of Chief Diing Akol at Madueny. Akwak Ayat of Chief Lual Dau was at Marialbaai. Ajak of chief Wek Ateny at Malekalel. Kongder area of Chief Dut Jok at Romaluel. Boonchaai of Chief Araith Kon at Taralait.

---

2       Chief A/ Bagi Akol Agany of Dinka Malual community, an interview, Khartoum, April 2004.

The east bank was further divided into the Korok area of the Chief Yor Wal at Wathok but later, divided into two chieftainships. Chief Diing Majok branched away and stationed at Koyom.

Atokthou of Chief Diing Wol at Majok. Diluit of Chief Deng Geng was at Mayom Adhel. Pawac Weng of Chief Anyuon Aturjong at Gogmachar. Makem area of Chief Ngang Jongkor branched away and stationed at Kuc Anyduk-dit. Majak Baai area of Chief Daungbar Anei at Majak Amandit. Diluit Kuc Ngor of Chief Kuc Ngor at Ayaii Dheb.

Wundiing of Chief Ngong Gau at Riengmal. Ajoungthii of Chief Tong Tong at Mareng. Apouth of Chief Makuac Kuol at Wanyjok. Later on Wun Anei of Chief Anei Angok Wein branched away at Malualkon. Ajoungdit of Chief Yor Deng at Madhol. Luo of Chief Aguer Geng at Ajerraik. Later other areas were further divided into small chieftainships[3] The administrative relationship between these chiefs was horizontal and the colonial administrator was their head, as illustrated in Figure (1.1) opposite.

## 1.1.2 Climate

The annual rainfall range is very long, covering April to November and the average rainfall ranges from 800 to 1500 mm. Summer is characterized by high temperatures, especially in the months of Febuary, March and April which make it possible to rain early in April. December and January are very cold winter months characterized by the end of the rains.

## 1.1.3 Vegetation

Dinka land has long tall grasses and huge trees, including savanna timbers like mahogany and teak. Usually, there are wild animals in the southern part of the area which attract the Baggara tribesmen who come to hunt in the area. Besides pastoral activities, Dinka practice agriculture; they cultivate crops like sorghum (dura), sesame, groundnuts, and many other vegetables.

---

3  J.M. Stubb, (Captain), Notes on Malual Section, Khartoum, Central Record Office, 1930.

*Figure (1.1) The Administrative Relationship Between District Commissioner and Dinka Malual Chiefs*

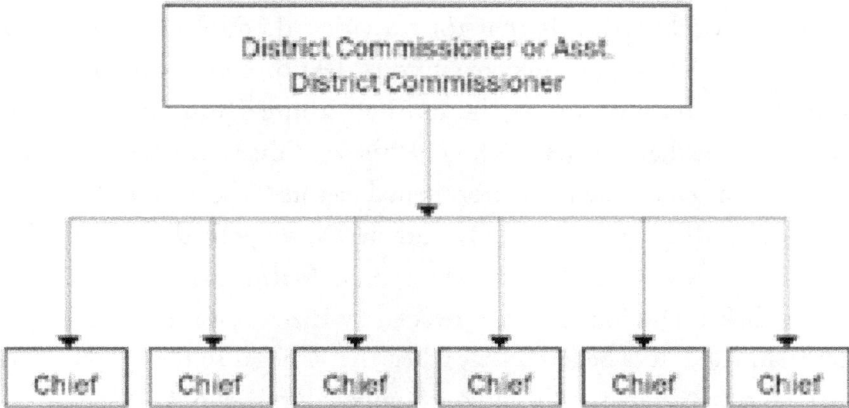

*Source: Khartoum Central Records Office, Khartoum*

## 1.1.4 Drainage System and Water Sources

Apart from rainfall, there are many rivers and streams in Dinka land which are considered the main sources of water. In the north is the Kiir River shared with Baggara. In the center is the Lol River which divides the area between west and east. In the east, are three rivers, Akuem, Wakabiel and Wardit. In the south, there are the Koum and Alok rivers whereas the Makadhek and Shel are found in the west coming from Central Africa. There are many toucs occupying different areas that are considered the source of water for animals in the dry seasons.

## 1.2 Riziegat: The Land and the People

The area occupied by Riziegat on the Sudan map is between latitude 12° - 100° and longitude 26° - 28°. The Riziegat are one of the Arab tribes that entered Sudan from Morocco through Chad into Darfur during the collapse of the Arab empire in Andulus (Spain) in the 14th century. Some writers say they entered Sudan through Egypt and the Red Sea because there is a section of Riziegat in Gina Province in Egypt.

There are two versions of the story about their movement to Darfur.

The first was that the whole Riziegat tribe entered into Northern Darfur, but the Baggara migrated to the south because of herding. Those who herd camels, (Aballa), remained in Northern Darfur.

The second version is that they divided themselves before they entered into Sudan. The first group took the northern route to Darfur and the second group took the southern route. Those in the north became camel herders, (Aballa), while those of the south became cattle herders (Baggara), due to environmental factors.[4] The area of the study is the south Riziegat (Baggara) in Southern Darfur; who share the border with Dinka Malual at the Kiir River (Bahr Arab). Like Dinka Malual before their migration, the area invaded by Riziegat was inhabited by a Chadian tribe. It is believed that when the Riziegat settled in the area, they increased dramatically and outnumbered indigenous people in the area. Consequently, they waged war against them who were defeated and forced to enter Central Africa, Chad, and Western Bahr el Ghazal.

The word Riziegat originated from Ziriag the ancestor of the tribe, and they are divided into three sections, and a fourth section is said to be that of Hiriag, the younger brother of Ziriag. The first section is al Nawaba, their town was Adhan Humar, now changed to al Firdos. The second section is Mahameed; their main town was Gimelia, and changed to Asallia. The last one is Mahiria their main towns are Abu Jabir and Abu Matarik.

This section is further divided into two sub-sections: Um Dhaia and Um Ahmed. The Um Dhaia section shared a border, particularly with Dinka Malual. Their town, Abu Matarik, is the nearest town to the Northern Bahr el Ghazal. It was also said that the majority of people from Um Dhaia and Um Ahmed are pro-Dinka or are of Dinka Malual origin.

Although there were serious struggles for leadership of the Riziegat tribe over a long period, the family of Midibo managed to maintain the Nizara. The tribal administration was based on a centralized system unlike that of the Dinka.

---

4    Interview with Mohamed Issa of Riziegat Consultative Council, Khartoum, May 2004.

Under Nazir were the Omdas. The most prominent Omdas were: Salam Abu Kalm of Um Ahmed, Ahmed Buram of Mahmeed, Yahia Musa of Um Dhaia, and Yagoub Ahmed of al Ghadinia and Khalid Mohamed Nour. There were other Omdas from different tribes but considered to be part of the Riziegat community like, Issa el Nur of Borigat, Abdel Rahman Wadodo and Adam Sherif Kilikli, both of Mahalla.[5]

*Figure 1. 2: Tribal Administration of Riziegat*

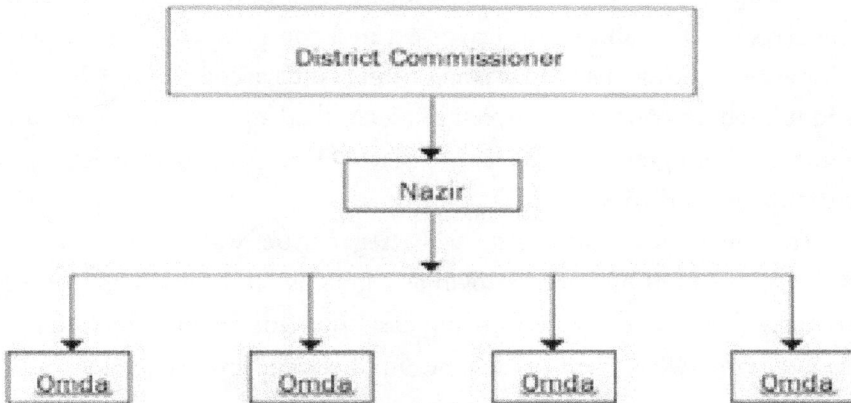

*Source: Khartoum Central Records Office, Khartoum.*

## 1.2.1 Geology, Topography and Soils

Riziegat land has three different environmental zones, each with its own features. The fourth is said to be in the Dinka land. It is necessary to indicate these four zones:

The first zone is called Goz (an Arab word meaning semi-desert); it is mostly an aeolian sandy soil sheet and dune complex with alluvial transition zones and valley complexes. Dominant soils are red, yellowish red and loamy sands. These features of the environment occupy larger parts of the area from the east to the west through the major cities. Also, this feature of environment is found in the North to the South

---

5    Mohamed Issa of the Riziegat Consultative Council An interview , Khartoum, May 200.

from al Fashir into Riziegat land in South Darfur up to al Ragab village in the South.

The second zone is called al Ragaba area; it begins where the first zone ends in the south and continues towards the Kiir River (Bahr Arab). The soil here is semi-clay mixed with sand. It is an alluvial levee and black swamp complex. Soils are dominantly calcareous, dark-coloured, silty clay loams, and clay. The cities which are found in this area are al Ragab Buno, al Quez, and Umm Koroba.

The third zone is called al Bahr area. It is an alluvial sand wash plain with basins, dunes and levee complexes. Soils range from sands to cracking clays with medium and heavy-textured compact soils dominance. This area was known as dry season grazing lands according to Riziegat, and it has been contested between Dinka Malual and Riziegat. There are short trees and grasses from place to place. Here, people of the Riziegat tribe spend most time with their cattle.

The fourth zone, according to Riziegat tribe, was called "al Boriya." This area has not been known as a grazing land for Riziegat until recently. They used it as a hunting area, but due to environ- mental degradation, the Riziegat people began to use the area as grazing land.

### 1.2.2 Climate

Here, the main annual rainfall ranges between 800 mm to 300 mm from south to north. The rainfall is confined to the five months of June, July, August, September and October.

### 1.2.3 Vegetation

The vegetation in Riziegat lands complies with the nature of the environment and drainage system. The trees are scattered from place to place in the northern parts of the area while in the south there are short trees and grasses especially towards the Kiir River (Bahr Arab). The trees found here are of the savanna type and the main crops cultivated by Riziegat tribe are millet, sorghum, sesame, groundnuts, and, hibiscus (karkadi).

## 1.2.4 Drainage System and Water Sources

Rainfall and hand-dug wells are the main sources of water supply in the area. Water is obtained from boreholes, hand-dug wells, excavated reservoirs, and seasonal water courses are called "khors" by the Arab, (meaning pool).

However, the khors and pools are the main sources of water supply during the rainy season. In addition, there are some "al Ragab" (under soils) alongside the Kiir River (Bahr Arab).

## 1.3 Conclusion

"Indeed, stock ownership is a determinant of nomadism, for it imposes a certain environment than a nomadic existence."[6] In other words, nomadism is not one's choice but dictated by environment. This statement is a real description of the situation in Baggara land, probably because Dinkas are partially sedentary tribes; their movements are sometimes for entertainment. Young people need to be away from the family for some time. In the case of Baggara actually, nomadic movement is a situation where a person is following the animals instead of animals following them.

It is a reverse situation for the case of Dinka. In other words, animals may not let the owner settle unless the sources of water and grazing are made available. It is a challenge facing governments in Darfur and Kordofan regions calling for an immediate addressing of the situation.

The disorganized movements of animals bring conflicts among cattle owners and between the cattle owners and the farmers, sometimes escalating into a tribal conflict. Elites of both tribes have exploited the situation for political ends, forming a political agenda that runs out of the control of tribal leadership. This is the exact situation in the Darfur region of Sudan currently.

In the author's unpublished dissertation for Master of Arts in Peace and Development, he concluded that the real cause of the problem between Dinka Malual and Riziegat tribes has been the competition

---

6       Ahmed, Abdel Gaffar Mohamed(ed) Management of crises in the Sudan, 1989,pp. 65.

over natural resources of water and land for grazing, fishing, and hunting. But the third party element escalates it into a political issue by introducing other causes of the conflict like the militarisation of tribes against each other as a way of defending their interests in the central government.

The time the Riziegat spend in Dinka land is much more than what they spend in their land. This usually causes a lot of problems in the absence of responsible authorities to organize these movements. It may be recalled that the Riziegat nomads move between North Darfur and Northern Bhar el Ghazal throughout the year.[7]

The tribe spends seven months in Northern Bahr el Ghazal from December to June. Likewise, Dinka Malual crosses the River during the rainy seasons to north of Kiir (Bahr Arab). These movements were managed by tribal administration.[8]

This book explores the role of the tribal administration of the Dinka Malual and Reizegat in managing the relations between the two tribes is discussed in Chapter Three.

---

7        Dhieu Mathok Diing Wol, Dinka Malual-Riziegat Relations: The Role of Third Party (unpublished M. A. Thesis), University of Juba, Khartoum, 2003, pp. 167-170.

8        Abdel Ghaffar M. Ahmed (edit , Management of Crises in the Suda , 1989, pp. 65 op cit.

# CHAPTER 2

## 2.1 Evolution of the Dinka Malual-Riziegat Tribal Relations

The known history of Dinka Malual and Riziegat tribal relations dates back to the period of the first kingdom of Fur, in Darfur, when Riziegat tribes settled in their current locations. Since that time, their relations with the Dinka in various aspects of life have been unstable. During the period of the kingdom of Fur, no systematic relationship between Dinka Malual and Riziegat existed, but the kingdom assumed a theoretical attachment of Bahr el Ghazal to its authority.

Dinka communities were not organized in an administrative manner but there were collective efforts to face whatever confronted them led by spiritual leaders. It was said that some Darfur tribes that migrated to Western Bahr el Ghazal practiced Arab and Islamic customs but the Dinka Malual community, although nearer to Darfur was not affected by this culture being practiced in the western part of Bahr el Ghazal (Reja and surrounding areas).[9]

During Turko-Egyptian rule (1821-1885) Bahr el Ghazal was governed as part of Darfur under one governor for the first time. The administration of Turko-Egyptian period started in the South in 1869, but Bahr el Ghazal and Darfur were not part of this administration until 1874 when al Zubier Pasha became the governor of the two provinces.

---

9      Abdel Ghaffar M. Ahmed, Management of Crises in the Sudan, 1989, pp. 65, op cit.

During this period, Arabic language became officially secularised in the South as a medium of communication, although not given priority by the colonial authorities because the new government's concern was on economic rather than social or cultural aspects.

In this period, the role of Dinka Malulal-Riziegat relations was significant as the headquarters of the new administration was based at Deim al Zubier near Raja. The little cooperation between al Zubier with the Dinka leader called Dengdit "Autiak Majok," based at Chak Chak near Nyanlath, and later relocated to Nymelel, was said to be involved in the slave trade and bilateral cooperation between the two political entities.[10]

When the Mahdist Government assumed power (1885-1899), it was less concerned with the South because its policies were more focused on the Middle East. For this reason, the administration in the South was very weak. Mahdi was supported by tribes with Islamic ideology, particularly in the Upper Nile and Bahr el Ghazal.[11]

The support for Mahdi by Dinka Malual was faced with many difficulties, among them; Islam was unpopular in Dinka Malual areas, and the dependency of Mahdi on Riziegat leaders to preach Mahdism in the Malual area was not welcomed because it appeared as a continuation of the dispute between the two tribes. Some personalities who were prominent in the conflict were made to lead the campaign for recruitment into the Mahdist army in Northern Bahr el Ghazal.

It was said that Mahdi sent two battalions to the Malual areas, the first to the West and the second to the East (Malual and Abiem respectively). The forces to the West via Path, Gomjewer, Makem, Korok, and Atokthou were led by Abu Marum. While those to the East via Abiem, Twic, Ngok Dinka were led by Osman. Both of them were Riziegat commanders in the Mahdist movement.

The mission of these two battalions was recruitment, but due to the fact that the leadership was from the known enemy, the West Malual

---

10     Douglas Johnson, The Root Causes of Sudan's Civil Wars, 2002.

11     An interview with chief A/Bagi Akol of Dinka Malual, April 2004.

Dinka misunderstood the mission and confronted Abu Marum at Wathok in the Korok area, killed him and destroyed his forces. Among Dinka Malual prominent leaders who participated in this war were Wol Reec Lual (Wol Aromjok), Wal Acien Anei (Wal Dorjok), and others.

The Eastern mission managed to obtain its objectives successfully, and most of the leaders from this part of the Malual Dinka area gave their support to and recognition of the Mahdist movement. They joined the forces on their way to Kadir where Mahdi was stationed.

They were brainwashed and told to preach Mahdism in their land and within their communities. They became Muslims though on returning to their areas some abandoned the Islam. Among the leaders who continued with Islam as their religion were Chief Arop Boing and Chief Manwher Rahan. Chief Aguer Geng abandoned the idea when he returned home. It can be recalled that Islam is more concentrated in the eastern part of Dinka Malual area than in any other area in Northern Bhar el Ghazal.

During the Madhist period, the relations between the two tribes were worsened by continuous raids from both sides. The fighting over pastoral resources, water, and fishing in the Kiir/Bahr Arab increased. The war took on different dimensions by adding new elements, such as abducting children and women. The intention was something less than slavery; it was a matter of treating those war victims in such a way that they would become part of their new community.

When a captive left the battle area and reached the enemy territory, he/she felt quite secure. For Dinkas, ladies were treated as daughters and sisters. It was prohibited to marry a girl or woman captured by your immediate family or clan. Men automatically became members of that community. They got married and were treated as part of the family. At Dar Riziegat, war victims and those captured reaching their area were considered as family members; nobody was allowed to assault them or even point them out, otherwise he/ she faced legal measures from the tribal leadership.

A report by the Assistant District Commissioner, Baggara states:

"A Riziegat whose father was a Dinka was fined for assault of a Dinka."[12] About slaves the report further states:"It might be true that cases of Dinka slaves in Arab hands and vice versa would be the most difficult to deal with. In reality, they are the easiest of all because both tribes realize that it is useless to claim the return of a relative long in Arab hands as the slave will not agree to return to his own people. It is the same with Arabs in Dinka hands. They become Arabicized and Dinkaized after a few years."

In Anglo-Egyptian Condominium rule (1899-1955), the colonial reconquest of the Sudan took different dimensions in the North and the South. In the North there was a fairly quick transition from military occupation to civil administration before World War I.

British civilian officials replaced all military governors in the Northern provinces, and police took over responsibilities for rural security from the army. There was recruitment of northerners in the police and army units.

It was not the case in the South. The civil secretary, focusing on "Southern Policy" in 1930, declared that the administration of the South was to be developed along "African" rather than "Arab" lines and that the Southern Sudan might ultimately lie with countries of British East African rather than with the Middle East.[13] In the field of native administration, the British administrators gave powers to those families who had held authority under Turko-Egyptian rule. The practice was regularised and such chiefs were given specific judicial and administrative powers. There was a much later assimilation of indigenous structures into administration in the South than in the North. This was mainly because British administrators could not find the same range of executive authority in the South as they had in their northern Sheikhs and Omdas, but in only few kingdoms such as the Shilluk and Azande.

Two different patterns of administration were developed within the

---

12    A/District commissioner Baggara Report to Governor of Darfur, Khartoum Central Records Office, 1926.

13    Ibid.

South, one for the pastoralists, who were found mainly in the central clay plains in the Upper Nile and Bahr el Ghazal, and another for the sedentary agricultural communities found in what is now Equatoria and on the iron stone plateau of Bahr el Ghazal. In the plains, people were accessible only during the dry season, making the Colonial Administration think about annexing parts of vast areas, that were difficult to be managed, to the nearest administrative areas and this is how Abyei area of Ngok Dinka of Bahr el Ghazal became part of Kordofan in 1905.[14] Courts were mobile and dealt mainly with cattle cases and were empowered to collect fines and taxes. The office of a paramount chief with strong executive authority did not exist. The courts and hierarchies of the southerners in most regions were accessible to administrators most of the year.[15]

The Anglo-Egyptian era was marked by regular contacts and continuous meetings annually between the two tribes. The study examines some of these agreements and meetings.

## 2.2 Savile Burges-Watson Agreement, 1918

This agreement was made by the British administrators in both Bahr el Ghazal and Darfur provinces. Its purpose was to allow Riziegat cattle grazing at 40 miles south of the Kiir River (Bahr Arab) which was almost beyond 30 percent of the Malual Dinka area.

The agreement was condemned and rejected by the Dinka Malual tribal leadership, as it was considered an eviction from their land for Riziegat. The spiritual leader Araithdit (Bol Yel) revolted in 1921 in protest to the terms of the agreement and collection of fines and taxes in Dinka Malual land. He was arrested in 1923 and sent to prison in Port Sudan; he was released in 1928.

---

14    Douglas Johnson, The Root Causes of Sudan's Civil Wars, 2002.

15    Ibid.

## 2.3 Munro-Wheatley Agreement, 1924:

This agreement was a modification of the Savile Burges Watson Agreement of 1918. The meeting took place at Safaha on April 22, 1924. It was attended by the Governors of Bahr el Ghazal and Darfur Provinces besides the District Commissioners of Northern District, Western District, Bahr el Ghazal Province, the District Commissioner of Baggara, and Darfur District.[16]

It was also attended by tribal leaders from Riziegat; Nazir Ibrahim Musa, Omda Yahia Musa, and Amir el Mominin Omda Gawad Abu Khelik; Omda Abdullahi Abul Ghasim, W Omda Fadlalla Bombome, W Omda Mohamed el Nur Wad Hamid, Sheikh Beshir Abdullahi, Sheikh Younis Damass, Sheikh Mohamed Dom Fellati, and Sheikh Kheir el Nur. From the Dinka Malual side, the meeting was attended by Chief Autiak Akot, Chief Lual Dau Marac, Chief Anyuon Aturjong, Chief Diing Wol, Chief Agany Amash, Chief Tong Bek Gout, Chief Lual Habishe.[17]

## 2.4 Safaha Meeting, March 24, 1935:

This meeting was attended by C.B.E. Governor of Darfur Province, P. Lupleson, Governor of Bahr el Ghazal Province, Capt. J.M. Stubbs, D.C. Northern District Bahr el Ghazal, Lu. F. Crawford, D.C. Southern District, Darfur Province, E.G. Nightingale A/DC. Baggara, Darfur Province.

The meeting was convened with the aim of finding means to improve relations between Riziegat and Malual Dinka on the Kiir (Bahr Arab) grazing grounds after a series of violent attacks in the area. This meeting was significant because of the dissatisfaction of Malual Dinka with the M. W. Agreement of 1924.

The meeting was preceded by many correspondences between the incumbent British administration in Bahr el Ghazal, Darfur

---

16    Civil Secretary Files Khartoum Central Records Office, 1924, pp. 111.

17    The author tried to trace descendants of the last three chiefs within Dinka Malual but couldn't manage. Maybe their names were written wrongly.

and Equatoria with the Civil Secretary. The main documents which dominated discussion in this meeting were the proposals presented by Captain J.M. Stubbs of Northern Bahr el Ghazal District, 1930 to the Governor of Bahr el Ghazal who reported the issue to the Civil Secretary.

In his proposal were some alterations to the M.W. Agreement to accommodate certain weaknesses that emerged during implementation. These alterations were not accepted by the Civil Secretary because the issue of accommodating two previously excluded sections of Malual Dinka (Wun Anei and Wun Makuac) was instructed by him.

The meeting considered the ongoing situation and the difficulties that arose which included:

Inability on the part of the Malual Dinka to appreciate the ruling of M. W. Agreement that the boundary of Dar Riziegat lay 14 miles South of the river. They assumed that their boundary was North of the river and not the South bank.

The undoubted increase in the number of Malual's cattle using the South bank for grazing.

The Malual adverse contention - which the Riziegat denied that the Arab's habit of camping and grazing on the South bank had greatly increased since 1924.

The idea of Malual's increase was disputed by the District Commissioner of the Northern District who presented a comparative table in 1935 showing areas (Wot) allowed grazing by the Munro Wheatley (M.W.) Agreement in 1924 and those actually grazed at the time, 1935.

### Table 2.1: Areas Allowed for Grazing by the Munro-Wheatley (M.W.) Agreement, l924

| 1924 | 1935 |
|---|---|
| Path + Fajok (One Section) | Path + Fajok (One Section) |
| Makem | Makem |
| Dulit | Dulit |
| Korok | Korok |
| Athoukthuo | Athoukthuo |
| 1/2 Wun Anai | Wun Anai (Whole Section) |
| 1/2 Wun Makuac | Wun Makuac (Whole Section) |
| MajakBai | - - - - - - - - - - - |
| Part of Gomjuer | - - - - - - - - - - |

*Source: Civil Secretary Files, 1924*

Note: One effect of the agreement was the exclusion of a portion of Wun Anai and Wun Makuac Sections.

In the course of negotiations, three methods of approach were explored:

Territorial division of the South bank into Arab and common/ Arabs and Malual grazing area.

Allotment of a specified period at the beginning of each season during which the Arabs would have the sole right of grazing in the whole area, on the understanding that, on its expiration, they would withdraw entirely to the North bank and leave the Malual in sole enjoyment of the South bank's grazing for the remainder of the dry season.

A modification of (1) and (2) including the reservation of certain specified areas for Arab grazing and the recognition of the common areas of certain sites as customary Malual camping grounds.

It was felt that both methods (1) and (2), by separating Arabs and Malual into water-tight compartments, perhaps afforded a greater prospect of relief to present problems. Method (3) then was eventually adapted.

On March 29, 1935, the resolutions were presented to the Meglis.[18] which was a form of council of tribal leadership composed of Malual and Rezeigat, besides British officials. There were representatives from both of the two tribes as shown in Table (2-2) below:

*Table 2-2: Representatives of the Tribes in March, 1935.*

| Dinka Chiefs | Rezeigat Chief |
| --- | --- |
| Anyoun Atorjong | Nazir: Ibrahim Musa |
| Nyang Jongkor | Sheikh Mahmud Musa |
| Nyoul Deng | Omda: Yahia Musa. |
| Acien Yor | Omda: Abdullahi Hamdan. |
| Diing Majok | Omda: Fadlal Bamboon |
| Diing Wol | Omda: Amir el Mumin. |
| Agany Adhyiyg | Omda:Abdullahi Abu El Gasim |
| Akuei Ajou | Omda: Jawadi Abu Likeilik |
|  | Sheikh:Awafi Sherif Ed Din. |

*Source: Civil Secretary Files 1924*

Prior to the general Meglis, the Governor of Bahr el Ghazal briefed the Dinka chiefs and explained to them, for the first time, the terms of the agreement imposed on them. Since that time in 1924, the area has been laid down as Riziegat grazing land.

The chiefs expressed considerable dissatisfaction with this and the terms of the agreement, though at the same time, affirming their readiness to obey government orders by allowing Riziegat cattle to pasture

---

18    An Arab word meaning council.

in their areas. Chief Anyuon Aturjong declined to attend the general Meglis, until asked by the Governor.

After the reading of the agreement, the Dinka chiefs were given the opportunity to express their views. The gist of their remarks was totally dissatisfaction with the agreement and general situation in the area.

## 2.5 Wunrog Meeting, February, 1935

Wunrog is a town on the border between Twic, Ngok and Dinka Malual. The meeting was held for the purpose of solving the problems of native affairs as well as the possibility of solving the problem of the two Malual sections of Wun Anai and Wun Makuac who were denied the right of grazing in the 14 miles zones South of the River Kiir (Bahr Arab).

The meeting was attended by the D.Cs of Western Kordofan, Eastern and Northern Bahr el Ghazal, and all chiefs concerned. The grazing rights in the areas between the Allal and Kiir were defined and arrangements were made whereby certain Malual Wots would graze in the area. The main provisions of the agreement were as follows:

The Ngok have full grazing rights South of the Allal and Twic (of Eastern District) Bahr el Ghazal, North of the Kiir laws defined as the common grazing area of the Twic and the Ngok.

The Owen-Blackley agreement concerning Malual grazing was cancelled as uncooperative.

The Ngok and the Twic chiefs agreed to admit nine specified Wots into their common grazing area. The Malual Wots would remain on the western border of the grazing area (no later than December). Kuol Arob, Chief of the Ngok, and Mohweir Rahan Chief of Twic had met the chiefs of the Wots[19] concerned and arranged grazing areas.

Cases arising between Malual and Ngok or Malual and Twic were to be heard by the Ngok and Twic chiefs respectively, with the Malual chief concerned sitting with them.

Any Malual Wot who repeatedly proved troublesome would be excluded from the area by arrangement between the D.Cs.

---

19      Wot is a Dinka word meaning cattle camp.

The administrative question of intercourse between the tribes of the two provinces was also generally discussed (with the consent of the Governor of Kordofan) and tentative proposals subject to further discussion between the governors were arrived at. The tentative proposals were:

1. That the grazing permits to Arabs to visit Bahr el Ghazal should be delegated to Nazirs or relative native authorities. Until such proposals were discussed and ratified, such as permits were to be issued by the D.Cs, in person.

2. That permits for Dinkas would be issued by chiefs' courts for specific purposes.

3. Permits would not be granted for the cultivation season.

4. Intercourse except with Ngok was then forbidden.

5. Persons without permits would be returned whenever traced.

6. A convenient date before the cultivation season Dinkas straying would be rounded and sent back to cultivate (and Arabs also if they showed signs).

There were other less important meetings held annually at Safaha to review Malual-Riziegat interrelations and to try to solve some grievances arising out of river and grazing land. Among these meetings are:

## 2.6 Safaha Meeting on March 10, 1939

In this meeting there was the issue of Riziegat hunting within 14 miles South of Bahr el Arab. There was a thought from the British administrators on whether the limited area should be extended up to the Lol River, 35 miles North of Aweil, such that a practical boundary would be fixed for hunting instead of an imaginary one of 14 miles South of Kiir (Bahr Arab). This clearly showed the policy intention of colonial rule in the area.

## 2.7 Safaha Meeting on March 5th-6th, 1943

Another similarly important meeting was held at Safaha during the above-mentioned period. It was attended by British administrators at both sides of Dinka Malual and Riziegat areas. Among those present were Captain Stubbs, Mr. Balfour, Mr. Mitchell-Inne, and Mr. Wordworth.

In this meeting, the situation was reported to be improving. It was noted in the meeting that the date fixed for Arabs to cross the river - January 15th - proved rather too early. Furthermore, it was agreed that a combined patrol of the Dinka and their Wots should be undertaken at the time for the next year to prevent "cream-grazing" which was otherwise difficult to check. The area to be supervised was too small, extending from the Rigl el Bagheili (Kangabar to the Rigl el Sileim (Buraping), and that two men from each side would be enough. Other minor issues such as the shortage of grain in Dinka areas were also discussed.

## 2.8 Social and Cultural Relations

It was reported in Addis Ababa during the meetings of Dinka, Misseriya and Riziegat (DMR) dialogue in February 2004 that the positive interactions between these tribes existed before the introduction of colonial laws, and there were many ways in which communities were linked and intertwined.

They shared a similar lifestyle as agro-pastoralists and there were numerous cases of intermarriage. There was never any restriction on movement, and communities would settle in proximity to others. Exchange of visits of friendship used to occur, and neighbouring groups cooperated in catching criminals evading detection on either side. In more recent times, communities participated in cross- border peace councils to resolve conflicts and assist cross-border trading.

During the same meeting of the tribes in Addis Ababa, it was agreed that the DMR communities were seen to have been divided recently by the unchecked promotion of discrimination and exclusion.

Ethnic exclusion, racial discrimination and violence were promoted at various levels by the tribes. Often fostered by the spread of harmful rumours rather than peaceful co-existence, the relationships between the DMR communities became negatively influenced physical and verbal violence, political exploitation, provocation, incitement of violence, and encroachment of tribal territories by neighbours, lack of respect for human rights, intolerance and exploitation of religious beliefs. Cattle theft and looting, abduction and killing were also common.[20]

It can also be pointed out that the overall result of these factors and causes was that the previous historical good relations between the DMR had been seriously constrained, and there was little ability to coordinate and to create mutual interest. The prevalence of physical and emotional violence meant that there was little confidence between the DMR communities. Each community had suffered serious loss in its cultural heritage and customs, due to the breakdown of the inter-community relationships and their traditional leadership.

The contacts between the two tribes were very weak during the Condominium period. It can be recalled that the policy of Closed Districts played a big role in the isolation of the South from the Northern merchants.

It was very clear in the area inhabited by Arabized and Islamised tribes of Western District (Bahr el Ghazal, Raga). As a result, some of the tribes migrated to Darfur and some were brought to the area nearer to Wau by the British colonial administration. The policy tried to isolate Bahr el Ghazal from Darfur, Arab language and Arab dresses were forbidden. In Wau and Aweil towns, notions of importing goods were raised to discourage trading with Arab traders.

The only interaction was at the Kiir (Bahr Arab), but with negative results that involved fighting over water and fishing, kidnapping and abduction of children and women, looting of cattle, forced marriages which were sometimes reported to the courts after illegal intercourse.

There were many Riziegat ladies married to Dinka and bore children, among some notable leaders in Dinka Malual, but those wives were

---

20      Report of the DMR meetings in Addis Ababa, Ethiopia, 2004.

not married off by their biological fathers, they were either captured in a battle or abducted and adopted by new fathers who married them to other people. Young men captured in battles were not killed; they were integrated into the community as soon as they reached Dar Dinka.

On the other side, Riziegats by all means tried to assimilate Dinkas, who were captured in a battle in their society. They treated them well and gave them the option to choose the section they wanted to belong to. When they did, their protection then belonged to that section. In an interview, Mohamed Issa, Chairman of the Consultative Council for Riziegat, said: "It is a crime to point out a person of Dinka or other tribe origins in Riziegat community, any Reziegi, who does this is punishable. So, it is a crime even for me to mention in this interview the names of those families with Dinka origins."

Umm Ahmed section of Mahiria, inhabiting Abu Matharik, was reported to include some Dinka origin families. This has been significant in bringing peace to the area.

The author's great-grandmother was abducted with twin daughters and taken to the Riziegat homeland in the early 19th Century. They were never seen again, but it is believed they formed a family within the Riziegat tribe.

The positive aspect characterizing this conflict between the two tribes in the past was that the issue of religion was not considered as a part of the conflict in the area. Although British administrators tried to make it an issue together with other factors in the policy of closed districts in the South, no religious conflicts existed between the two tribes at the grassroots level during the Condominium rule.

Though there were cultural differences between the two tribes recognized by British administrators, it did not contribute to escalation of the conflict in the area. The religious conflict between the two communities started after independence of the country in 1956.

In his report in 1926 to the Governor of Darfur the A/D.C. of Baggara said: "Apart from that, being an Arab, he looks down on the Jnghe (Janang) as of a lower order of creation than himself and on a visibly lower plane of civilization, and I believe that this is the secret of another difficulty to be overcome in dealings between the tribes."

There was nothing mentioned about religious conflict between the two communities except the Arabism.

"These Dinkas have never been subdued by the Arabs when it comes to fighting, they gave as good as they got, and the recent history of their wars is that they invaded Dar Rezeigat as Um Dessoussa," the A/D.C of Baggara added.

This feeling from both tribes should be the point of strength in their social and cultural relations, not a weakness.

Another common factor was the circumcision of men which was said to have been adopted by the Dinka Malual community through their contacts with Riziegat and Misseriya. Other people think that it came to Northern Bahr el Ghazal through certain people from Dinka Malual who had come to the north during Mahdiiya, and stayed there for a long time. When they returned to the South, they took with them this Islamic practice.

## 2.9 Economic and Commercial Relations

The main objective of Mohamed Ali Pasha in conquering Sudan was to get men and wealth. Although the mission was not so successful in getting commercial commodities, they could transport wood, timber, honey, and ivory from Sudan to Egypt. The practice of slave trade was intensified in the areas especially, in the western part of Bahr el Ghazal where there was al Zubier Pasha.

It was alleged that Chief Autiak Majak, a Dinka tribal leader, was quite cooperative with al Zubier Pasha in the practice of the slave trade in the area of Dinka Malual. During British rule in the Sudan, many changes occurred. First, the practice of the slave trade was stopped and prohibited. Secondly, there were Closed District laws or regulations which prohibited the Arab merchants (Jallaba) from going to the South for purposes of trade.

Despite all these, economic and commercial relations between Dinka Malual and Riziegat were prominent. Dinkas are known for practising both grazing and cultivation of subsistence crops. After sowing their crops in June, they go on a journey to Dar Rezeigat to cultivate what they called *magomas*, in return for cows or money or portion of the produce. Riziegat, as pastoral nomads, they do not cultivate but depend on what is known as Jnghe (Jnghe means Dinka according to Baggara) to cultivate their area in the months of July and August. Cleaning and harvesting of crops at Dar Dinka (Wak Wak) are left to a group of selected people, individually or collectively. This practice is known as Nafir according to Rezeigat.

Dr. Francis Deng stated: "The economic activities of the Dinka are very much conditioned by the four seasons which they recognize, but which do not correspond exactly to the Western seasons. They allow some overlap of the months. Ker, the season begins from May to early July, and Ruel (from July to October) from the wet season but, extends from November to February, and Mai (from February to May) from the dry season. During Ker during the early rains fall, the fields which had been cleared earlier are planted, and the cattle gradually returned to camp near the villages while some cows are kept in the villages to provide milk.

In July, mosquitoes increase and it becomes necessary to bring the cattle home to be protected in the cattle byres at night. Ruel is the period of heavy rains and locals take permanent residence in the villages. Agricultural work, including the harvest, falls in this season.

The end of the rains is referred to as anomic, the period when crops are ripe and the cattle begin to graze further away from the villages but are brought back during the harvest of the second crop. This is a period when the fields have to be properly protected from the cattle as they crave the flavor of this second crop. Conflicts often occur between the owners of cattle when they stray into the fields and destroy the crop. Ruel is also the season for selection of young men to go to their rest period, leaving cultivation to be done by the women and older men."[21]

This shows that Dinka carried out both pastoralism and agriculture concurrently in their economy.

---

21    Francis Mading Deng, The Dinka of the Sudan, New York, Holt Rinehart and Winston, 1972, pp.109.

The shortage of food production from Dar Riziegat was solved by bringing grain (dura) from Dinka land. The A/D.C. of the Baggara was reporting to the Governor of the Baggara about this matter. He wrote under the title, *Difficulty of Obtaining Grain on the River:*

"Riziegats on the river in the direction of Safaha and further to the East have to go on a four-day journey to obtain grain from their villages. Its supply is a real difficulty with them. I suggested to Bimb Owen that his Dinka might be induced to sell grain to the Riziegat, their villages being within a day of the river. He appeared to doubt the immediate feasibility of this but said he had 200,000 rotles stored at Nyemlell which had been collected as payment of taxes in a kind. Thus, he stated, he would be very pleased to sell to the Arabs provided that the necessary approval could be obtained and that a satisfactory price could be fixed."[22] Although Riziegat prefers dukhun (Arabic word for millet), in this situation of shortage in food, it was recommended to use grain (dura).

In the commercial aspect, although there were restrictions against Arab traders entering markets in Southern Sudan, there were still chances of exchanging commodities between the two tribes. The charges levied for going to Dinka towns were increased to reduce Arabs going to those towns.

At the same report presented to the Governor of Darfur, Baggara A/D.C. in 1925, put forward the complaint raised by Nazir Ibrahim Musa of Riziegat thus: "Nazir Ibrahim Musa brought forward this question saying that it was a general complaint among his people that they were charged very heavily on going to markets in the Bahr el Ghazal. He had previously told me that it seemed to him that the Bahr el Ghazal authorities did not want Arabs to go to their markets at all."

He further states: "I later found a man returning from Wau market. He went there via Aweil taking 70 rotles of "Semmin" and a bull of dried fish. He said he was charged p.t.27 at Meding and p.t. 14 at Wau, a part from p.t.10 charged for the sale of his bull."

---

22    A/District Commissioner of Baggara Reports to Darfur Governor, op cit, pp. 14-15.

This practice was before the declaration of the Close District Law, however, the intention to isolate the South began from that time by discouraging Arab traders and mistreating them in order to stop them from going to the South. Nonetheless, the exchange of goods continued in Northern Bahr el Ghazal with Arab merchants. They brought with them horses, cows, sugar, and salt, in exchange items like hides, dura, sesame, oil, and honey.

In addition to the issue of higher taxes and charges, there were other difficulties hindering trade between the two tribes. First, the policies were rigid. Secondly, facilities like transport and banking were lacking. Even during the first national government in the Sudan, goods were carried by camels, horses, cows, and people between internal markets within Northern Bahr el Ghazal and into other markets outside the area.

All these were obstacles in promoting economic and market expansion. However, according to a DMR report in Addis Ababa in 2004, economic and environmental factors were identified as contributing to the causes of the conflict; among these were erratic rainfall and drought which aggravated the competition over natural resources like grazing land and water for cattle. The spread of diseases in cattle from one tribe to another had also caused conflict in the past.

The overall decline in the economic status of the DMR communities, which was reflected in increasing poverty, increasing illiteracy, decreased holdings of cattle, high unemployment and lack of access to basic services, was noted as an important factor in enhancing the atmosphere for conflict between the communities. These economic factors were noted to be clearly related to the isolation and marginalisation of the border area and the DMR communities from the central authorities.

## 2.10 Political and Security Relations

From the onset, there was no coordination of politics and security matters between the two tribes as the authorities seemed to undermine the need to protect mutual interests of the communities.

During Mahdiya, it was reported that when al Mahdi declared a policy of recruitment in his army, some Riziegat escaped from their homeland to Dinka areas but were mistreated and considered to be enemies. In a report to the Governor of Darfur, A/D.C. of Baggara wrote:

"When the Riziegat were rounded up to go to the Mahdi some fled to Dar Dinka and were enslaved by Jinghe. A well-known Riziegat called Adam Maki is one of those who were so mistreated."

Authenticity of this story is questionable as it is not on par with the Dinka customs. Customarily, the Dinka tend to defend the defenseless to the point of death. They have ingrained this value in every generation.

In the words of Francis Deng: "In character, a Dinka is a socially conscious yet individualistic person, gentle and humorous, but sensitive, temperamental, and prone to violent reaction when his sense of pride and dignity is hurt — and that may not take much. Dinka society is an exceedingly violent society, and from a very early age, one of the central values in a boy's education is valor and physical strength. Determination and readiness to fight for one's honour and right against anyone of whatever strength merits high esteem in children and youth. Fighting with clubs between individuals and local groups leaves many a Dinka with scars on the head; and fighting with spears between tribal segments leaves many a feud to continue in perpetuity."[23]

It was reported that in the course of recruitment to his army, al Mahdi sent two forces to Dinka Malual land. One of the forces was commanded by soldiers from the Riziegat tribe. The mission of this particular force failed because of the acrimony between the two tribes in the area.

The chief Autiak Majak, who was said to be working with al Zubier Pasha on slave trade, and was famed to own more than 20 rifles from the French, sent his support to Mahdi. The message was taken by his men together with his daughter, Awuet Autiak, as a gift to Mahdi. Mahdi accepted the gift, and gave her to one of his men from the Fur tribe and the lady was given a new name "Magbolla" which means "accepted."One of Magboll's daughters was married to the Mahdi's

---

son Abdelrahman, the grandfather of late Asadig Al Madhi and this is how the relationship between the Madhi's family and the family of Akotjokngeth was established. During the untimely death of Imam al Sadig al Mahdi, the family of Akotjokngeth organized a funeral rite in Juba and attended by many dignitors from the government of South Sudan.

Nothing was mentioned about joint political and security moves between the two tribes during the Anglo-Egyptian period. Darfur was under Sultan Ali Dinnar up to 1915. Some writers think that the capture of Darfur by colonial rule in 1916 came from the southern part, via Dar Dinka and Dar Fertit. Zubier Pasha was stationed at the western part of Bahr el Ghazal. There was fighting between Dinka Malual and Anglo-Egyptian forces in Alok in 1922 and Araithdit, the leader of the Dinka forces was arrested and sent to prison in Port Sudan.

The explanation given by colonial administrators for the battle was that; firstly, Dinkas were unhappy with the new grazing boundary made by the Savile Burges-Waston Agreement of 1918 which extended the Riziegat grazing territory up to 40 miles south of the River Kiir (Bahr Arab). The second explanation given by the British Administrator was that the protest came as a consequence of high taxes which were imposed dramatically. However, the reason for the revolution was attributed to a quest for an immediate evacuation of the colonial regime and declaration of total independence of the country. Unfortunately, due to a lack of ideological support, the revolution failed.

At the local level, there were committees between the two tribes which met at the border areas, mostly at Safaha (Adiem), under the supervision of British administrators in both Bahr el Ghazal and Darfur provinces to coordinate security matters between the two tribes. It is reported that even these local committees were not left to resolve their disputes without the intervention of British administrators. They insisted that anything should be brought to them first. The report of A/D.C. of Baggara District to the Governor of Darfur on this matter is quoted: "I informed Bimbo Owen that no settlement of a dispute be allowed between the parties interested without reference to the D. C. in the first place. In this, even in Dinka to Dinka disputes, the danger being that in the attempt to come to an agreement, they will probably come to blows."[24]

This shows native institutions played a minor role in solving disputes of its people. The usurping of powers by the colonial masters is a sign of control and use of native administration for the purposes of controlling and collection of taxes.

According to DMR in Addis Ababa in 2004, the volatile political environment in Sudan, with its inherent institutes and unpredictable change in policies and practices, was considered as an important factor in the conflict between the communities. Successive regimes, as well as political parties regularly intruded in the tribal relationships, which resulted in increased conflict locally and a chronic weakening of traditional leadership.

This trend, combined with resistance and ineffectiveness of policy, provided an environment where violence and criminal activities were carried out with impunity.

A further result of the economic, social, and political marginalization was the increasing militarisation of communities. Tribal militia, armed with heavy guns rather than the traditional knives, were established to protect tribes and political interests in the absence of effective local authority, structures, and traditional authorities who were unable to control these militias and their victims were most often civilians.

The movements and activities of the militias were generally undisciplined, but were often supported in their activities by the previous warring parties, the SAF and SPLA, reciprocation as a means of, and creating instability.

The militias were also seen to have been used by the elements of the tribes seeking advantage for themselves within the context of SPLA-SAF fighting and received arms from many sources.

The increased availability of small arms led to increasing random and uncontrolled use of grazing herds, without recourse to the indigenous

---

24      A/District Commission of Baggara Reports, op cit, pp. 14-15.

owners of the land. Furthermore, the militarisation of the tribe and its use in the war against SPLA was used by the Riziegat elites as a mechanism of seeking political accommodation in Government institutions in Khartoum. The same was done by SPLA in order to remove the Khartoum-based government from power.

## 2.11 Conclusion

Although there was difficulty in communication, the British Administration was very concerned about peace in the area. The application of the Native Administration Act in 1922 and the subsequent organisation of tribes were very helpful to Dinka Malual and Riziegat tribes. There was no political agenda between the two tribes; their problems were grazing land and water for their animals and the fishing grounds. These problems were managed annually by the colonial administration through organisation of peace conferences between the two tribes. The colonial rule was very concerned with the life of Baggara animals. This made them frequently create what they called grazing boundaries between the North and the South.

In the past, it was very clear that the issue of religion did not come up as a problem between Dinka Malual and Riziegat tribes, although there were abductions within these two tribes. The intention was not for slaves as perceived. The war captives and the abducted women and children were for the purpose of assimilation. After capture they were treated as a part of family or clan.

The colonial rule had been accused by Dinka Malual's notables of favouring the position of Riziegat tribes because of their rebellion against colonial authority in the area in 1918 under the leadership of Bol Yel (Araith Makuei). The rebellion was believed to be the reason why British authorities, in their various meetings with the two tribes, tried to support the stance of Riziegat. This happened in 1918 and 1924 during the grazing boundaries agreements between the two communities leading to creation of a14 mile grazing area for Riziegat.

# CHAPTER 3

## 3.1 The Role of the Successive National Governments in Dinka Malual-Riziegat Relations

The period after the Anglo-Egyptian era in Sudan was long and oppressive. Although the British administration seized major towns in the South in the 1900s, they were only able to penetrate through to the local population until 1930 with the enactment of the Native Administration Ordinance in 1922. The ordinance divided the country into chiefdoms and pro-colonial chiefs were appointed to make the natives more submissive to colonizers. The 54 years of colonization left a lasting effect on the South Sudanese national identity. However, The British should be commended for their efforts in protecting cultures and norms of the South Sudanese. The administration went as far as formulating a law to safeguard the cultures of the people called The Closed District Ordinance. This was contrary to the Sudan government policies which focused on Arabizing and Islamizing the South Sudanese which national unity would be achieved through Arabization and Islamization. The chiefs in Southern Sudan were urged to change their names and adopt Arab ones and convert to Islam. The Arabic language was introduced and made compulsory in the schools. *Jallabiya*[25] and *Toub*[26] were introduced as national dresses for male and female respectively. Christians

---

25      *Jallabiyia* is a long dress wears by man demonstrating Arab culture.

26      *Toub* is a loose dress to cover all of a women's body including her head.

were not allowed to marry Muslim girls unless they were circumcised and converted to Islam. Even those that were not interested in such unions were still forced to go through circumcision. This mistreatment escalated the rebellion and migration of the southerners to East Africa and other neighbouring countries in a quest for arms in order to fight the regime in Khartoum.

Post-independent Sudan has had a number of successive national governments from the period 1956 up to the Government of National Salvation which transformed itself to the Government of National Unity (GoUN) as a result of signing the Comprehensive Peace Agreement with SPLM/A in 2005. Each government has had a role in the political events in Sudan. The era after the Bashir regime was not discussed as the Sudanese masses are still struggling for a credible system of governance in Khartoum.

This study, therefore, confines itself to the era before signing the peace agreement with predictions of the future of the country which were made before the referendum in 2011. This issue of the referendum has been addressed in Chapter Seven thoroughly using a designed questionnaire. The focus is directed towards the role played by all these governments in the issues related to Malual Dinka-Riziegat relations. It covers the period of the Azhari Government 1956 – 1958; the first military government of General Abboud 1958 – 1964; the second Democratic Government 1965 – 1969; the May Revolution 1969 – 1984; the third Democratic government 1985 – 1989, and the government of National Salvation that started in June 1989, but accounted for, up to July 2005, the time of formation of the GoUN. There are other issues related to the post-referendum era discussed in Chapter Eight which constitute the reasons for publication of this Second Edition.

## 3.1 Azhari Government 1956–1958

After independence in 1956, the policy drawn by the new government was focusing on the 1953 Sudanisation of all institutions in the North and the South. The Sudanisation policy was considered by southerners as neo-colonialism. A lot of things happened as Northern administrators replaced their colonial counterparts, including the English language being replaced by Arabic and missionaries being asked to leave the South.

These processes were preceded by a mutiny at Torit in 1955 as a result of the Sudanisation policy, and rumours circulated about transferring Equatorial Forces into the North. It was considered as a taking away of the indigenous army and replacing it with one run by northerners. The rapid increase of northerners in the South as administrators, senior officers in the army and the police, teachers in government schools, and merchants, increased southerners' fear of the Northern domination and colonization.

The failure of the national governments to formulate a permanent constitution that could accommodate the views of Southerners on federation was a setback in the South – North relationship. This led to the formation of the Federal Party in the South and mobilization of the rest of the regions to join the demand for a federal system in the country.

## 3.2 Abboud Regime 1958–1964

The elected government of Ismail el Azhari didn't last long because of conspiracies between his party, the Democratic Unionist Party (DUP) and the Umma party of Abdalla Khalil. The Southern representatives mobilized other members of parliament to support their demand for federal governance. This weakened the government which was over-thrown by the Umma party supported by the army led by General Ibrahim Abboud. Abboud's reign is well remembered in Southern Sudan for its forced Arabization and Islamization policy. As well as the intro-duction of the Islamic schools in the major towns of Southern Sudan, the government ordered the closure of the missionaries operating in the region. Before the popular uprising in 1964, about 300 missionaries were shutdown both in Southern Sudan and Nuba Mountains, (Arop, 2012) and the personnel were asked to leave the country. He (Arop) categorically quoted the regime's governor in the Equatoria province Mr. Ali Baldo as saying "Thank God, by virtue of the marvelous efforts of the revolution government, the country will remain forever united."

However, the regime was wrong about the efficacy of their assimilation policies in the Southern, so their attempts were unsuccessful.

The second democratic government under the Umma Party 1965-1968 caused more bloodshed in the South. In June 1965 the Assembly passed a resolution to restore law and order in Southern Sudan. According to Arop (2012), the security forces were given free hand to act in pursuit of that goal. Massacres were executed in Juba, Bor, Wau and many towns. Some schools were either closed or transferred to the North. Rumbek Secondary School and Juba Commercial were operating in Khartoum. Many students and intellectuals fled the country and joined the rebellion or lived in the exile as refugees. Some pan-Arabist politicians in the North had this wrong belief that Southern Sudan had no identity and should be assimilated by the Arab culture and identity.

### 3.3 The Second Democratic Government 1965–1969

After the overthrow of General Abboud in 1964, the interim government, dominated by leftist elements, took the most apparent policy which negatively affected Dinka Malual and Riziegat communities indirectly. The government took measures against the native administration considering it a colonial institution, and declared war against it.

The government passed a resolution to resolve all Native Administrators. The leaders of the nationalism movements, who were urbanized and Western educated perceived Native Administrators as "colonial stooges" founded to help foreign rule by pacifying the rural population and prolonging their existence. Radical political elements had always felt that Native Administrators blocked their access to rural masses. They considered Native Administrators as influential supporters of conservative and sectarian political parties in the rural areas.[27] The elected government of Sadig Al Mahdi in 1966 did not favour the resolution of liquidating Native Administration. This stand led to accusation by leftist elements of the sectarian political parties' support and sympathy with Native Administration.

---

27      Bakheit, G.M.A Native Administration in Sudan and its significance to Africa, in: Hassan Y.F. (ed) Sudan in Africa, 2nd ed, 1985, pp. 54-94.

Bakheit (1985) believed that the interim government was short-lived. The sectarian government that succeeded it ignored the implementation of the liquidation resolution of native administration but the harm had already been done. Native Administrators lost credibility in the eyes of their followers and lost interest in performing their traditional responsibilities.

## 3.4 The May Revolution 1969 – 1984

Though there was no direct involvement in Dinka Malual-Rezeigat conflict until mid-1970s by President Nimeiry, the liquidation of Native Administration in 1970 led to the most effective traditional conflict resolution mechanisms in Sudan. Actors in the May Revolution, when assuming power, was known for its sympathy with socialist ideology. Hence, it wanted to build the programme of leftists which had failed in finding a way of liquidating native administration during the democratic government of al Mahdi.[28]

The liquidation of Native Administration in Western Sudan reflected itself negatively during the tribal conferences which were held between Misseriya, Riziegat, and Dinka in the South-North Sudan border. There was no representation of tribal leadership in the conferences. Disputes arose over resources of grazing land, water, fishing, and even social matters without trial. The absence of this important institution from the community created the absence of a peaceful resolution of the disputes.

The responsibility of grassroots affairs in Kordofan and Darfur was given to the Sudan Socialist Union's (SSU) members, especially in the rural areas Native Administration leaders, but their experience in the field of tribal conflict resolution was limited. According to Bakheit (l985), a more serious blow to Native Administration came in 1970 when the Second Radical Government (1969-1985) dissolved the system, unseating the paramount chiefs. Although further attempts have been made by subsequent governments to reinstall the system, it has not been possible to make it perform the same functions.

---

28      Ibid.

The absence of Riziegat chiefs in the tribal conferences on the part of was condemned by the chiefs of Dinka Malual considering the resolutions of conferences as meaningless, without their participation.

Chief Riny Lual Dau of Marial Baai, in one of the conferences in 1974, commented on members of SSU who were brought to attend the conference, saying: "How can we negotiate the important issues of the area with lay people."

He meant that the members of SSU who represented Rezeigat in the peace conferences were not the right people to negotiate with. This comment was confirmed later because resolutions and recommendations of the conferences were not respected and not implemented.

Though Nimeiry stepped down from his position of liquidating Native Administration as a result of pressure from the traditional political parties after the national reconciliation, Native Administration still suffered from losing credibility with their communities, particularly in the rural areas.

National reconciliation with traditional political parties in 1977 provided advantages to the Native Administration in the North, but at the same time created another problem in the South. The leaders of these political parties opposed the May Government for making peace in the South. After they came in, they exerted a lot of pressure for the Addis Ababa Agreement (1972) not to be implemented.

The issue of the borders which was addressed by the Agreement, like Abyei and Kafi Agangi, had stopped. Instead, the grazing borders of 1918 between Dinka Malual and Rezeigat were revived by the Central Government claiming the part of the Northern Bahr el Ghazal up to 40 miles south of the River Kiir (Bahr Arab) as Southern Darfur.

The Nimeiry Government began to provide guns and necessary logistics to Rezeigat forces to occupy Dinka Malual territories. Anya Nya One army commanders at Mathiang Garrison responded and provided guns to their people to protect themselves and their cattle. Many battles were fought in the period between 1974 and 1984.

Then, the May Regime was brought down by popular uprising after the SPLM/A manifested itself in 1983.

## 3.5 The Third Democratic Government 1985 – 1989

In 1984, before al Sadig took over the government as an elected Prime Minister, the conflict between Dinka Malual and Rezeigat was at its peak. The Transitional Military Council (TMC) was led by Lieutenant General Swar al Dahab and it included Major General Fadlalla Burma Nasir, a Misseriya from Southern Kordofan, who had been associated with the conflict in the area. Although TMC called for a general solution of the Sudan conflict with the SPLM/A, Major General Burma made use of his position to arm Rezeigat and Misseriya people as a clear indication of their intention to occupy Dinka land. The government of al Sadig took over in 1985 and unfortunately General Burma was appointed again as State Minister in the Ministry of Defense. General Burma was not given this important portfolio to carry on national functions, but as a continuation of the initial plan of massive displacement and genocide against Dinka and non-Arab tribes in the area.

The appointment of Major General Burma escalated the conflict into a war which took different dimensions from traditional rivalry over grazing resources with traditional and non-complicated weapons to an organized conventional warfare with the participation of the national army from both sides.

Leaders of the Anya Nya army in Mathiang, upon realising the matter had taken that form, decided to involve themselves to protect their people from organized raiding, displacement, and genocide.

Among the dead bodies found in the battlefield at Safaha were some actors from General Military Headquarters in Khartoum disguised as civilians.

There was no proper explanation that could be given by the Prime Minister, other than telling people that it was a reaction against what had been done in the area by the SPLA, undermining the fact that the victims who were killed were innocent citizens of his own country. He went further to support mass killing of displaced people at Daien despite the fact that this act undermined Islamic teaching. He said: "The indigenous Muslim populace must protect non-Muslim immigrants (Muhjireen)."

He even went ahead to blame SPLM/A for the massacre which took place in Daien in 1986. The al Mahdi and the Coalition Government, agreed to give the Native Administration an effective role but with defined duties. A ministerial committee was formed to study and give proposals on the issue. Some recommendations given by this committee were:

1. Reinstatement of Native Administration in the pastoral and semi-pastoral areas with full administrative, judicial, and security powers;
2. Reinstatement of Native Administration in the stabilized rural areas with administrative and semi-judicial powers; and
3. Reinstatement of Native Administration in towns and modern productive areas but with limited administrative powers at the level of Sheikh.

There were a lot of restrictions over the selection, supervision and the type of relationship between the Native Administration and regional authorities. However, no action was taken on these resolutions until the National Salvation Government came to power in 1989.

## 3.6 National Salvation Government 1989-2005

This period covers the era before the signing of the CPA and the formation of the Government of National Unity (GONU) in the Sudan. The post-independence issues related to this regime will be discussed in Chapter Eight.

Before taking over power on June 30th 1989, a big part of Southern Sudan was under control of the SPLA/M forces. The government authority was confined to the provincial cities of Juba, Malakal, Wau and other small towns in the South, including Aweil, Raja, and Yei. Not only was the South threatened to be overrun by the SPLM/A forces, but the war had also shifted to the North, losing the areas at the border known as "contact areas" like Kurmuk and Giesan.

At the same time, fighting was taking place in Nuba Mountains, West Kordofan and Darfur. Security deteriorated even in big towns.

There were rumours coming from Port Sudan that some officers in the SAF were planning a *coup 'detat* to cut off Port Sudan from Khartoum. There was also fear that SPLA/M would take over power by over running Damazein, Wad Medani and Khartoum.

In his policy statement, the justification given by the Chairperson of the Revolutionary Council Brigadier: Omer Hassan Ahmed al Bashir, for taking over power from the elected government was the negligence of the army by the democratic government, resulting in the deterioration of security all over the country.

Bashir blamed the traditional political parties of neglecting national interests while fighting for their own narrow agenda. He described the Garang-Marghani peace initiative signed between SPLA/M and DUP as a sign of surrender to the rebels and not a durable peace initiative.

Consequently, he proposed his own peace initiative called "Peace Within" and created the Peace and Development Corporation to promote it. He promised to implement Islamic laws in the country. The policy was appreciated by majority of Northern Sudanese people who considered the new government a real salvation because the situation in all aspects of life was difficult. There was a shortage in food, fuel, medicine, education, water and electricity, as well as deterioration in security.

To restore security the new government concentrated its limited resources on military supplies. The National Army was equipped to perform its functions adequately. There was a "national call" that the public must contribute to the maintenance of security and participate in war against infidels in Southern Sudan.

The conflict was transformed to a Jihad (Holy) war and as such all Muslims were required to participate in protecting their religion and country. The already existing tribal militias were organized to face the threat imposed by the enemies of God in the South.

The Popular Defense Forces (PDF) Act was enacted and passed by the Revolutionary Council in 1989 and later taken to the Transitional Assembly for endorsement in 1992. Training centres were opened for students, government officials, and citizens. Military training was made compulsory and a condition for getting employment, a trading licence, or a visas to travel outside the country. The tribal militia institutions in the Upper Nile, Equatoria, Bahr el Ghazal, Kordofan, Khartoum, el-Jazeera, White Nile and Darfur were empowered besides the national army to confront the rebellion in the South, which was perceived as a Dinka affair.

The Khartoum governments have pursued this campaign of terror mostly in the Dinka region because of the assumption that the SPLA/M was a Dinka organisation.

The mission given to Riziegat and Misseriya militias was to crush the movement in Northern Bahr el Ghazal by destroying its base, killing, and looting properties. In the holy war Jihad, confiscation of enemy property is legal.

Riziegat and Misseriya tribal militias were assisted with necessary facilities including train transport to Bahr el Ghazal in South Sudan. The element of remunerating them as a reward was introduced to encourage the majority from these two tribes to participate in the war.

In spite of all these activities, Riziegat and Misseriya were not at all motivated by the Jihad, their intention was only to loot and abduct women and children in order to use them on farms, a confirmation that the conflict was not a religious one.

In his mobilization speech in South Kordofan, (the late) First Leuitenant General al Zubier Mohamed Salih, the then first Vice-President of the Sudan in 1996 was reported to have called on the Misseriya people, especially those whose ancestors supported the Islamic Movement of Mahdist, to come out and give their support to the National Salvation Government as a proposition of the Mahdist Islamic ideology and asked them to participate effectively in the war in Southern Sudan against animists, but a notable from Misseriya, replied to al Zubier saying: "We do not have a hard religion that can make us fight Jineghe (Dinka)."

Many human right circles consider the use of the train by Murahaleen as a direct involvement of the government in the abduction of women and children.

The report of the International Eminent Persons Group (IEPG) on slavery, abduction and forced servitude in Sudan in 2002 wrote: "A large number of Murahaleen raids on villages in Bahr el Ghazal is associated with seasonal movement of the military train that travels between Babanousa and Wau."

The report further states: "As Baggara pastoralists move North with livestock to wet season pastures the military train prepared to move south. The purpose of the train, which is run by the military, is twofold: to supply government garrison towns along the railway line and to establish Northern Bahr el Ghazal. The government recruits Murahaleen in South Darfur and West Kordofan to protect the train. The recruits are registered and provided with guns and often with horse-mounted Murahaleen to create a security cordon several kilometers wide on either side of the line. The cordon was created for raiding and burning villages deep into Dinka and Luo territory. The raids are brutal, with killing, rape and amputations reported, in addition to the looting of cattle and other property and abduction of civilians. Abduction is generally worse as the train returns north."[29]

It was noted, when the train moves to the South, the main target of Riziegat and Misseriya militias was cattle raiding. During the train time, the price of a cow in Aweil and Wau towns goes down to Ls.50,000 (50,000 Sudanese Pounds) equal to $20.[30]

On their way back to the North, the main targets were women and children. It was said, some of those women and children were not abducted, but due to the devastating situation of war, those who had lost their parents or husbands might have decided to accompany the trains to the North assuming life would be better there. When they reached the North, they were assumed to be among those that had been abducted and some were forced to take-up arms as members of Murahaleen forces.

---

29      International Eminent People Group, Report on Abducting, Slavery and Servitude in the Sudan, 2002.

30      Ibid.

This is true, because the children abducted in their earlier ages became part of Murahaleen forces. Also, some SPLA soldiers who committed crimes in the Movement and escaped to towns decided to join Murahaleen forces in the area, not only to seek wealth through looting but revenge for previous deeds against them and/or their families. This turned the confrontation into a South-South conflict.

In 1998, a war plan set by the government to destroy SPLA/M areas in Northern Bahr el Ghazal was repulsed. The government forces raided Nyamlel and Fariak, which were SPLA headquarters in the West and East Malual Dinka areas respectively.

Intensive and extensive mobilization to capture Nyamlel was carried out in 1998 when Riziegat and Misseriya were mobilized by the government to conduct joint operations with the SAF and PDF.

Nyamlel town was captured, burnt down and looted. Many people were killed; among them were SPLA senior officers and soldiers in the garrison. There were massive abductions of women and children who were taken to Daien Town. Within a short time the captured town of Nyamlel was visited by senior government officials from Southern Darfur including the Commissioner of Daien Province.

The loss of the headquarters of SPLA/M at Aweil West County, was agonizing to the leadership because it was a strategic garrison that linked Darfur and Western Bahr el Ghazal. The town was however, re-captured within a few days.

Another attempt to capture Pariak at Aweil East in 2000 was repulsed by SPLA forces at Gair area about 10 miles from Aweil town. Murahaleen forces escorted a train and upon reaching Aweil town, they decided to attack Pariak Garrison. However, before reaching Pariak they fell into an ambush of SPLA forces at Gair. Many of them were killed, wounded and captured. They were not able to move ahead but returned to Aweil town. Senior SAF commanders visited them in Aweil town and the wounded were taken to Khartoum by a military plane after receiving their remuneration.

The facilitation that Murahaleen got from the government justified the accusation that the government was behind the activities of these forces. Many human rights agencies accused the government of human rights violations. The government laid the blame and responsibility of abductions on the Murahaleen directly.

In an interview carried out by IEPG, the military commanders denied the use of the train by the Murahaleen, or that they were at all responsible for their actions. Other government officials heaped the blame on tribal leaders. They considered the Murahaleen as irresponsible elements that they were unable to control and who were attracted by the incentives offered by the government.

It was, after all, they explained, "a government train." The same report indicates: "In the past two years, however, many of the Misseriya and Riziegat leaders had sought to distance themselves from the Murahaleen and discouraged their youth from joining militias that escorted the train." The gains, however, from looting property and abducting people had been proven too lucrative.

Since late 2000, there has been substantial evidence that the Ministry of Defense had also begun to pay incentives to militia members to escort the train.

Due to these allegations, the International Community held the government responsible for human rights violations and the revival of slave institutions in the Sudan. The United Nations sent Special Rapporteurs on Human Rights in 1993 who continuously reported to United Nations Annual Meeting of the Commission on Human Rights.

Sudan was considered an uncooperative country in the field of human rights. Abduction of women and children in Dinka Malual areas by Riziegat and Misseriya tribes reached a worrying state by the time of the intervention of Christian International Solidarity (CIS) mobilized the Western community and drew their attention the to slave trade which had revived in the Sudan in the 21st century.

Western media launched a campaign to mobilize all human rights circles against the Sudan Government. The organized efforts to identify and free abducted persons began in the early 1990s when Malual Dinka chiefs in the North formed a group which became known as the Dinka Chief Committee (DCC) to identify and negotiate the release of abducted persons. Their work was dangerous and undertaken in secrecy.

In 1996, Save the Children United Kingdom (SCUK) began to provide small-scale support to the committee's work. In early 1999, as a result of publicity by international organisations and a report by the U.N. Special Rapporteur on Human Rights, discussions started between the Sudan Government and European Union (EU) to change the term "slavery" and adopt the term "abduction." The discussion arrived at measures to be taken to eradicate the practice, starting with the creation of a committee known as the Committee for Eradication of Abduction of Women and Children (CEAWC) by the government in May 1999. The provision of the establishment was issued by the Minister of Justice who was a Chairperson of the Advisory Council for Human Rights. Again the organisation was re-established by the Presidential Decree No. 14/2002 to give it more powers and support, and affiliated it directly to the Presidency. Its mandates were:[31]

1. To investigate reports of the abduction of women and children and to bring to trial any person(s) suspected of supporting or partici-pating in such activities and not cooperating with CEAWC.
2. To investigate the cases of the abduction of women and children subjected to forced labour or similar conditions and recommend ways and means to eradicate this practice.
   1. The membership of CEAWC includes representatives from the following:[32]
   2. Relevant government authority, the Ministry of Justice, Police, army and security.
   3. Civil Society (Bar Association, Women Union)
   4. Parliament.
   5. Non-Governmental Organisations (NGOs)
   6. Concerned tribes.

---

31     Ahmed El Mufti, Experience of CEAWC in Gathering Information, Training, and Reunification of Persons Abducted during Armed Conflict, Khartoum, 2003.

32     Ibid.

CEAWC has official organs at national, state, provincal and local levels. For the organisation to work effectively, committees were formed and composed of representatives from the office of the Director of Public Prosecution, police, armed forces, security, and state government.

It also has tribal organs at the grassroots levels composed of 22 joint tribal committees (JTCs) all over the affected areas. Those committees were the executive arm of CEAWC and its members were selected by the tribes. The top management of the organisation had no power to change the membership of the committees nominated by their constituencies. CEAWC worked closely with the International Community, especially SC/UK and UNICEF.

Upon its establishment in 1999, CEAWC conducted a number of operations through JTC. The organ worked at the grassroots level. One of the problems CEAWC faced was the screening of exact figures of the abductees. There was disagreement on the total number of the identified abductees and those reunited with their families by the concerned organisations as it is shown in Table 3:1.

*Table 3.1: Estimated, Identified and returned abducted women and children by different NGOs working in the field of human rights.*

| Organisation | Estimated total persons abducted | Total No. of abducted persons identified | Total No. of abducted persons returned or recruited |
|---|---|---|---|
| CEAWC | 14,000 | 1.500 | 1.000 |
| Dinka Chief Committee (DCC) | 14,000 | 1.127 | 1.000 |
| UNICEF/SC U. K | 10,000-17,000 Estimated children and women abducted.6,000-7,000 missing | 1,570 | 1,034 |
| CIS-Switzerland | Over 100,000 CIS also quote estimate of 200,000 by Dinka chiefs Bahr el Ghazal (SPLA/M areas) | | 65,000-70,000 |

*Source: International Eminent Groups Persons Report, 2002.*

The National Salvation Government, upon taking power, declared war against a set of enemies in the North and the South. In the North the Revolutionary Military Council issued the Second Constitutional Decree dissolving all political parties and trade unions in the country.

A statement by its leader Brigadier Omer Hassan read: "The revolution shall wage war against sectarianism in the Sudan." It was known that the sectarian parties (Umma Party and DUP) constituencies in

North Sudan were basically supported by Native Administration. Specifically, tribal leaders in Western Sudan supported the Umma Party and in east and north of the country people supported DUP. In the south, there was the SPLA/M, which had been labelled a Dinka or pro-Dinka organisation and a set of procedures was taken against the movement.

Douglas Johnson argued: "Much of the fighting in the civil war has been reported by external observers in tribal terms and for years the SPLM/A was perceived as a Dinka army."[33]

This is how the successive governments of Sudan viewed the SPLM/A. Tribal institutions suffered from the war of ethnic discrimination between the North and the South. There were attempts to weaken the role of tribal leaders on the ground by creating new Nizara[34] in Western Sudan.

In Dar Riziegat the number Omdas[35] which was only 10 in 1989, was increased to more than 50. The move was aimed at creating loyalty to the Government. In Northern Bahr el Ghazal, tribal leaders who were known for their support of the SPLM/A, were sent to live in camps in Khartoum and in slum towns in the North in order to weaken the movement.

The displaced Chiefs in Khartoum were not recognised, instead a new leadership in tribal hierarchy was created to support the government. Northern Bahr el Ghazal alone had more than 500 chiefs around Khartoum. They were provided with identity cards by Internal Displaced Persons (IDPs) administration in Khartoum State and were used in political mobilization and demonstrations supporting government policies.

Hamid Bashier was convinced that the government substituted the traditional tribal leaders by appointing new leaders loyal to its fundamental ideology.

---

33      Johnson Douglas H, op cit, pp. 67.

34      Nazir is a Paramount Chief.

35      Omda is a sub Chief.

Islamic ideology had not been common in the rural areas so, the government had to see to it that it created strong followers in the Native Administration.

The practices resulted in the collapse of tribal institutions in the armed zones of Darfur and Bahr el Ghazal which in turn led to deterioration of security, especially on the border of Dinka Malual and Riziegat tribes.

The idea of joint committees and meetings was abandoned. There were no annual conferences being held, and conflicts remained unresolved. Continuous supervision on the border to manage the shared pastoral resources was stopped, and no annual appeal courts sat to deal with cases of abduction, compensation and illegal marriages among the two tribes.

The only joint programme carried on by the two tribes was the work of CEAWC but with less cooperation from the leaders of the Riziegat and Misseriya tribes.

The programme of reuniting abducted children with their families started well but faced some problems. For example, some children did not know where their families were. Some hardly knew names of their parents, because they had been abducted when they were young. Some children decided not to go back to their families. Others were raped, forced to marry and became housewives.

The cooperation between the two tribes became possible after a number of workshops conducted by the NGOs working in the field of human rights.

Problems facing native administration during National Salvation Government are not confined to the area of Dinka Malual and Riziegat only, but all over the country.

In 1998, a law was passed in the National Assembly to democratize the Native Administration. However, the idea was not welcomed in many states due to coerciveness and the tribal position of traditional chiefs in their areas.

The new Localities Act of 2002 which was passed by the National Assembly gave a strong provision for popular administration at grassroots level as a means of weakening native administration.

On September 9, 2001 the President Bush Administration nominated a priest, John Danforth as a Special Envoy in Sudan (Discussed
in detail in Chapter Five).

Followed by the 11/9/2001 terrorists attack on New York City, in
which hundreds of US citizens died in the International Trade Towers,
there was a wave of changes in the global political environment which
placed Sudan on the USA list as a country that supported Islamic terrorism. The government was compelled to sign the peace protocol with
SPLM/A in Machakos, in July 2002 championed by the US Special
Envoy to Peace in Sudan, John Danforth.

This protocol legalized sovereignty for the people of Southern Sudan
to be determined through a referendum scheduled after a period of
six years. In the 2011 referendum, the people would choose either to
stay united or separate Southern Sudan from Sudan in 2011. Other
important elements of the Machakos Protocol related to the issue, were
the exemption of South Sudan from Islamic laws and the provision of
an autonomous government in the South during the interim period
of six years.

After the Machakos Protocol was signed serious negotiations began
and the agreement was signed between the Government of Sudan
represented by the National Congress Party (NCP) and Sudan People's
Liberation Movement/Army SPLM/A in Nairobi on January 9, 2005.

Consequently, violations by the NCP of the agreement were noted
during implementation that would affect it yet a number of issues
remained to be resolved before the referendum. Among these issues
were the withdrawal of SAF forces to the North boundary of 1/1/1956,
SAF militias who are still in the South, the demarcation of the South
- North boundaries, distribution of proceeds from the oil produced
in the South, Sudan's population census and the demarcation of the
Abyei boundary.

In Southern Darfur, many previous government militias from
Rezeigat and Misseriya tribes declared their allegiance to the SPLA, a step
which was considered by the government as detrimental to peace and
security.

The government had been in efforts to evacuate the forces from the area to south of the 1/1/1956 boundaries. The efforts were not fruitful and instead there were indications of a resumption of the war if the issues were not addressed. The US Administration and UN Secretary General's (UN/SG) office expressed concern over the same and the UN/SG visited South Sudan to forge a way forward with its leaders for implementation of the Comprehensive Peace Agreement (CPA). The same was done by the former President Bushs' Special Envoy to Sudan, Andrew Natsios in October 2007 before he resigned and left the task to Mr. Robert Peterson and subsequently to Scott Gration.

### 3.7 Conclusion

The role of the successive national governments in the Dinka Malual-Riziegat conflict has been persistent. The major reason was that the North-based governments needed to exploit the Riziegat tribe to sustain its power in Khartoum against the frequent rebellion in the South.

Dinka Malual, as one of those tribes on the border with the North and also as a strong harbour of the rebels found themselves targeted by the authorities in Khartoum using SAF, PDF and sometimes tribal militia of Riziegat and Misseriya. It can be deduced that all governments which took power in Khartoum had contributed directly toward escalation of the conflict between the two tribes. However, it is clear, according to the proceedings in Chapter Three, that the democratic governments led by al Sadig al Mahdi, the Transitional Government of 1985 and the National Salvation Government of 1989 had a big stake in the escalation of tensions between Dinka Malual and Rezgiegat.

During the Transitional Government of General Swar al Dahab, the Riziegat tribe received guns from government. The idea of training them as semi-soldiers was intimated by the government of al Mahdi in 1986, but during the National Salvation Government, the tribal militia was institutionalized by a law called Popular Defense Forces Act which concentrated on the Riziegat and Misseriya tribes because of their geographical location with the South.

The use of ethnic politics by the Khartoum-based government as a strategy to sustain power, has very clearly manifested as detrimental to unity of Sudanese people.

Though the real source of this conflict were communities competing over natural resources like grazing land, water and fishing prospects, the power struggle overrode the matter, turning the tribes into agents of the policies that the Khartoum government wanted to implement.

# CHAPTER 4

**4. The Impact of the Liberation Movements in Southern Sudan on the Dinka Malual and Riziegat Tribal Relations**

Liberation movements in Southern Sudan were accused by some tribes and individuals in the North of causing disunity in the country with their frequent rebellions which were against Arabs and Islam in the Sudan.

This chapter examines the role played by the Southern Sudanese armed struggle movements. This includes Anya Nya One Movement, Anya Nya Two Movement, and the SPLA/M.

## 4.1 Anya Nya One Movement 1955-1972

Anya Nya was an armed wing of the Southern Sudan Liberation Movement (SSLM), the armed struggle which started in Torit in August, 1955. Although the Movement took different names along the period, the longest lasting was Anya Nya. The movement started as a mutiny from Equatoria forces protesting against hostile post-independence policies in the country.

Southerners were marginalized in the process of Sudanisation and the attempt to transfer Equatoria forces to the North fueled the crisis. Due to the serious grievances felt by the South, the conflict took on different dimensions; instead of calling for justice, it called for separation from the North. Surprisingly, during the peace negotiation in Addis

Ababa that culminated in the Peace Accord in 1972, the Movement stepped down from secession to local autonomy which brought an unsustainable peaceful settlement in the South.

The Movement which started in Equatoria did not spread quickly in Bahr el Ghazal until ten years later when the government of al Sadig al Mahdi killed more than 100 people at a wedding party in Wau. Similar incident happened in Bor town. These mass killings could be categorized as genocide.

William Deng the leader of SANU Party, decided to transfer his political activities inside the country instead of East Africa. He was supported by many southerners. Although he was advocating for a peaceful resolution of the conflict by giving the South federation, the North considered this demand a crime. Many of his followers in major towns were arrested and killed by the security organs in the South which motivated many people to join the armed movement in the South.

Anya Nya was not organized on a functional basis, rather its organisation was based on tribal groupings in Bahr el Ghazal, Upper Nile and Equatoria, each tribe or ethnic group trying to protect its territory from what they thought and considered as an enemy.

Although the Movement was basically a protest against Northern domination, the position of Malual Dinka rebels was surprising in the Dinka, Riziegat and Misseriya borders.

Major General Albino Akol, a former Anya Nya officer, and a former Governor of Bahr el Ghazal Administrative Area (BGAA) during the Swar al Dahab Interim Government of 1985 and also a former Minister in the Government of Southern Sudan (GOSS) said:

"We were so friendly with Riziegat and Missseriya. When we started the movement in Northern Bahr el Ghazal in 1961, there was a question of how to cooperate with tribes in the area. Our patrol was seated at Gok Anour village. Some Dinka notables came and advised us not to target Baggara especially Riziegat and Misseriya in Darfur and Kordofan respectively. Riziegat and Dinka Malual relations were smooth as the two tribes integrated. Of course, the blood relationship existing between the two sub-sections of PAraith and Padhieu (these are subsections of

Malual Dinka tribe) of West Malual Dinka with Awlad Umm Dheia of Riziegat was exploited for the benefit of the two tribes. This was a social understanding, and nobody was really interested in destroying it. We became friendly to Riziegat to the extent that they protected us even from the army in their areas. Supplies and materials were brought from Dar Riziegat."[36]

Major General Albino went on: "The first meeting between Anya Nya One leaders in Northern Bahr el Ghazal and Riziegat native leaders at Gok Anour was very successful. When he saw us with machine guns, one of the notables from Riziegat said: 'Those people who gave Dinka machine guns must make peace now, because it is going to be a dangerous situation. Dinkas fought us with spears. What will then the situation be if they use a gun?'[37]

By warning the government of the dangerous situation that Dinka would create by having machine guns, he thought the only alternative to avoid a disastrous situation was by making peace in the area immediately. No fighting took place between Riziegat and Misseriya with Anya Nya until the time of the Agreement in 1972. It can be recalled that the period between 1962 and1972 was a stable period on the border between the two tribes despite the mass killings of southerners inside the towns of Baggara by the government. The grazing, watering and fishing were done mutually in the Kiir River (Bahr Arab).

It can be summarized that two factors contributed to stability in the area; first, unwillingness of the tribal leaders of Riziegat and Misseriya on one hand, and Anya Nya leaders on the other hand, to involve themselves in politics particularly the local politics. The second factor was that the balance of power between Riziegat, Misseriya and Dinka Malual was more or less the same and no tribe could overweigh the other.

---

36     An interview with Maj.General Alboino Akol Akol Khartoum, June 2004.

37     Ibid.

## 4.2 The Anya Nya Two Movement 1976-1983

Having signed an agreement with the Government of the Sudan in 1972, some Anya Nya officers protested, saying that the Movement did not realize its objectives. Some also were not satisfied with absorption policies and integration into SAF.

Those officers and soldiers who protested and rejected the peace agreement organised themselves in the Ethiopian border and declared themselves Anya Nya Two under leadership of Gai Tut, Akuot Atem, Vincent Kuany and William Abdalla Chuol of the former Anya Nya leaders from Upper Nile province.

In Bahr el Ghazal province, particularly at Wau Military Garrison (Gerinti), Captain Aguet mutinied with some soldiers in 1976. He withdrew to a village called Bour Madier near Kayanga, Aweil-Wau road. He protested against promotions and some administrative issues in the army. He was contacted by the commander of the garrison and second in command to Major General Joseph Lagu, Brigadier Emmanuel Abour and other officers, but refused to listen. He instead opened fire and killed Brigadier Abour and some officers while others escaped with wounds. This was a major setback to the whole peace process in the South.

In 1981, a good number of Aweil citizens including students of Nyamlel Secondary School rebelled, protesting what they considered an Arab invasion of their territory and the president Nimeiry policies in the South. After the arrival of Jamus battalion to the area, all the Anya Nya Two forces were rounded up and sent to Bilfam in Ethiopia for further military training where they became part of SPLA forces and were commissioned to a different task.

In carrying out its functions and trying to implement the Addis Ababa Peace Accord, the Regional Government brought up the issue of those areas contested in the South-North border, especially Kafi Akangi in the Bahr el Ghazal-Darfur border and Abyei in the Bahr el Ghazal-Kordofan border. This was counteracted by the Central Government by raising the same issue and more in the national parliament. Grazing borders between Riziegat and Dinka Malual, particularly the 1924 agreement made by Wheatly Munro was among those controversial debates between Southern MPs and their counterparts from the North in the National Parliament on the ground that the Central Government supplied Riziegat and Misseriya tribes with machine guns to wage war against Dinka in order to chase them away from their land and the North insisted that the Malual Dinka also received guns from Anya Nya.

The central and regional governments fueled this fire and each gave its support to the waring parties instead of advocating for peaceful resolution to the conflict; they fought by proxy through the tribes on the border. It can be categorically said that the 14 Mile has never been part of any peace agreement until the Government of Sudan included it during the negotiations of the post-independence issues in Addis Ababa in 2012.

There was an attack on the Ngok Dinka as well. The period between 1972 and1982 was a hard time for both the Dinka Malual and Ngok Dinka. It appeared as a confrontation between the North and the South, taking a racial and ethnic twist between Arabs and Africans and sometimes the regime in Khartoum portrayed it as a religious conflict between Muslims and Christians.

Some Anya Nya officers, soldiers and chiefs' guards decided to go back to the armed struggle; citizens from Northern Bahr el Ghazal went to Azande land and Central Africa Republic to purchase guns to protect themselves, their children, women and cattle from Murahaleen.

In 1985, Nimeiry was overthrown by a popular uprising. Swar al Dahab who was the army chief of staff in his government took over power and formed a military council called TMC. Fadlalla Burama, a Messeri by tribe from Kordofan became a member of TMC.

The policy of supplying Riziegat and Misseriya with guns became institutionalized in the central government, escalating the revival of Anya Nya Two and consequently turning the conflict into a North-South confrontation in the contact areas.[38]

---

38

Many Arab traders were killed at Araith town by Anya Nya Two soldiers. The raiding and abduction of children and women, and the looting of cattle continued from both sides, especially, in mid-1980s, until the manifestation of SPLA/M on May 16, 1983. The balance of power was very weak on the side of Dinka Malual, something which encouraged many people to join the new movement in order to acquire guns for their protection.

Sudan People's Liberation Army and Sudan People's Liberation Movement (SPLA/M)

SPLA/M is a product of all accumulated grievances that the South and marginalized people of the Sudan experienced during the post-independence era. Without entering into details about the political circumstances under which the South passed in the beginning of the 1980s, the May Regime prepared ground for the Movement to thrive. Among the political differences between the South and the North was the issue of the borders, which was subsequently raised in the Regional and National Assemblies.

Another factor, was the issue of the oil refinery which was supposed to be installed in Kosti rather than Bentiu, and the issue of the Jonglei Canal which the Central Government decided would be dug without the consent of the South. Many demonstrations took place in the major towns of the South. The division of the South into three regions and implementation of Sharia laws by Nimeiry in September 1983, increased the percentage of those who believed the conflict could not be resolved through dialogue.

When the force from the Southern Army Command Headquarters in Juba attacked Bor, the Battalion 105 mutinied and went to the bush under the command of Major Kerubino Kuanyin Bol on May 16th 1983. The attacking force was commanded by Colonel Dominic Cassiano, a former Anya Nya officer. His mission was to quell, by force, the Bor military garrison.[39]

Under Major Bol the force in Bor, put up stiff resistance before it

---

39    Lam Akol , SPLM/A: Inside an African Revolution, 2001. pp, 12-20.

was dislodged and withdrew into the bush.[40] Major Kerubino was from Bahr el Ghazal, Twic Dinka.

Another small unit at Pibor and Pochalla joined Major Kerubino in the bush. On June 6, 1983, Major William Nyuon Bany, a friend to Kerabino and a former Anya Nya officer, killed Arab soldiers in Ayod and withdrew into the bush with his Battalion 104.

There was a plan that all Anya Nya garrisons in the South should move at the same time and capture the towns. This resulted in a move at Rumbek garrison by Battalion 111, but the action was taken by a junior officer, First Lieutenant Abengo Majak, leading to the failure of the plan.

Also, Battalion 110 of Mathiang garrison at Aweil was supposed to react on the fixed date, but due to the differences in the rank of its commanders, the mission failed. The suggestion given by some officers was that the rebellion should be delayed so the younger officers were trained to manage modern warfare. Mathiang garrison forces were transferred to Darfur and the mutiny failed.

There were already existing camps at the Ethiopian border controlled by Anya Nya Two. The mutineers joined them and training centers were opened for the new soldiers. In order to join the revolt, students, workers and government officials trekked to the Ethiopian borders where the soldiers had withdrawn to regroup and reorganize.[41]

These groups linked up with some elements of the Anya Nya Two in Itang, Ethiopia in order to form an organisation that would wage an armed struggle against Khartoum. Colonel John Garang, who was in Bor with his family for annual leave withdrew, together with the forces, when the war broke out. As a senior officer among junior officers Colonel Garang was made to lead the struggle, to win support from Ethiopia and Eastern bloc.[42] The Movement adopted a socialist ideology and its manifesto was advocating for the liberation of the whole of Sudan

---

40      Ibid.

41      Ibid.

42      Ibid.

instead of just Southern Sudan. The following points were significant: [43]

1. Fight for the creation of a new united Sudan that would give the marginalized areas of the Sudan equality and justice.
2. Adopt a socialist system of rule.
3. The fighting forces scattered all over the South, including Anya Nya Two to regroup, train and then start the war.

The new trend was opposed by Anya Nya Two officers; who went to meet the President Mengistu Haille Mariam of Ethiopia together with Colonel John Garang. They thought that the Movement had to struggle for secession of the South. When the team came back to the camps, Akuot Atem (as the leader of the delegation) was asked to write the position paper. This was because Akuot Atem had already shown some suspicion against John Garang.

The hurried document was revealed that fighting took place and the Anya Nya elements, with support from President Mengistu, were defeated. John Garang became Chairman and Commander-in-Chief (C.I.C.) of the Movement. Major Kerubino was promoted to Lieutenant Colonel and was made Deputy Chairman and Deputy C.I.C. Major William Nyuon was also promoted and made Chief-of-Staff in the Movement. Captain Salva Kiir Mayardit, who was an intelligence officer at Malakal garrison before he joined the rebellion, was made a Major and responsible for security and operations in the Movement. [44]

When the Anya Nya Two forces from Northern Bahr el Ghazal came to join the Movement, they found the structure of the Movement already established. Colonel Garang told them that no further organisation should be made, but he promised Major Kawac Makuei, (Dinka Malual) after promoting him to the rank of Lieutenant Colonel and commissioning him to command the Battalion, that further organisation would be done when he (Kawac) returned from a recruitment mobilization in Bahr el Ghazal.

---

43    Arop, Maut Arop, Sudan Painful Road to Peace, 2006, pp. 67-71.

44    Ibid.

Lt. Col. Kawac managed to perform his duty perfectly. On his way back to Ethiopia, Lt. Col. Kawac met Major Arok Thon, who had been promoted to Lieutenant Colonel, and was responsible for training and logistics as number five in the Movement hierarchy. Innocently, without knowing that the man had become senior to him, Kawac demanded a military salute, an act considered by Arok as insubordination; the charges for which in the military amounted to an arrest and fine. However, Lt. Col. Kawac was left to proceed.

Finding out about the promotion of Lt. Col. Arok to number five in the Movement's military hierarchy, Lt. Col. Kawac protested and differed to Dr. Garang as the Chairman of the Movement and

C.I.C of SPLA. He was arrested and sent to prison in 1984 from where he escaped in 1993 and returned to Sudan.

The politicians who arrived from Northern Bahr el Ghazal to Ethiopia in November 1983 with Lt. Col. Kawac Makuei included, CDR Lual Diing Wol, Sultan Gitano Kom Geng, Aluk Akec, CDR Lual Riny Lual, CDR George Kuac, and many other students from Nyamlel Senior Secondary School. All these people, and soldiers, were taken for military training in Ethiopia.

## 4.4 The Mission of Jamous Battalion in Bahr el Ghazal

Most officers and soldiers of Jamous Battalion were from Upper Nile, especially from Nuer tribe, with a few from the Dinka tribe. Although they had joined Anya Nya Two, they supported Colonel Garang in his war against what he called separatists in the South.

There were more than 50,000 Anya Nya Two forces in the area. The overall commander of the area was CDR Lual Riny Lual (Lual Makong) who was the first to decide to use the guns of his father, Chief Riny Lual, and formed an army at Marial Baai to protect their people from Riziegat militia.

During the time of Anya Nya's operations in the South, Chief Riny Lual, (who was fighting Anya Nya forces), migrated to Daien, and made friends with Chief Mohamud Musa Madibo. They formed a joint court at Daien. Later, Chief Riny Lual returned to his area of Marial Bai after the peace agreement was signed in 1972.

He was accompanied by some friends from the Riziegat who came along with their cattle to the area for grazing. Riziegat herders used Achana Park (One of the National Wildlife Reservation Park) for hunting. Fighting took place between Riziegat and the wildlife forces. Riziegat killed all the Wildlife Park forces except for one person who reported to Nyamlel army garrison. The garrison sent forces to investigate the situation immediately. Another battle took place, and the Riziegat were defeated.

News reached Daien and a few days later there was an attack on Marial Baai area thus the war between the Riziegat and Malual Dinka was revived. Malual Dinka decided to deal with the new situation and one of the options available to them was mobilization of people to form a force that would prevent the Riziegat from entering into Northern Bahr el Ghazal. They decided to buy guns from Zande land, in Equatoria, but others went to Bilfam in Ethiopia. The situation was exploited by SPLA/M as the main source for recruitment for the liberation struggle in the Sudan.

This is when Lt. Col. Kawac Makuei was sent to Aweil for purposes of recruitment, and succeeded in mobilizing Anya Nya Two soldiers and students to join SPLA/M. They went to Ethiopia for further training and a supply of machine guns with the aim of returning home ready to fight Riziegat and Misseriya forces at the border, an objective which was completely different from that of SPLA/M. The Jamous Battalion conducted operations at Aweil in March 1983 aimed at getting citizens from the town to join them. In February 1983, the Anya Nya Two soldiers destroyed the Lol River Bridge, which connects Aweil to the Babanousa railway, so as to stop Murahaleen from using the train from Babanousa to Aweil-Wau and vice versa. The battalion reported back to Ethiopia after carrying out its mission satisfactorily, but its Lt. Col. Makuei was arrested by the leader of the Movement in early 1984. In 1993, after he escaped Lt. Col. Makuei formed a faction with other commanders and later joined the Khartoum Peace Agreement as a signatory with five other Southern Sudanese factions led by Riak Machar Tiny in 1997. The government still sought to weaken the SPLA/M by transforming the conflict into a South-South war. However, the plan was unsuccessful and most signatories of the Khartoum Peace Agreement went back and joined the SPLA/M including its leader Riek Machar.

## 4.5 The Role Played By Some Patriotic Aweil Officers And Soldiers In Protecting The Area

On his way to Bor town, alternate Commander and the then First Lieutenant, George Kuac Atuer, an ex-army soldier from Aweil, received the news that the Riziegat militia had invaded the area. They abducted children and women and looted Dinka resources and burnt down houses. This happened after taking away Anya Nya Two fighters from the area for further training in Ethiopia.

First Lieutenant Atuer decided to disobey orders from the high military authority of the SPLA, and diverted the mission to Aweil with a patrol composed mainly of Dinka Malual fighters. Among them were many young officers like First Lieutenant Atak Deng Mayen, Lieutenant Garang Maloudit, and many others who did not survive.

When they reached Gogrial, they met Murahaleen forces driving over 3,000 cows and a good number of women and children as slaves/ abductees and a battle took place at Buol Majak near Gogrial. The invading forces were destroyed; cows, women and children were taken back. First Lieutenant George and other officers decided to go and station at the frontier between Riziegat, Misseriya and Dinka tribes. On their way to this area, many battles were fought and both sides experienced severe causalities in men and materials.

In 1985, the Mour Mour battalion forces graduated and most were from Northern Bahr el Ghazal. They were deployed in the Central South Sudan war zone, exclusively Northern Bahr el Ghazal. It was alleged that, the policy of the Movement was that no battalion should be taken to Northern Bahr el Ghazal, because if the Murahaleen stopped attacking Dinka Malual, the recruitment from Northern Bahr el Ghazal to SPLA forces would stop and as such, protection to this community from Riziegat and Misseriya militias and SAF forces was considered unnecessary.

There is a famous statement, allegedly made by late John Garang: "The end of a cultivated field is usually eaten by monkeys, not harvested. So, Northern Bahr el Ghazal is the last part of our field, let Arabs destroy it." This allegation was concurrently rumoured in line with the news being circulated widely in Northern Bahr Ghazal that General Chief-of-Staff of SPLA, CDR Salva Kiir Mayardit wrote a message to his assistant for supply and logistics asking him not to send ammunition to Aweil. All these allegations were considered as a way of creating conflicts between the leadership and people of Northern Bahr Ghazal who constituted a majority of committed SPLA/M members and supporters.

The policy of not providing protection to the people of Northern el Ghazal and their properties, of course, contradicts the aims for which the Anya Nya Two took-up arms in the area. Some elements from various battalions decided to escape to Aweil and join 1st Liet. George Kuac. In1986, the operations were extended up to Safaha (Kiir Adiem) where many Riziegat were killed and their cows were looted and their women and children abducted. This forced them to retaliate, by killing the Internal Displaced Peoples (IDPs) in Daien town under the knowledge and in the presence of the government officials and police in 1987.

Many more officers decided to come back to the area, forcing the leadership to recognize Northern Bahr el Ghazal as an important SPLA military base. Some prominent commanders who contributed to this work, included CDR Lual Riny Lual, CDR Paul Malong Awan, CDR Dau Aturjong, CDR Sanito Ayuang, CDR Butrus Bol Bol, CDR James Ajounga Ungang, CDR Deng Wol, CDR Diing Diing Wol, Capt. Koul Diing Wol, Capt. Diing Malong Wol, Capt. Reec Malong Wol and many others who also lost their lives, while others were seriously wounded for the cause of South Sudan and the marginalized people of the Sudan. Their contributions to the liberation will be remembered forever. The blood of those who lost their lives was not shed in vain. Instead it shall stand as an energizing factor that drives us to our destination and prosperity.

It's worth mentioning that H.E. President Salva Kiir read the First

Edition of this book and he categorically dismissed the allegations of ordering commanding officers to not supply arms and ammunitions to Northern Bahr el Ghazal considering it as mere propaganda from the enemy.

## 4.6 The Mission of Khil-Weing Forces in the Northern Bahr el Ghazal

The Khil-Weing was a part of the SPLA and not a separate force. The word Khil-Weing in Dinka Malual language means cattle protection. The force was led by one of the SPLA officers. The reason behind its formation was partially to protect the area from Riziegat and Misseriya militia who used to raid the area and partially to back up the SPLA/M in the area. As mentioned earlier, a good number of former Anya Nya Two fighters who joined the Movement did so for the reason of securing guns to protect themselves, their children, women, and cattle. Unfortunately, they were taken on different missions in other war zones.

Khil-Weing forces were formed in all villages and deployed at the border with Riziegat and Misseriya during the dry season under the overall command of CDR Jal Maluith Jal. The commanders of the forces were officers from the SPLA troops, transferred regularly from various units.

Khil-Weing from Atokthou deployed at War Painy; Khil-Weing from Dulit deployed at Siake; those from Makem deployed at Masora-Safaha, Khil-Weing from Akwak Ayat deployed at Ajok and Majok Dengdit at Raja road, Khil-Weing from Korok at Gok Anour near the Kiir River (Bahr Arab), Khil-Weing from Makuac deployed at Malek Alek Yai near Miaraim. The purpose of this distribution was to place the forces at the frontiers of the enemy in such a way that the war was not fought in the Dinka territory, so as to curtail collateral damage (abduction of women and children).

Other Khil-Weing forces from South Aweil areas, specifically those from Paleit and Paleupiny, were stationed around the railway along the Wau-Aweil road.

An SPLA soldier, who was interviewed before the signing of the CPA said that the mission of Khil-Weing was not just to protect the cattle as such, but it included participation in any operation when the enemy garrison was attacked. Also in the event of the enemy garrison falling into the hands of SPLA forces, it was the responsibility of Khil-Weing to maintain the security and order in the town. That is to say, Khil-Weing was to assume the function of police in the liberated areas. They would also engage the enemy until re-enforcement came to the nearest garrison of the SPLA forces.

They were also responsible for providing logistics and ammunition in the battle field and the withdrawal of whatever had been captured from the town in case SPLA forces were defeated.

Khil-Weing participated in the battles of Majok Dengdit in 1994 and Matwic in 1995, Lol Kau in 1996, and Araith, Wad-Weil, and Nyamlel in 1998. It can be recalled that in the mid-1990s the activities of the Riziegat and Misseriya militias became restricted, but continued at certain places, especially at Malual West. The East was fully secured by SPLA forces, resulting into the formation of peace markets.

## 4.7 Formation of Peace Markets with Riziegat and Misseriya

SPLA/M leadership and the local authorities of Riziegat, Misseriya and Dinka Malual people realized that the war had cost the people dearly and those suffering the most were innocent people living on the border. This motivated them to devise means of making people- to-people grass-roots peace. They made local peace agreements without the consent of the government or the SPLA/M leadership.

They maintained their contacts in the peace markets, setting up administration units of the markets between the tribes. The markets became an effective unifier for the Dinka Malual, Misseriya, and Riziegat people. The exchange of goods and materials went on smoothly. Sometimes the traders came from Khartoum and other big towns to purchase from the peace markets.

There were various peace markets at Malual North like Manyial Akok and Machar Adut, and in Aweil East at Warawar. Transport was available in those areas between Dinka Malual, Riziegat and Misseriya either by car, cows, horses, or camels and sometimes people walked.

## 4.8 Conclusion

Comparatively the situation between Dinka Malual, Riziegat and Misseryia, during the Anya Nya was contrary to the condition during SPLA/M because relations between the two tribes remained volatile. The government of Sudan continued supporting Rezeigat while the SPLA/M recruited Dinka Malual and used them in different missions to consolidate its stance against the government in Khartoum. Although the movement stated publically that it was fighting for the cause of marginalized people of Sudan in its manifesto, most of its fighting forces were from Southern Sudan.

The ethnic differences were used by the Government of Sudan to support Riziegat tribe by giving them necessary arms and logistics to invade Dinka Malual. The SPLA/M had done the same to support Dinka Malual in order to defend themselves from Murahaleen, the tribal militia of the government.

It can be recalled that the Government of Sudan and SPLA/M were fighting the war by proxy using ethnic differences existing between the two tribes. This policy was not understood by the two tribes until the tribal leaders decided to form the peace markets on the borders as a means of fostering mutual interests. The contribution of the two tribes in North–South relations, considering their geographical setting, is significantly important.

# CHAPTER 5

## 5. The Role of the International Community in Management of the Dinka Malual-Riziegat Conflict

The involvement of the international community especially, those bodies concerned with human rights values in Sudanese affairs, started early after the National Salvation Revolution (NSR) came to power in 1989.

Slavery was top on the agenda of international intervention in internal affairs. Slave trading, servitude and forced labour were cited in the western part of Sudan. The Dinka Malual, and their neighbours, the Riziegat and Misseriya tribes became part of international politics.

These global concerns were expressed by Western governments, NGOs, and other international agencies like the UN and international media.

This study examines the role of the USA, UN, international media, NGOs, and the role of some Western countries, in addressing the key issues that sparked the Dinka Malual and Riziegat conflict. It also explores how the issue of slavery/abduction became a matter of international concern.

### 5.1 The United States and the Dinka Malual-Riziegat Conflict

The United States policy on Sudan can be seen in a broader context of its interests in the entire region. Alternatively it can also be looked at in comparison with the U.S Middle East policy.

The Bill Clinton administration declared a policy of isolation and containment of the Government of Khartoum, because the Sudanese Government was perceived to be against the rule of law and democracy in Sudan.

Also, upon its seizure of power in the country in 1989, the regime supported Islamic international terrorism. The U.S Administration then directed its attention to four issues in the region; international terrorism as a threat to international peace and security, regional destabilization caused by illegal governments formed without the mandate of the citizens, human rights abuses, and the need for humanitarian assistance, generated by natural and/or human factors.

The study confines itself to the issues which connect areas of the research with those factors justifying the involvement of the U.S in the conflict between Dinka Malual and Riziegat. This is the examination of the activities related to slavery/abduction in the area.

The US strongly condemned the Sudan government and tried to intervene in its policies. From 1991, the US spearheaded a campaign among international development partners, pointing out issues of human rights violations in the Sudan, until 1998 when the US bombed a pharmaceutical plant at Shifa, Khartoum. This decision backfired against the US as the Sudan used this as a scapegoat to get away with its atrocities. Consequently, the US representative backed down leaving European countries to lead the move against the regime in Khartoum.

A briefing paper by the Washington Office on Africa 1999 (25.2) reads: "Still until 1998 the US took the lead. In developing the bombing of the factory in Khartoum; the US tended to yield to European initiatives. The issue of slavery in Sudan has secured some attention and resolutions in the General Assembly and Commission on Human Rights citing the Government of Sudan's disregard for human rights when it found itself isolated diplomatically."[45]

It was very unfortunate for the U.S to see the Commission of Human Rights pass the resolution dropping the term slavery and adopting the

---

45    Washington office on Africa, Briefing Paper issue: Slavery, War and Peace in Sudan, 25/2/1999.

word abduction. The resolution was considered by the U.S as unfair and declared its reservation on it.

Assuming the Presidency, George W. Bush Junior, inherited an explosive situation: Sudan vs regional and international politics.

The Sudan Government alleged that the Clinton Administration had deployed in neighboring countries and gave financial and material support to SPLA/M. Attacks on Kassala in 2003 and Torit in 2004 were alleged to have been masterminded by Eritrea and Uganda respectively but with logistical support from the US.

Internationally, there were attempts to impose sanctions on Sudan by accusing it of planning to kill President Husni Mubarak of Egypt. All financial assistance from the West to the Sudan government was cut off. The Sudan government reacted by closing doors on Western companies, especially those that had developed interest in investing in the oil sector. Eastern Asian countries, like, China, Malaysia, India and Korea, took that opportunity to invest in Sudan.

The Clinton policy to oust the Khartoum government failed especially after the bombing of the pharmaceutical plant. Instead a new objective was set to forge cooperation between the US and Sudan to bring peace as a prime human value.

A paper presented by the Strategic Studies Institute in the US proposed how the new policy would be conducted, with peaceful settlement being a top priority. Yet President Clinton was unwilling to step back from his declared policy of containment.

The Bush Administration faced two constraints. The first group demanded changes in the previous policy of direct confrontation. This position was advocated for by the business community who reasoned that the new policy allowed them to invest in Sudan.

The second group believed that, the cooperation with Sudan, which is the biggest human rights violator in the world, contradicts America's values; they therefore opposed cooperation with the Islamic government in Khartoum. This confrontational policy was led mostly by religious groups. Bush himself was said to be pro this group.

Between this conservative position from churches and the flexible attitude from business enterprises, the new administration found a place to set up its own policies that addressed the interests of both groups. The administration accepted cooperation with Sudan with conditions.

The US led war against terrorism necessitated wider cooperation, especially with Middle East countries, including Sudan which had better knowledge about Islamic terrorism. As such the areas of cooperation with the Sudan government were drawn to include war against terrorism, improvement of human rights conditions, peaceful settlement of the conflict in the South, and restoration of democracy.

The immediate concern here was the US involvement on humanitarian grounds in internal Sudanese affairs, particularly the issue of the conflict between Malual Dinka and Rezeigat on the border.

On September 9, 2001, just 48 hours before the September 11 attack, the former senator John Danforth, who was a religious and Episcopal clergy, was appointed as envoy of President Bush on peace in Sudan. This indicated that the church accepted the new policy on the Sudan and played a role in the nomination of the special envoy.

During his visit, Senator Danforth proposed an end to abductions and slavery among a series of steps aimed at building confidence between the two sides. As a matter of fact, the proposed measures were not aimed at building confidence between the government of the Sudan and SPLM/A as such, but it was a reconciliation of the interests between the US community and the government in Khartoum.

To end slavery/abduction immediately as proposed by Senator Danforth, the government issued a Presidential Decree to empower CEAWC and entrusted it with this responsibility.

Though CEAWC had been working closely with international organisations in the field of eradication of abduction of women and children, the view of the US was that no serious steps were taken. This was in compliance with its old position in the UN agencies.

It was even difficult to persuade US delegations to adopt the term abduction and drop the word slavery, until the two words were used concurrently in the text signed between the Government of Sudan and the US delegation that negotiated confidence-building measures in Khartoum in January 2002.

Four months before appointing Danforth as special envoy in May 2001, President Bush named Andrew Natsios as Head of the US Agency for International Development to be his "humanitarian coordinator" for genocidal, slavery-ridden, war-ravaged Sudan." In this respect, President Bush stated that, "This is a first step, more will follow. Our actions begin today and my Administration will continue to speak and act for as long as the persecution and atrocities in Sudan last."[46]

He continued: "Women and children have been abducted and sold into slavery. UNICEF estimates that more than 12,000 to 15,000 people are now held in bondage in Sudan."[47]

The dramatic change in the policy by appointing Danforth instead of Natsios, was also an indication of the role of the faith-based organizations in the US, in regard to the conflict in the Sudan.

Despite the efforts exerted to bring slavery/abduction to an end, there was still a belief in the US administration that the practice of slavery, slave trade, servitude, and forced labour was going on. As such Sudan was left on the list of those countries that refused to cooperate in ending human rights violations. It was hoped that the diplomatic relations would be resumed by the two countries after the CPA was signed in Nairobi on January 9, 2005, but the US went back on its promises that a new page would be opened after the improvement of the human rights situation in the Darfur region of Western Sudan.

There were no diplomatic contacts between the two countries until August 2007 when a high delegation from the Ministry of Foreign Affairs in Sudan visited the US to resume dialogue on normalization of relations on request of the government in Khartoum.

Another session was conducted in France which agreed to meet again in Khartoum, but due to developments in Abyei which led to the killing and displacement of the citizens by SAF in May 2008, the talks did not proceed. However, the USA kept pushing for the implementation of the CPA and independence until South Sudan seceded from Sudan officially on July, 2011.

---

46      Bush, New max.com, UIRES, Saturday, May 5th 2001.

47      Ibid.

## 5.2 The Role of the United Nations in Management of Dinka Malual-Riziegat Conflict

Issues of human rights violations in the Sudan came to the forefront in 1987 when a big massacre took place at Daien town in Southern Darfur. A report written by two lecturers from the University of Khartoum indicated the murder of more than 1,000 persons from Dinka Malual. Quoting the report; "On March 28, more than 1,000 Dinka children, women and men were killed by some Riziegat Arabs."

According to eyewitness, the attackers raided a wooden wagon in which more than 200 Dinkas were travelling. They threw thatch and burning mattresses into it and burnt all the Dinkas to death.[48]

It should be recalled that the massacre was executed for three consecutive days from March 27 to 29, 1987.

The report went on to say that the massacre was supervised by government officials, and some policemen participated in the killing of the innocent people. A series of events surrounding the attack confirm their suspicions. First government officials chose to move the thousands of Dinkas who spent the night in Hillat Sikka Hadid to the railway station following an attack by the Riziegat and others on the Dinkas. Then government officials and the police met at the train station to evaluate the situation, later these same officials disappeared when the massacre was taking place.[49]

In his statement to BBC radio, the Prime Minister Sadig al Mahdi said: "The act was one of revenge for what SPLM/A did at Safaha."[50]

The Minister of Interior Affairs Sid Ahmed al-Hussain gave a similar explanation. It should be recalled that SPLA attacked Safaha in January 1987 and defeated the Riziegat militia with heavy casualties.

The Prime Minister and the Minister of Interior Affairs' statements indicated government involvement in the tribal conflict and its plan

---

48    Suliman and Ushari, Human Rights Violations in the Sudan: The Daein Massacre: Slavery in the Sudan, 1987 pp. 1-16.

49    Ibid.

50    Ibid.

to kill Dinka displaced people at Daien.[51]

Following the massacre of innocent people and the response of the government, the two lecturers from the University of Khartoum visited the scene of the incident to investigate and expose the culprits.

No practical step was taken on human rights violations in the Sudan until 1992 when Gaspar Biro visited the country. He submitted a report to the Commission of Human Rights in 1992 in his capacity as an independent expert. Biro was then appointed as a Special Rapporteur on Rights in the Sudan by the High Commission of Human Rights in 1993. He paid several visits to the country and submitted his reports on human rights violations, including slavery, the slave trade, servitude and forced labour, until he resigned in 1999. During his time, there was severe deterioration of Sudanese relations with the international organisations.

He was succeeded by Mr. Leonardo Franco in 1999, who visited the country in the same year and submitted his report to the Commission of Human Rights.

Before Mr. Franco took over in 1998, a delegation from the office of the High Commission of Human Rights visited Sudan to discuss cooperation in the areas of human rights with the government and the United Nations agencies in the Sudan.

During this period, there were intensive contacts between the government and the UN agencies to resolve the issue of human rights violations. The Sudan government tendered a report to the UN Committee on Economic, Social and Cultural Rights (ICESCR) denying the existence of any kind of discrimination.

Another report on children's rights through the National Council on Child Welfare to the UN Committee on the Rights of the Child confirmed its position that children were well taken care of.

A third report was submitted to the UN Committee on Racial Discrimination, claiming that there was no ethnic and racial discrimination. Other similar reports were prepared and submitted.

_____

51      Ibid.

The international organisations involvement in government activities were preceded by the visit of Lord McNair of the British House of Lords, who visited Sudan to investigate the allegations of slavery. Lord McNair inspected many locations and released his report in November 1997.[52] Part of it read: "I have recently returned from a working visit to Sudan from 4-11 October 1997. This visit was the culmination of an examination of slavery allegations made against the Government of Sudan and took me to the states of South and North Kordofan. My overall impression was that there was something contrived about some of these reports which suggested to me the possibility of a deliberate campaign from some quarters to discredit the government."

Although Lord McNair did not visit the area of Dinka Malual and Riziegat, it is very clear from what he saw in Kordofan the homeland of Misseriya tribe who partnered with the Riziegat in carrying out slavery. Many Dinka children and women were taken by trains to Western Kordofan. According to the report, Lord McNair found abducted women and children but their situation was not that of slavery.

This sparked a great debate in European communities whether the practice was a slavery or abduction. Finally, the resolution came out in favour of abduction, and the government was tasked to exert more efforts to eradicate it.

In compliance with instructions from the International Community, the government established the Committee for Eradication of Abduction of Women and Children (CEAWC), an institution charged to eradicate the abduction of women and children in the area of inter-tribal conflicts. CEAWC was formed in 1999 with the full consent of international NGOs working in the field of children's rights and protection like UNICEF and Save the Children U.K. These NGOs gave some funding to assist CEAWC in carrying out its duty.

During the time of Senator John Danforth's mission to Sudan as Special Envoy of President George W. Bush on Peace in the Sudan in 2001, CEAWC was empowered by the Presidential Decree and

---

52      Ibid.

delegated powers of the Minister of Justice to enable it deal with the eradication of abduction of women and children in the armed conflict areas.

Reports submitted to the U.N. Commission on Human Rights by Mr. Leonardo after the establishment of CEAWC indicated progress on the human rights situation in Sudan. However, the reports called for more freedom of press, freedom to form associations, religious freedom to Christians, and rule of law and democracy.

The report also called for an end to the war in Sudan and the establishment of peace in the country as a way of addressing the source of human rights violations.

Mr. Leonardo was replaced by Mr. Gerhart Baum in 2001 who visited the country three times to evaluate the progress of the human rights situation. In the 58th session of the High Commission for Human Rights in October 2002, the Council's resolution included the Sudan in "The Chairman Text" which was issued, meaning that the country should exert more efforts to improve human rights situation. It also called for material and moral support from the international organisations in this regard.

In March 2003, the Human Rights Commission voted in favour of the Sudan and it was removed from the list of "Chairman's Text" to the list of those countries which cooperated fully in the field of human rights. The decision was criticized by the US, but it did not vote against it due to the consensus in the UN Security Council (UNSC).

To show its concern with the peaceful resolution of conflict in the South, the UN held its first meeting in Africa in Nairobi, Kenya in November 2004. The meeting urged the two warring parties to stop fighting and work for peace.

This eventually led to the signing of the CPA on January 9, 2005. In April 2005, the UNSC held in its sitting a special session on Peace in the Sudan, and made several resolutions to support peace, including the deployment of the UN forces, United Nation Mission in Sudan (UNMIS), as peace keepers.

Jan Bronk was nominated to head the mission and was later expelled by the government and replaced by Mr. Ashraf Jehangir Qazi. In October 2007, the Secretary General of the UN visited Juba to discuss the implementation of the CPA in the Sudan where he urged the parties to work for the implementation of CPA.

### 5.3 The Views of the International Media on Dinka Malual-Riziegat Conflict

The issue of slavery in the Sudan came to be highlighted, particularly, in the Western media in the mid-1980s through the former government minister and well-known journalist, Bona Malual Madut. From Dinka Twic of Bahr el Ghazal region, and Chief Editor of *The Sudan Times*, the English-language newspaper, Madut exposed the practice in the Sudanese community. Exiled in England, Madut started publishing articles in the *Sudan Democratic Gazette* focusing on slavery in Sudan.

In 1987, Ushari Mohamed and Suliman Ali Baldo from the University of Khartoum wrote their famous book; *The Violation of Human Rights in the Sudan: The Daein Massacre and Slavery in Sudan.* The findings of this investigation were published in many international media outlets and broadcast by BBC Radio on 23rd May, 1987.

In the 1990s the issue of slavery in the Sudan became dominant in the field of journalism. *The New Yorker, The Los Angeles Times, The Washington Post, The Washington Times, The Boston Globe, The New York Times, The Irish Times, The Independent on Sunday, The International Herald Tribune,* as well as other monthly magazines like *The Atlantic Monthly, The Economist* and many other Western, Middle East and African press publications expressed concern about the practice of slavery in the Sudan.

Some views were that SPLM/A senior commanders used the situation to fraudulently buy the freedom of slaves in areas under their control.

Also, many of these newspapers exposed the role of the government in the practice. Other organisations, especially Christian International Solidarity (CIS) and Anti-Slavery International (ASI) worked hard to break international silence about slavery in the Sudan.

While the campaign was on-going, other publications denounced the existence of slavery. This contrary campaign was led by the European-Sudanese Public Affairs Council based in London. Mr. David Hoile the Director of this Council published many works in the field of human rights in the Sudan, peace, US-Sudan policy and articles of a similar kind in newspapers and magazines.

Apart from the anti-slavery campaign, Sudan faced international condemnation following the allegation that some officials in government attempted to kill President Mubarak of Egypt in 1996.

The United Nations Security Council issued many resolutions considering the Sudan government as a violator of human rights. Many human rights circles visited the Sudan to investigate the allegations on slavery. No agreement came out among those circles for the simple fact that those who decided to visit Southern Sudan and areas under the control of the Movement, came out with findings of the existence of slavery, then recommended the slave redemption process.

However, those who visited Khartoum, reported a different situation, and they called for support of the government to eradicate it. The example is the visit of Lord McNair to North Sudan.

The war divided the country into two parts; a person that wanted to fly to Khartoum was required to seek a visa from the Sudan government. But if someone was interested in visiting the occupied territory in South Sudan, permission was granted by SPLM/A offices abroad.

The government attempted to convince the human rights investigators that what had been going on was abduction resulting from inter-tribal conflict over pastoral resources in the contact areas. For the SPLM/A, the visitors to their areas had to be convinced that what had been going on was slavery and a slave trade, sponsored by the government.

This situation by itself was detrimental to human rights values since the two parties rivaled for power in the same country. However, obviously, it was also a competition to win international support and sympathy.

Compelled by videos showing the CIS and ASI buying back enslaved women and children from Arab slave traders, school children in the United States donated the cost of their breakfast meals to the suffering children of Southern Sudan. The propaganda by CIS and ASI got support from civil society within the US especially Christian organisations and in Congress.

Father Mario Riva, an Italian priest who spent more than 20 years in Southern Sudan and had managed to learn local languages including Dinka, appeared on CNN TV programme, "CBS 60 Minutes." The topic under discussion was the redemption of the slaves by CIS in Southern Sudan. He said:

"The translators he saw at Eibner redemption purposely misinterpreted the words. For example I tell him, please ask the people if they are - they were slaves, or they are slaves or not. And the translator says, 'Are you coming from home? And they say yes', and the white man sees them nodding but he doesn't know what for."[53]

He added: "The slave traders are local people; they are given money to round up villagers and bring them to redemption. As for the people who may be playing the part of a slave, they may get a few coins to fill an empty belly." Father Riva thinks Eibner (CIS) and others must know that a scam is occurring. "They know" he says, "They want to save the Sudanese. But this is the wrong way."[54]

John Eibner, an American human rights activist and one of CIS personnel stated that the criticism was unfounded: "I am absolutely sure that what we do is credible. That money which is sent to us for this purpose is used for that purpose, and that women and children are freed from the terrible abuse, the rape, the beatings. The forceful conversions, all of the horrors are an inherited part of slavery in Sudan."[55]

Late Samson Kwaje, the former SPLA/M spokesman and former minister in the GOSS, advised an Ontario-based church group called

---

53    CNN T.V. An Interview with Rev. Mario Riva through the programme CB 60 Minutes, February 2002.

54    Ibid.

55    Ibid.

"Crossroads" to give up redemption and spend its contributions on other projects such as digging wells. Kwaje said: "There is the moral issue of people being abducted and the Movement being seen as insensitive to its own people."[56]

Declan Walsh, the reporter of the *Independent News* U.K., on 24th February 2002, wrote an article entitled "Scam in Sudan—An Elaborate Hoax Involving taking African Slaves." He wrote; "High profile western campaigners who spent millions of dollars buying the freedom of slaves in war-time Sudan have been the victims of a scam, it is alleged. Anti-slavery organisations have 'redeemed' more than 65,000 Sudanese slaves from their Arab masters over the past seven years, usually for $50 (Ls.35) for a head."[57]

The leading charities were the Swiss-based Christian Solidarity International (CSI) and Christian Solidarity World Wide (CSW), founded by Baroness Caroline Cox, the Deputy Speaker of the House of Lords. Although slavery was a reality, *The Independent on Sunday* claimed that "redemption" had often been carefully orchestrated by the charities.[58]

According to witnesses interviewed by the Independent in Sudan: "Local villagers are rounded up to pose as slaves when Christian groups arrive with briefcases full of money. Rebel soldiers from the SPLM were sometimes disguised as "slave traders."[59]

A retired Italian missionary told the CSI that he saw his own parishioners posing as slaves. A European aid worker saw children she knew were pretending to be in bondage. Also, a former rebel commander said that his relative, a soldier in SPLM/A, had been forced to pose as a slave trader.

Baroness Caroline Cox who had been an member of the CSI,

---

56    Vick, Ripping off the Redeemers" Washington Post, Tuesday, February 26, 2002.

57    Independent on Sunday "Scam in Sudan-An Elaborate Hoax involving take African slaves," The Independent on Sunday, 24 February, 2002.

58    Ibid.

59    Ibid.

broke away and formed a new organisation called Christian Solidarity Worldwide (CSW) in 1997. She left the activities of CSI to John Eibner and Jim Jacobson and came to the South on her own. Other Christian groups decided to distance themselves from the practice of redemption. Even the newly formed CSW of Lady Cox stopped the practice and worked in the field, supplying medical items into Sudan's ravaged South instead of cash for redemption of slaves. *The Irish Times* on February 23rd 2002 published:

"In Sudan, the slave trade countries and western charities have collected millions of dollars to free women and children enslaved in the North."[60]

However, the high profile redemption of thousands of slaves was often a corrupt racket. In a major investigation, Walsh talked to witnesses of the sale of fake slaves by fake slave traders;

"The slave redemption made for powerful human drama. A line of children emerged from the African bush. A slave trader in front wrapped in the white robes of an Arab. Furthermore, before them, waiting with a bag of money at his feet, was a white, Christian man. The procession halted under the shade of a tree. There was discussion, then money changed hands. Suddenly, the trader gave a nod, the slaves walked free and there were the cries of joy as families were re-united in freedom at last."[61]

Many newspapers focused their attention on this issue.

*The Washington Post* on February 26, 2002, stated: "this coincides with descriptions of the scam offered by Sudanese officials and Western aid workers who said the sheer volume of money flowing into the south made corruption inevitable."[62]

In one of its articles, *The Independent on Sunday* stated that "interpretation was key to the deception."

Some commanders in the SPLM/A rank responded by condemning

---

60    Ibid.

61    Vick, op cit.

62    Ibid.

the practice of fake redemption as a humiliation of their principles and its leadership.

In a meeting in December 1999, the issue of slave redemption was brought up by late CDR Mario Mour Mour, the Deputy Commander of Sudan Relief and Rehabilitation Association (SRRA), the SPLM/A's aid wing. The meeting of senior SPLM/A commanders condemned the practice and asked for its immediate end. CDR Mario in October 2001 stated that; "a number of Southern Sudanese accompanying CSI, John Eibner's organisation into Southern Sudan – mostly SPLM/A officials – were selling donated medicines as well as being involved in redemption frauds. Redemption is just a scandalous act."

However, CDR Dr. Justin Yaac, admitted that the rebels made exorbitant profits selling Sudanese pounds to CSI up to the end of 1999, enough to buy thousands of gallons of fuel, 27 secondhand Land Cruisers and 10,000 uniforms for the army. The dispute over scandalous redemptions made previous friends enemies of the day.

Bona Malual, a man described by Baroness Cox as one of the well-respected elders of the Dinka tribe, in a letter to European-Sudanese Public Council, directly challenged Cox's claims to have redeemed slaves.

The head of the Land Mine Clearing Agency, former SPLM/A Commander, Aleu Ayieng Aleu, said his relative who was a captain in the Movement was forced to play the role of a slave trader as an Arab middleman accusing SPLM/A officers in the cash for slave redemption for personal interests. "It was a hoax," said Aleu. The SPLM/A leader, John Garang made a written order forbidding Bona and others from traveling on future redemptions to Southern Sudan. UNICEF believed that the process of paying money to the slave master would encourage the practice rather than discouraging it.

On February 2002 CSI announced, for the first time that it had liberated 14,500 slaves without payment. They claimed the slaves were freed through negotiations between Southern and Northern tribal elders.

## 5.4 The position of International Non-Governmental Organisations (INGOs) On the Dinka Malual Rezeigat Conflict

The role of INGOs, human rights agencies, and the issues discussed in this chapter cannot be handled in isolation. The significant difference is how a particular organisation or an agency viewed the situation of human rights in Sudan.

Some groups believed there was slavery in the Sudanese communities while others considered it a by-product of war and hence did not regard it as an serious matter that would end once the war ended. The third group was torn between, giving explanations that the practice was abduction, known in the Sudanese community, caused especially by inter-tribal conflicts at the tribal border between the North and the South and sometimes between the South-South communities.

The great difference was the absence of a clear definition of what was taking place. Was it slavery or abduction? This conceptual difference resulted in serious disagreements among the human rights groups and indicated how communities would deal with the phenomenon.

UNICEF thought the best way to deal with this phenomenon was to cooperate with the government, through CEAWC, to stop the practice, and then eradicate the abduction of women and children.

It considered the buy-back policy of slaves by some human rights organisations as an encouragement and incentive at the same time for the slave masters to continue with their activities, and that the money used to buy-back slaves could even constitute revolving funds in the slave markets. As such, the situation was complicated.

In Geneva, in February, 1999 UNICEF stated that the Sudanese had invited the agency for the first time to investigate the charges, adding that the authorities had left the door wide open for a full investigation. They accepted Khartoum's request for a detailed report on the issue. The agency expressed its hope that other organisations, both the Sudanese and the international organisations, would join the inquiry.

The invitation was followed by the new allegations against the government that the slavery/abduction still persisted but the government denied it.

The Christian groups claimed that they had bought back the freedom of more than 5,000 slaves in the South for $52,000 by the beginning of 1995. CSI urged the immediate intervention of the UN to end this unacceptable inhuman practice.

However, UNICEF considered Khartoum's acceptance of an investigation, instead of the usual denial of the practice, as a step forward which needed to be considered on its part. UNICEF launched a blistering attack on CSI's practice of buying back, asserting that it encouraged slavery as well as the trade in arms in a region torn by war.

UNICEF was also attacked by several human rights bodies especially the religious groups based in the United States. They considered its position, of refusing to support the process of buying back of slaves, as sympathizing with the Government of Sudan.

In a statement on March 16, 1999, the American Anti-slavery Group (AASG) accused UNICEF of inaction on slavery in the Sudan, and of moral obtuseness. The AASG was established in 1994 and was not connected with ASI, which in turn did not support the American group's accusation against UNICEF in any way.

ASI was quoted as saying: "One aim is to put an end to patterns of slavery altogether and to ensure that no one is subjected to slavery in the first place." Mike Dottridge, the Director General of ASI, stated: "We realize it is tempting to pay ransoms or pay off loans which keep people in slavery. However, when anti-slavery activists paid money to the owners of slaves in the past, we often realized afterwards that the same owners used the money they had received to acquire more slaves replacing those who had been released. Because of this danger, we do not support schemes to pay the release of slaves."[63]

Commenting further on the situation, Dottridge added: "The current rumpus about paying for slaves in Sudan is preventing the real issues from being addressed; the Government of Sudan is continuing with its policy of supporting militia raids and captives are still being enslaved. In view of the Government's refusal to change this policy,

---

63      Statement by Dattridge, the Director General of ASI on Sudan, Washington, March 3, 1999.

U.N. agencies such as UNICEF should be encouraged to intervene to secure the release of slaves. It is completely unacceptable but because no solutions have been found to end Sudan's civil war, slavery is going to continue into the next century."[64]

Commenting on the issue of slavery in Sudan, the Sudan's Undersecretary for Foreign Affairs, Hassan Abdin was quoted on March 17, 1999, saying: "Negative practices arising from conditions of civil war and tribal conflict cannot be classified as a sort of slavery."[65]

This statement provoked ASI to say: "When people are held by force and made to work, it is ridiculous to quibble about words and pretend that it is not slavery."[66] There have been consistent reports over the past 12 years that government armed militia have taken women and children captive during raids and have forced them to work. Attempts by the Government of Sudan to dismiss this as tribal practices and to deny that it amounts to slavery do not convince us or anyone else. This is simply an excuse for not taking action against illegal imprisonment and slavery, and means that the Government is quilty of condoning slavery. CSI's Policy on Sudan since 1995 has consistently agitated for international intervention to stop what it called organized systematic genocide and slave practice in Sudan.[67]

Baroness Cox, before branching away from the CSI, was working together with John Eibner, the Executive Director on the redemption of slaves. They paid slave masters to release slaves, an action which created differences between them and UNICEF administration.

CSI said that it was able to release more than 65,000 persons, and there were more than 200,000 persons still enslaved in the North. The organisation (CSI) criticized the position of UNICEF to cooperate with the government in the process of CEAWC.

---

64    Ibid.

65    Abiden (Undersecretary for Foreign Affairs Ministry/Sudan) comment on the issue of slavery in Sudan, London, The Independent newspaper on 14/7/ 1999.

66    Mike Dottridge Op cit.

67    Ibid.

On his return from a fact-finding visit to Sudan in July 2001, Eibner encouraged President Bush to use the current window of opportunity to support Sudanese civil society's efforts to free the slaves immediately, he believed, "There can be no true peace in Sudan as long as black African women and children are enslaved."

In January 1999, a new Sudanese slave documentation programme was launched, undertaken jointly by CSI, AASG and National Black Leadership (NBL). The documentation project targeted enabling the government, human rights organisations, and the public to understand better the extent both quantitatively and qualitatively of Sudan's revived slave trade. CSI declared that it managed to release slaves from Arabs without paying money but through negotiations.

In June 2003, in a conference at Mabil, Northern Bahr el Ghazal, CSI called for continuation of dialogue with UNICEF on the issue of slavery in Sudan. It was the first dialogue between CSI and UNICEF since 1999. In its briefing paper, on May 25, 2000, The Washington Office on Africa said:

"Slavery's resurgence in Sudan is rooted in the civil war. Hard evidence of this resurgence dates from the mid-1980s. Slavery has historically been a feature of ethnic rivalry in Sudan but they revived and increased the practice. With support from UNICEF and Save the Children Fund (SCF), the government of Sudan which continues to deny the existence of slavery, agreed to establish a committee for the eradication of slavery and abduction of "women and children under the auspices of their Ministry of Justice in May 1999."[68]

Slave raids were carried out primarily in the province of Bahr el Ghazal by an agreement between the government of Sudan and armed militia of the Baggara ethnic group-nomadic cattle- owning Arabized people-known as the Murahaleen. A number of international groups, church members, and US schools tried to end slavery in Sudan by buying back those who have been enslaved. International intervention was welcomed by the families of the slaves and their chiefs who longed to be reunited with family members.

---

68     Washington Office on Africa Briefing Paper, op cit.

However, according to David Hoile, head of the European-Sudanese Relations Council (ESPRC); "There have been accusations of fraud where unscrupulous southerners are said to have borrowed children who have never been abducted offering them as slaves to augment the proceeds from the redemption. Some observers suggest that the SPLA/M and other local government structures are implicated. Concern continues that the enterprise of slave redemption could increase funds for combat rents, guaranteeing the purchase of more arms to fuel the war. Highly publicized international intervention may undercut Southern Sudan's efforts to find their own solutions for this problem."[69]

Human Rights Watch, released in March 2002 an updated report on slavery and slave redemption in the Sudan, denounced slavery in Sudan in the context of the 19-year civil war. They described this contemporary form of slavery, conducted by government-backed armed militias of the Baggara tribes who raided to capture children and women who were then held in conditions of slavery in Western Sudan and elsewhere. They were forced to work for free in homes and fields; they were punished when they refused, and were abused physically and sometimes sexually. Raids were directed mostly at the civilian Dinka population in Bahr el Ghazal. Human Rights Watch called on the Government of Sudan to take firm measures to stamp out slavery and prosecute those responsible for it, including law enforcement officers who were paid to assist. The victims and their families had consistently complained that local government officials, including police, rarely helped them when they traveled to Western Sudan in an attempt to locate and free their abducted children. Thus, the Government of Sudan was responsible not only for knowingly arming, transporting and assisting the slave-raiding militia, but it was also responsible for not enforcing its own laws against kidnapping, assault, and forced labour.

Religious organisations which were concerned with the issue of slavery in the Sudan were; We Hold This Truth (WHTT), National Association of Evangelicals (NAE), Southern Baptist Church (SBC), Lutheran

---

69    David Haile, Force Majeure: The Clinton Administration's Sudan Policy, 1993-2002, London. The European-Sudanese Public Affairs Council, 2002.

Church Missionary (LCM), Front Line Fellowship (FLF) and many other organisations.

Contrary to what has been advocated by CSI, ASI and other organisations, especially based in USA, UNICEF and SCF took a moderate position and developed working programmes with the Government of Sudan in the process of the eradication of the abduction of women and children by giving technical and financial support to CEAWC.

UNICEF conducted many workshops in the field and drew a strategy on how to deal with the practice of abduction. Unlike UNICEF, the involvement of SCI, U.K. in the programme of eradication of abduction was less intensive.

The official position prevented the organisation from going into the internal affairs and looking for children but they were brought to the organisation's care and were given assistance. The position of UNICEF not to consider the case of children above 18 years was highly criticized by the families of the victims who argued that the children were abducted when they were young and they should not be forgotten and left as slaves in the hands of Arabs just because they had become adults.

Although its mandate did not allow it to engage directly in this process, many people argued that the organisation should have allowed others to engage in redemption of the victims if its mandate did not allow its engagement.

In 1999, SCUK retrieved 400 children through police and tribal leaders. It also gave financial support to JCC to facilitate the movement in the area of abduction.

The UNDP, in collaboration with UNICEF and MOHE, presented a paper on conflict surveys and mapping analysis in August 2002, considering the conflict between Malual Dinka and Baggara (Riziegat and Misseriya) as a competition over natural resources but became politicized with racial overtones.

UNDP suggested programme dialogues for sustainable human development in the war-torn Sudan. It aimed at confidence building between the key parties of the conflict by providing an opportunity for discussing technical and developmental issues that had direct relations with political negotiations.[70]

Other civil organisations, like European-Sudanese Relations Council (ESPRC), took a stand by supporting the Government of Sudan against propaganda launched by the religious groups. The organisation considered the propaganda as something planned by the previous US administration to bring down the government in Khartoum.

David Hoile continued to criticize the practice by saying; "it was clear the US Administration had used these allegations as anti-Sudan government propaganda within the international community. The propaganda still persists against the present government in Sudan." According to him, tribal raids and abductions were presented by Christian fundamentalist groups, such as CSI and other activists, as slavery. Although, the Dinkas are overwhelmingly humanists, these groups had additionally presented the conflict between the Dinka and the Arabized Baggara as a religious one.[71]

Hoile justified the non-involvement of the government in the North in the practice of slavery by saying: "If these people were as much at risk of being enslaved by northerners (as alleged by CSI), Khartoum would have been their last place of refuge. It would make as little sense to go there as would have for Jews in Nazi-occupied Europe to have sought refuge in Berlin. Khartoum was their first place of refuge which must be taken as important evidence against the CSI claim."[72]

This kind of statement was not new, there were rumours saying that Mr. Hoile was employed and paid by the regime in Khartoum to protect its interests.

## 5.5 The Issue of Slavery/Abduction in CPA

The relevance of this topic to this Chapter comes from the fact that the CPA was a product of the regional and international efforts and pressure on the warring parties in the Sudan. It was clear how the

---

70    UNICEF, UNDP, MOHE. Conflict Survey and Mapping Analysis, August, 2002.

71    Hoile, David, op cit.

72    Ibid.

International Community, NGOs, Governments in Western countries, and international media and press, were concerned about the issue of slavery/abduction in the Sudan. US President's special envoy, Senator John Danforth, placed the issue of slavery/abduction in the South on the top of his agenda when he was negotiating what he termed "confidence-building" steps between the Sudan Government and SPLM in 2002.

The concern that the issue of slavery/abduction revived in the mid-1990s and early 2000s by international communities and INGOs was absent during the negotiations of the peace agreement between Sudan Government and SPLM/A.

The prevention of slavery/abduction was among the issues discussed and an agreement was reached in 2002 as confidence- building steps. However, during the negotiations at Naivasha the issue of slavery/abduction did not come up. Rev. Danforth placed it as one of the fundamental issues leading to peace in the Sudan, but, it was dropped during the discussions.

No clear explanation was given, but presumably, the differences which existed between INGO's about the nature of the practice and the way the Government of Sudan had responded to the situation can be assumed as the reason why the mediators did not bother themselves with the issue and its controversies.

Northern Bhar el Ghazal elders in the Movement discussed the issue of the inclusion of slavery in peace negotiations with John Garang but the SPLA/M delegation on the table did not discuss the issue with the Government's delegation.

The SPLA/M delegation might have ignored it because of the efforts of CEWAC members who wanted the practice to be considered as abduction and were supporting its eradication. They were moving between Khartoum and Nairobi seeking more powers in order to solve the problem by the reintegration of those children separated from their families with the support of the parties to the peace agreement. CEWAC obtained support and managed to reunite more than 1,500 children with their families by the end of the year 2005.

All these reasons made the CPA silent on the practice of slavery/ abduction in South Sudan and only mentioned it as a part of a bill of rights criminalized by international laws.

There was no clear official position, whether in GONU or GoSS about the fate of children and women captured/abducted by Baggara in Northern Bhar el Ghazal, Northern and Western Upper Nile during the war in the South. The little effort which was exerted was from private and personal initiatives of the Dinka Malual chiefs' council which did not eliminate or eradicate the phenomena once and for all.

In the grassroots peace conference between Dinka Malual and Misseriya in Aweil town in May 2008, the members of the two communities called the government to finalise the process of eradication of the slavery/abduction of women and children by financing CEWAC programmes. The GOSS pledged $1m but the project needed $7m. The project collapsed after the independence of South Sudan although there are more than 50,000 persons still in bondage in Sudan.

## 5.7 Conclusion

The Western communities were unhappy with the Government of National Salvation represented by the National Congress Party (NCP). This government had essential ideological differences with the West. The differences came from three basic principles; the first is that the West believes in the rule of democracy, but the National Salvation Government removed the elected democratic government of the Prime Minister al Sadig al Mahdi from power.

The second principle is the position of the Government of National Salvation on human rights. Many human rights actors believed that the government did not respect human rights. The United Nations sent many special envoys to investigate the situation of human rights in the Sudan, unfortunately their reports showed no improvement. The issue of slavery/abduction falls under this principle which is the focus of this study. The Rezeigat tribe had been accused of enslaving/ abducting Dinka Malual children and women.

The third principle is the issue of terrorism; the government has been accused of supporting Islamic organisations which are considered terrorist organisations. The effort made by the Western governments and civil societies was supposed to be reflected in the CPA, but surprisingly all these efforts were not considered in the peace agreement and the CPA was silent about the issue of slavery/abduction. The Dinka Malual citizens thought the CPA should not neglect this important issue because more than 50,000 women and children were believed to be in bondage in the area of Riziegat and Massiria tribes.

# CHAPTER 6

## 6.1 Impact of Ethnicity and Politics on Unity of Sudan

Most severe and persistent threats to global peace and stability arise not only from conflicts between major political entities, but also from increased discord within states, societies, and civilizations along ethnic, racial, religious, caste, or class line. The spread of internal discord is a product of powerful stresses on communities, economic, demographic, sociological, and environmental concerns.[73]

Sudan, the largest African country occupies a total area of one million square miles with a population estimated to be more than 30 million people before 2005, which means each one square mile for three people. This area is inhabited by more than 500 tribes that speak more than 100 languages and has great diversity in terms of cultures, religions, origins and environments. It has also been in conflict since independence in 1956.

In other countries, like Malaysia for example, the element of diversity was managed and used for welfare of the people through application of a good system of governance and democracy where every citizen feels at home with the same rights and performs duties which are supposed to be carried out as a citizen.

Diversity of nations has not been a problem, but if people are denied

---

73      Michael Klare, War, Weapons and Sustainability in Post-Cold War Era 1996 pawss.hampshire.edu.

their rights and live in a situation of political exclusion then, it will turn into a problem. This may result sometimes in a rebellion or a military coup in some countries. For this reason, Sudan has been witnessing a long political struggle between the South, whose largest population is Christian and of African ethnic origin, with the North whose origins are Arab and Muslim by religion. Douglas

H. Johnson describes the conflict in the Sudan by saying: "The conflict between the Northern and Southern Sudan has usually been misunderstood, because the historical roots of the conflict have been misrepresented."[74]

He continued; "two contrary explanations are frequently given for the continuing rift:"[75]

1. That the division between the North and the South is based on centuries of exploitation and slave raiding by the "Arab" North against the "African" South; or

2. That the Sudan was artificially split by imperialist meddling, since Sudanese Islam, being both African and Arab, imposes no natural or historical division between the two regions. Certainly there is broad agreement that the Sudan has been undergoing a process of Arabization and Islamization since the invasion of the Sudan by Arab tribes from Upper Egypt and across the Red Sea during the middle ages."

In simple terms, politics in the Sudan has been based on ethnic and religious lines where some tribes and other non-Muslims feel politically excluded in their own country causing political unrest in the country.

As such it was such imperative that political leaders in South Sudan carefully addressed the issues of ethnic and religious minorities so that the same situation would not occur in South Sudan after its secession in 2011. The new government in South Sudan was charged with introducing a political system where citizens have a right to participate fully in major decisions affecting their lives.

---

74      Douglas Johnson, The Root Cause of Sudan's Civil Wars, 2002, pp.1.

75      Ibid.

Johnson believes that: "Northern Sudan has been united by Islam, and therefore confronts the South with a political and cultural unity which the South itself lacks."[76]

This may not be the case, because Southern Sudan is mainly African; these African nationalities have African culture, traditions, and a common history. Existing tribal misconceptions were caused by the North to create differences among southerners to enable it win the war of liberation in the country.

Some people may think it was unwise to advocate for secession, but the unity of the country was under threat by many factors such as competition over identity and territorial claims, instrumentalization of ethnicity in the pursuit of power, exploitation of religion for political ends and recurring border conflicts and their impact on unity of Sudan. The implications of the forced unity by the North are discussed in detail below.

## 6.2 Competition over identity, and Territorial Claims

The Sudan is one of the African countries which has not realized peace since its inception as a sovereign entity in 1956. Before independence in 1956, the rebellion erupted in the South in August 1955 at Torit military garrison.

The fighting took place between Southerners in the army against their colleagues from the North. The majority of victims were Northern Sudanese traders who were in the town. The rebellion was a reaction against the serious marginalization the South underwent at the hands of the North during the process of independence of the country.

As Johnson said the conflict between the South and the North has been misunderstood, hence misrepresented.[77]

It is very important to know the reasons beyond the North's marginalization of the South. Among those asserted issues was the competition over the identity of the country. The North believes in Arabization of

---

76      Ibid.

77      Ibid.

the country contrary to what the South considers as an African entity.

These conceptual differences between the North and the South created competition over political power in the country. This scenario had clearly manifested in 1954 during the Sudanisation of civil service positions when the North were allocated 99 percent of civil servant positions.

In terms of constitutional posts, Southerners never occupied what politicians knew as sovereign portfolios like the presidency, defense, interior, foreign affairs and others, since independence up to the era of CPA. Only in 1964 when the popular uprising took place, did Trade Unions elect Mr. Sir al Khatim al Khalifa, who was a teacher in the South before the war erupted, to lead the Transitional Government in Sudan. Clement Umboro, a veteran politician from South Sudan, was appointed as Minister for Interior Affairs in the period from 1964 to 1965 before the general elections of the second democratic era.

Many people think that the assimilation policy of Arabization and Islamization, introduced in the South by the former President Ibrahim Abboud in 1958 when he came into power, was mainly meant to resolve the issue of identity in the country. In their responses to the questions during interviews some participants thought that the regime was mistaken in believing that if somebody is a Muslim and speaks Arabic then they can easily change their origin to become an Arab.

This is exactly what has been taking place in the Blue Nile, Nuba Mountains, Beja land in Eastern Sudan and Darfur where Africans are forced to become Arabs. A nation may adopt Arabic as its official language and Islam as a religion of the majority, but it does not amount to an automatic Arab nationhood.

For example, Somalia, before its current crisis, was a member of the Arab league but maintained its African entity. Likewise, Mauritania is a member of the Arab League, and most of its citizens are Muslims and speak Arabic language, yet, they identify as Africans. The majority of the citizens in Nigeria are Muslims but this has not made the state an Arab country.

According to Mohamed Suliman Mohamed: "The Northern elites

who dominated the state and the market were of Arab and Arabized Muslims originating from central Sudan living along the Nile River. As they imposed their domination on economic and political power, they intended to impose their Arabization-Islamization identity over the rest of the Sudanese people."[78]

Many people consider this domination to be the reason some of the citizens are considered second-class citizens in their own country, causing a lot of trouble in Sudan which may lead to the fragmentation of some parts.

The South has been considered as an obstacle to Islamization and Arabization in Sudan since independence in 1956. It is surprising to see some people from Darfur – which has been considered a centre of Islam in Sudan – changing their tone to speak up against what is known to be ethnic domination and yet they consider themselves as having nothing to do with the Arabic identity and an Islamic state in Sudan. Many people from Western Sudan believed the war in Darfur as a competition over political identity in the region. Al Bagir Mukhtar Senior Fellow, US Institute of Peace, says: "the Arab identity constructed by Northerners places Darfurians on the fringe. Northerners neither "fit" the prototype for Arab identity nor do the Darfurians in the Northern constructed illusion."[79]

It can be recalled that the issue of identity posed a threat to the unity of the country. The fear is that, the seceded Southern Sudan would cause further secession in the Sudan, with the West and the East following as well. Many issues to do with identity and the role of religion in politics hindered the agreement during the negotiations in Kenya. The leader of SPLM/A late Dr. John Garang believed that the competition over identity had been the problem of the Sudan. Talking to *The Washington Post* on February 11, 2005, Dr. Garang said: "It was in 1974 when we came to the United States with my colleague, who

---

78    محمد سليمان محمد ، السودان حروب الموارد والهوية ، دار كمبردج للنشر ، كمبردج ، المملكة المتحدة ، الطبعة الأولى ، 2000م.

79    Albagir Mukhtar, Report on the Fringes of Northern identity: What's Missing in the Darfur Peace Process? Institute of Peace. Washington, DC. July 2006.

was a Major in the Sudanese Army, from the North with hundreds of other people from around the world, for military training at Fort Benning. The group spent a week of orientation in Washington studying United States history, the constitution, and the government. During one session, the Africans in the group were asked to stand up and be counted but the two Sudanese remained seated. When the Middle Eastern members were called on, they still stayed put. At the end, we were the only two left."[80]

It was believed that the confusion over identity had been adequately addressed by CPA, but it seems that the Ruling Party in Khartoum (the National Congress) did not see the danger facing the country through its divisive policies since the time of peace negotiations in Abuja in 1992. It required that the Sharia be the centre of any agreement that must be concluded with the South. The same argument was advanced by the GoS until the concept of "one country, two systems" was introduced in Naivasha as a temporary arrangement for the six-year and half interim period, 2005 - 2011. This led the SPLM to opt for self-determination as a fall-back position.

The intransigence of the Islamic Government in Khartoum posed a major hindrance to the unity of the country at the end of the interim period. There was continued confrontation between SPLM and NCP over the implementation of some issues in the CPA including security arrangements, Abyei protocols and the South-North 1956 Boundaries Demarcation some of which are still outstanding today.

Many political analysts were convinced that the result of the referendum would be secession of the South. Before he died in the plane crash, on May 15 2005 in Rumbek town, the late Dr. Garang the Chairman of SPLM and SPLA C.I.C, was quoted as warning Southern Sudanese people not to be second class citizens when the time of the referendum came. He urged those who did not taste bush life to do their best when their turn came in 2011. A request which Southerners honoured on January 9, by voting for their freedom and becoming first class citizens in their own country.

---

80      John Garang De Mabior, Interview, Washington Post, February 11, 2005.

The outcome of the referendum raised other questions: What is the future of other marginalized areas, like Nuba Mountains, South Blue Nile and Darfur regions and will the separation of the South bring stability into the country? For these questions and other related aspects, the study provides the answers in Chapter Eight. However, part of theses questions were addressed by President Salva Kiir during the Independence Day on July 9, 2011 when he publically declared in his speech that they were not going to betray the cause of marginalized people of Sudan in Nuba Mountain, Blue Nile and Darfur. He then worked tirelessly to achieve peace in Sudan on October, 2020 and some of the former comrades in the struggle joined the Transitional Government of Sudan. According to the 1983 SPLM Manifesto, amended in 2008, 65% of the population in the country was of African origins as per the 1956 Population Census, yet the country was considered as an Arab state by sectarian parties.[81]

Sudan People's Liberation Movement (SPLM) viewed the aspect of marginalization in Sudan as a systematic process based on ethnic exploitation by Arabized tribes along the Nile in central Sudan. This ethnic exploitation misrepresented the country's identity by declaring Sudan an Arab state, an idea which was resisted by the South since independence in 1956.

The Anya Nya in the 1950s also undermined the issue into a Southern problem which could be solved by separating the South from the North. However, the SPLM defined the magnitude of the problem, as generated by the ignorance of successive governments in Khartoum, about the reality of Sudan's historical and contemporary diversity.

These governments failed to evolve a Sudanese identity, a Sudanese commonality, or a Sudanese commonwealth that includes all Sudanese and to which all Sudanese pledge a united loyalty to, irrespective of their religion, race, or tribe.[82]

The formation of a democratic Sudan based on the principles of

---

81      SPLM Manifesto 1983, Amended 2008.

82      Ibid.

justice, freedom, rule of law, human rights, peace, and good governance is what SPLM called the "New Sudan." They viewed this as the solution for the paradigm of the "Old Sudan" characterised by injustice, inequality, racial and ethnic discrimination.[83]

In simple terms, the reality had to be accepted that the Sudan was an African dominated country, whose identity is not Arab but rather African. This notwithstanding, many political analysts considered this trend not free from potential crises because of influences from Arab minorities in the country who could have opposed the idea of a New Sudan.

The matter of the North refusing to accept reality reached the climax during the Sudan Fifth Population Census and House Counts when the NCP refused to include information on ethnicity and religious background in the census forms in order not to be confronted with the reality of Sudan – which would compel them to revise the identity of the country from an Arab and an Islamic state.

If unity was to prevail, Sudan needed to face reality and create a real Sudanese identity that could accommodate all citizens and suit its people and land.

## 6.3 Instrumentalization of Ethnicity in Pursuit of Power

Ethnic mobilization has been the main source of conflict in sub- Saharan Africa since independence, and constitutes one of the major barriers to human and economic development in African societies.[84]

Countries like Rwanda, Cote d'Ivoire, Burundi, Democratic Republic of Congo, Chad, and many others experience political crises because of ethnic divisions that lead to socio-economic segregation, and political exclusion.

Ethnic identity has been used by some elites in the continent since the time of decolonization to get political power. It has been done either

---

83      Ibid.

84      Alexis Rawlinson, The Political Mobilisation of Ethnicity in Africa, 2003. www.insolens.org.

through military coups or through oriented democracy based on tribe, clan and sub-section affiliations and sometimes through rebellions.

This continuous struggle over political power and wealth of the state in Africa is deemed necessary by the elites to capture the centre of authority in states. Sometimes the process resulted in genocides in some countries.

This instrumental use of ethnicity dominates political contestation and it undermines efforts for nation building since it is largely an artificial construct. This tribalism may be reduced through responsible conduct by elites.[85]

The issue of ethnic mobilization and conflict has not only been a challenge to the democratic transformation but it has also been a factor of instability and a threat to unification in Africa.[86]

People should see the danger of ethnic mobilization to pursue power during what Marina Ottaway called "Political Openings."[87]

"The political opening situation prevails when the country is opened to a system partially pluralist and partially dictatorist," she states, further arguing that, "Political openings not only change the balance between the State and existing organisations of civil society, but also create the space for new organisations to form."[88]

This situation is considered as fair because political stability in many African countries is a dream. Sometimes change comes overnight, and all institutions which were built are burned down and a new era starts. By doing so, new civil society organisations emerge, and the old ones may or may not appear, either in the same form or in a different shape.

Sometimes the new leaders do not like existing civil society organisations and begin to form new organisations which are considered to be the basis for emerging political participation.

Ethnic identity does not always lead to ethnic conflict. People who

---

85    Ibid.

86    Ibid.

87    Marina Ottaway, Challenge of Democracy in Africa, 2003.

88    Ibid.

belong to different ethnic groups can live together without problems much of the time. However, in a rapidly changing situation in which power is up for grabs, ethnic identities can easily become instruments of power and thus lead to conflicts.

As a matter of fact, many African leaders recently came to realize the danger of exploiting ethnicity for political gains and have begun calling for nation-building, overcoming differences and development of a common identity among all citizens of the state. Colonial borders were declared sacred and separatist movements were denied recognition. Efforts have been made towards the unification of Africa through the African Union (AU).

Sudan was no exception. Ethnically, it was divided into two major sections; Africans and Arabs. Since its independence, the Arabs and Arabized tribes living along the Nile in central Sudan were in power, controlling most significant government institutions and the wealth of the state. They used this privilege against Black Africans and non-Arab tribes all over the country.

The marginalized people of Sudan were left without choice but to rebel in order to claim their rights in South Sudan, Nuba Mountains, South Blue Nile, Eastern Sudan and Darfur. Sometimes unsuccessful coup attempts in Khartoum were described by the regimes as racist attacks.

The coup led by Hassan Hussein from Kordofan in 1976 and the other led by Bol Jok from Southern Sudan in 1985 were said to be racist movements. Meanwhile, this description was not applied to the coups led by General Ibrahim Abboud, Colonel Gaafar Nimeiry, and Brigadier Omer Hassan in 1958, 1969 and 1989 respectively.

When he assumed power in 1958, General Ibrahim Abboud introduced policies which were meant to strengthen Arab nationhood in the Sudan. He changed the language of instructions in South Sudan from English to Arabic; he also changed all syllabi and ordered the evacuation of Christian missionaries from the country immediately.

The regime was viewed as working to exclude African nationalities from political power, weaken them and deprive them of wealth. These policies increased insecurity among southerners and other Christians around the world who concluded that there was no alternative to these policies except giving support to the rebels in the South.

When it seized power, the May Regime started as a leftist movement with neither an Arab identity nor Islamic leanings. This strengthened the Southern Sudan cause and led to the signing of the Peace Accord in Addis Ababa in 1972.

The agreement gave the South regional autonomy but still had minimal participation in the central government. It was locked out of all the portfolios like defense, interior, finance, foreign affairs which went to the North. The presidency too had been put aside for Muslims of Arab origin, particularly those residing along the Nile River.

The Addis Ababa Agreement was viewed as insensitive to the cause of marginalized people of the Sudan. In addition, President Nimeiry violated contents of the Addis Ababa peace accord by declaring the re-division of the South into three regions instead of one region. These injustices started another rebellion; the Sudan People's Liberation Movement and Sudan People's Liberation Army (SPLM/A) in 1983.

When Nimeiry was removed from power, the Northern Sudanese political parties that assumed power in Khartoum followed in the footsteps of the May Regime which caused more wars.

In 1989, the Salvation Regime took over power in Khartoum. The regime was strong on Islamic fundamentalism and it gave Muslims with Arab origin special treatment. This caused conflicts between non-Arab and Arab Muslims especially those in Darfur which was considered as the fortress of Islam. Political analysts say the government supported Arab militia, the Janjaweed, in its war with

Black African Muslims of Darfur, to invade the land and change their African identity.[89]

Not only did they cause conflict between the Muslim brotherhood but also tried to pit African tribes against each other in order to maintain power in Khartoum as evidenced during the war of liberation in South Sudan (1983-2005).

---

89    Albagir Mukhtar, Report on the Fringes of Northern identity: What's Missing in the Darfur Peace Process? Institute of Peace. Washington, DC. July 2006e.

Arab tribes, like Riziegat of Southern Darfur and Misseriya of Southern Kordofan, were used in order to fight their neighbors in Northern Bahr el Ghazal and Northern Upper Nile, resulting into soured tribal relations at the South-North border, and undermining the fact that there are common interests between these tribes.

The neighborhood between the Dinka tribe in the South and Baggara tribes in the North will not change because of separation or unity between South and North Sudan. So, it is important for these tribes to bear in mind that political institutions do change but neighborhoods do not, unless someone decides to move to another place. Something that is not possible for tribes like the Dinka Malual or Riziegat.

The political strategy of relying on tribal conflicts to gain power played a major role in the secessions in Sudan. Because the country was racked by divisions, the government was not strong enough to maintain its status quo in the centre, making it difficult to defend the peripheries.

## 6.4 Exploitation of Religion for Political Ends

The idea of placing religion at the centre of politics is not man-made according to Islam. Ali Hassan Shawory categorically emphasizes that it originates from the Holy Qur'an "makes you inheritors of the earth (an-Naml 62[90])." The theocratic statement was adopted for the first time in the Islamic system of governance in Madina State which was ruled by prophet Mohamed bin Abdullahi. The first constitution for this Islamic state was known as "Madina Gazettes," which organized political, social, and economic relations in the State. Other non-Muslim minorities who were living in the State were cared for. God asked the rulers to consult on matters of public affairs. "whose affair is consultation among themselves (ash- shura 38)."[91]

Islam strongly prohibits the concept of separation of religion from a state. According to Muslims, a state is a political scene and its constitutional doctrine is populace, environment, geographical entity and

---

90      62. علي حسن الساوري ، لنصيص السياسي للشراكة السياسية ، دار افريقيا العالمية للطباعة والنشر ، الخرطوم 1999، سورة النمل الآية 62.

91      نفس المرجع سورة الشورى الآية 38.

governing authority. Meanwhile, religion is a set of norms, behaviours and laws generating from beliefs that one cannot separate them from the state.[92]

For this reason, in an Islamic state, non-Muslims do not have the same rights and duties as their Muslim counterparts. Rights of non-Muslims in the state are determined by the degree of their relationship with the ruler; 'Wali' or governor. This relationship in Islam is known as relationship between the governor and the governed.[93]

In an Islamic state, the governor decides what task to be assigned to whom among non-Muslims but these rights and duties are not inclusive. The position like a presidency, prime minister, head of the army and intelligence, and judges are not given to non-Muslims.

This marginalization of non-Muslims in an Islamic state is what caused conflicts in some Arab countries where non-Muslim minorities are denied their citizenship rights. The issue is sometimes picked up by external forces, as religious intolerance in order to promote their interests.[94] Conflicts stemming from religion are the most difficult to resolve because believers think non-believers are fighting against Almighty God, not human beings. They become fanatical about the believing that God shall guide them to victory. With this understanding, the only option for non-Muslims who want to enjoy equal rights and freedom in an Islamic state is either extended federation or separation.

War against terrorism becomes emotional. There is a belief among Islamic organisations that they are protecting their religion from invasion. When a conflict takes the form of religious discrimination, the chances of it getting out of internal players' hands are very high.

Al Nazir argued that the North tried to downplay the religious aspect in the conflict between the North and the South, in order to

92    علي عيسى عبدالرحمن، الحركة الاسلامية السودانية من التنظيم الي الدولة، 2000-1949، مطبعة التيسير ، الخرطوم، 2006.

93    النزير صالح الخليفة، الحقوق الدستورية للاقليات الدينية في الدولة الاسلامية بالتركيز علي السودان الخرطوم ، 2007، ص25.

94    نفس المرجع.

stop intervention by foreign players.[95]

But without a doubt this is what was taking place in the Sudan. The Government in Khartoum used double standards to serve different agendas internally and externally. With the Arab and Islamic worlds, the war was said to be a conflict between Christians and Muslims and with the external world, especially non-Islamic countries, the conflict was politically oriented for power and therefore, there was need for political solutions based on fair distribution of power and wealth between the South and the North.

In the opinion of Dr. John Garang, the founder of New Sudan: "Religion is a relationship between a human being and the creator. Hence this relationship is governed by religious legislations. Whereas the relation between a human being and their own made things like a car, hotel, state and so on, must be a different issue altogether, because the state is a socio-political institution made by a human being not God. However, God is the creator of human beings; therefore, the relationship should be different between what created us, and what we have created. These are two different distinct relations."[96]

It was believed that the issue of Islamization in Sudan caught the attention of many players when The National Islamic Front (NIF) promoted a very conservative brand of Islam as a central goal when it assumed power in 1989. The Government's "Civilization Project" whose original architect was al-Turabi, has a sweeping social agenda.[97]

The conflict in the Sudan is so multi-layered and multifaceted that it is really difficult to identify one dominant element. Religion is definitely one of the bigger issues. The ICG report in 2002 says: "The relationship between religion and state is perhaps the most controversial of all the forces driving conflict in Sudan. Islamists have dominated the current Government since it came to power. This has at times made the divergence between the interests of the Government and the secular-minded

---

95    نفس المرجع ص 228.

96    النشأة الكبرى ، جون قرنق رؤيته للسودان وجاعاو الجديد بناء دولة السودانية، مسرتر للطبيعة ص 2005 87.

97    ICG God, Oil and the Country, 2000.

SPLA appear irreconcilable."[98]

The SPLM manifesto defined the nature of conflict by saying: "The central problem of the Sudan is that its reality, both in its historical perspective and in its contemporary context, conflicts fundamentally with the policies of the various governments that have come and gone in Khartoum since independence in 1956. Those policies have been pursued with impunity and almost completely disregard the country's rich diversity, its history, geography, people, and cultures."[99] The eruption of war in Darfur and Eastern Sudan, where non-Muslims have equal rights supports the above observation.

Although Darfur has been Islamized for centuries, it found itself in conflict with the Government in Khartoum because of ethnic differences. Being a Muslim is not enough to give you the first-class citizen status in the Sudan; you also need to be of Arab origin. Politicians in Khartoum opined that the region should not be identified with Fur tribe, but be renamed as Arab land and rid it of whoever resisted this idea. Some had gone even further to claim that the government had been bringing in new settlers of Arab origins from neighbouring countries to displace the indigenous people but this information is still unverified.

Also continued war in other parts of the country, especially the Islamized ones waged by the Islamic government in Khartoum, stressed the SPLM argument that Sudan's causes of conflict were historical and contemporary diversities and not the Islamismization of the country alone. Conflict in Darfur is not a direct issue of this study, but only an example.

Let's examine the attempts made by the Northern political parties in Khartoum to bring the idea of an Islamic constitution into the State and how these attempts contributed to the conflict in South Sudan.

To begin with, the modern history of Sudan's political system started before the country's independence by the emergence of Northern

---

98      Ibid.

99      SSPLM Manifesto, op cit.

political parties advocating Islamic ideologies as a basis for rights and duties in the country rather than citizenship. This came from the fact that parties like Umma and DUP who claimed victory over independence of the country, had both been deep-rooted in Islamic sectarianisms like Ansar and Khatimiya. Later, a small group known as Jabha Messak emerged. The concern of all these political parties was how to chase away the colonizers in order to establish an Islamic state in Sudan, a task which was impossible after independence.

The first attempt was made during the Round Table Conference in 1965 when the Islamic parties proposed an Islamic constitution, as a solution for the participation of non-Muslim minorities in the country's institutions.[100]

This idea was rejected in its totality and considered as a means of intensifying the war against the South.

The proposal appeared again in the National Parliament in 1968 but faced a lot of resistance by the members from the South. The move was stalled by the dissolution of the parliament in the same year and the sudden capture of power by the May Regime in 1969.

The second attempt was made by Nimeiry in 1983 when he implemented some Islamic laws in the field of criminal law, known as "The September Laws." Those, who viewed the matter in a religious context, were convinced to join the rebellion in the South. When president Nimeiry attempted to revise his decision by canceling these Islamic laws, the Islamic parties spearheaded by National Islamic Front (NIF) and its leader Hussan Abdalla al Turabi mobilized the public against Nimeiry and overthrew him in the uprising of 1984.

The SPLM/A major transformation was the removal of Islamic laws as a prior step towards any peaceful settlement in the Sudan. This was noted in the Kokadam Declaration in 1986, and also during the Marghani-Garang Agreement in 1988. But the Umma party, which was by then a major political party in the Coalition Government had a different opinion about peace with SPLM/A.

---

100    علي عيسى عبد الرحمن ، المرجع السابق.

The liberation struggle continued until the Salvation Government came into power in 1989 and declared itself as an Islamic government in Sudan. During the Salvation Government, the Islamic agenda of the war in the South became clear to everybody. Al Turabi formulated an Islamic Constitution in 1998. One of its articles dwelt clearly on Sharia and Sunna as sources for formulating laws in the Sudan. Article (65) in the 1998 Constitution is quoted;

"The Islamic Sharia, the Sunna[101] and the National Consent through voting, the Constitution and Customs are the sources of law, and no law shall be enacted contrary to these sources, or without taking into account the nations' public opinion, and the efforts of the nations' scientists. Part of the supreme law of the land and legislation must take this reality into account."[102]

The war in the South was declared a Holy War Jihad against animists or infidels in the South. Women and children were abducted and property looted on the pretext of war-confiscated properties (Ganaim Harb) which is a legal act according to Islam. All these mistakes committed by individuals, groups and the government contributed to the growing of Southern Sudan's negative opinion on the chances of unity with the North.

Another important factor that pushed the South towards separation was the position of the government in the peace process. Since its inception in 1989, the issue of a relationship between state and religion occupied the centre of discussions in the peace talks. The government refused to allow any room for compromise on this issue until the idea of one country, two systems and autonomy for the people of Southern Sudan came up. The government was criticized for compromising the unity of the country because of the limited interests of its leadership. With these disagreements, many people believed there were no viable chances for unity.

---

101    *Sunna* is an Islamic teaching.

102    Sudan Constitution, 1998.

## 6.5 Recurring Border Conflicts and their Impact on Unity of Sudan

Disputes on border areas between the South and the North are ancient (see Appendix 2), but were brought to the forefront officially by Anya Nya during their negotiations with the May Regime in Addis Ababa 1972. But it could not be concluded that the issue did not exist in the minds of Southerners.

Since the 16th century, Dinka Malual and Riziegat tribes as an example of the South-North border conflict have been in dispute over grazing areas around the Kiir River (Bahr Arab). The same conflict has been ongoing in Western Bahr el Ghazal and Southern Darfur between the Hofra Nahas and Kafi Akangi, and in Warrap State and Kordofan over Abyei.

Bahr el Ghazal is severely affected by recurring border conflicts because the colonialists made the vast areas and huge population of Bhar el Ghazal and Equatoria into one provincial district in the 1940s. The British administrators moved some parts bordering Darfur and Kordofan provinces to the North away from Bhar el Ghazal.

Douglas Johnson, an expert brought in by the GOSS to advise the government on border issues argued: "the provincial boundaries of the Anglo-Egyptian Sudan were constructed bit by bit throughout the 54 years of Condominium Rule. The earlier boundaries were drawn on maps before the Government had a clear understanding of the geography, topography, and demography of the country, and were described in the most general terms in province reports."[103]

The three elements of geography, topography, and demography mentioned by Johnson are most essential for any border demarcations. These factors which were not put into account by the colonial rule when drawing the boundaries are very significant in the demarcation of boundaries. If these were to be taken into account, Dinka Ngok would not have gone to Kordofan and also the south Kiir River would not have been demarcated as a grazing land for Riziegat. Riziegat or any tribe can be allowed to graze in Dinka land without drawing grazing lines

---

103    Douglas Johnson, South Sudan Boundaries Report. Juba, August, 2007.

provided that there is a communal agreement that legalizes the practice.

The ignorance of the Colonial Administration on geography or the demographic setting of the people of Sudan created a political crisis after Independence in 1956. Knowing the demographic settings of the South would have helped even in suggesting the type of administration that the new Government, after the independence, would have taken in order to address the issues of exclusivity and avoid domination by one ethnic group.

Another important issue associated with border demarcations in the Sudan was the process of transferring power from the Anglo-Egyptian rule to the Sudanese leaders in 1954. The transfer of power did not take into account the issues of potential conflicts that would cause problems in the country, like participation of all ethnic groups in affairs of the nation, border demarcation between the Sudan and other neighbouring countries, and internal borders between the provinces and localities. Johnson was convinced: "This was done because the date of independence had been fixed by the parliament only a few days prior to January 1, 1956.

No survey had been made of internal provincial boundaries in anticipation of independence. There is some ambiguity about what the borders were on that date."[104]

Under normal circumstances, this issue of national boundaries would not have been a problem if the politicians had been genuine about the unity of the country, embarked on nation building and, promoted nationalism and unity by creating a good political system where citizens participated effectively without discrimination. Instead, the dominant major political parties of the time, who negotiated the independence, selfishly implemented political policies to exclude some of their fellow countrymen from the process of power and wealth sharing. This action has cost many lives and resources and will take a lot of time to be corrected.

Mismanagement of administrative issues at the grassroots has

---

104    Ibid.

potential to result in a war. There were some border issues which needed to be addressed thoroughly between those communities sharing the borders. These issues include, and are not restricted to, grazing land and water for Riziegat and Misseriya and their cattle in Bhar el Ghazal, border trading and fishing. These issues continue to create problems among the communities that share the borders.

Exploration of oil in some areas at the border between the South and the North was another element complicating relations in Sudan. This matter made governments in Khartoum keep changing boundaries southwards whenever there was extraction of oil in the South. The then First Vice-President of the Sudan and the President of the Government of Southern Sudan, H.E Salva Kiir Mayardit confirmed this in an interview with the National Television in the program called "Hot Line" presented by al Zubier Ahamed Hasan in 2006:

"The reaction on redrawing Unity-Kordofan Province Boundaries by the South in 1983 after exploration of oil in that area poses many questions whether Bentiu is not part of Sudan. And why Nimeiry thought the refinery must be in the North instead of the South while the South and the North constitute one entity? Are Jallaba genuinely interested in Unity?

All these questions were ringing in the minds of Southerners. When they failed to get answers, a good number of them decided to go to the bush and fight Nimeiry in 1983.

It is evident that the exploration of oil in Abyei was the cause for conflict in the area, making it impossible to reach a compromise between SPLM and NCP.

There was doubt that the agreement reached on Abyei by the presidency in June 2008 in Khartoum would be fully implemented especially if the distribution of the oil is not put into consideration. The ICG report in 2002 asserted: "Oil has raised the stakes of the war, and given both sides an increased commitment to the battlefield. Any equitable peace deal will require some form of oil revenue sharing."[105]

---

105    ICG. God, Oil and the Country, op cit, pp. 100-108.

Thus, the wealth sharing protocol took into account this issue, and the oil produced in the South was divided equally between the South and the North.

A young man who was interviewed for this study concluded that this would not make unity attractive between the South and the North; South. "Sudan will opt for separation to get all its oil revenues. Anyway we are buying our freedom," he concluded.

As a sensitive commodity, it was brought to the attention of many Sudanese that the exploration of oil would fuel war between the South and the North. Johnson asserted: "A prime reason why the North has always resisted Southern separation is the latter's natural resources wealth. Particularly central to the current equation is oil."[106] Some people who were interviewed thought that the Government in Khartoum was more concerned with the land than the people in the South.

The conflict at the borders between SPLM and NCP was a war over resources, which was bound to hinder a lasting solution if each party was not given its equal share.

Tribes were compelled to fight each other, as was the case in Northern Bhar el Ghazal between Dinka Malual and Misseriya in December 2007; in Unity State between Misseriya and Nuer in April 2008; and in Abyei between the Ngok Dinka and Misseriya in May 2008. In all these tribal clashes, the government forces (SAF) and SPLA troops were reported to be behind the fighting.

The partial purpose of this research was to suggest solutions to border disputes, and to examine how these types of conflicts contributed to issues of unity and/or separation in the Sudan.

In a situation where there was competition over resources by ethnic groups in one country, unity was at stake, and this could lead to the conclusion that the ultimate result of self-determination of the people of Southern Sudan in 2011 would be secession – as expressed by many participants in Chapter Seven.

---

106    Douglas Johnson, The Root Causes of the Sudan's Civil Wars, 2002.

The question which still lingered then was: Would separation bring peace in contact areas between the South and the North especially on borders? This remained a big challenge for peace researchers in the area to address, asking the Almighty God to help in bringing peace to the people.

## 6.6 Conclusion

The issues discussed in this chapter are of importance: Identity and territorial claims, instrumentalization of ethnicity in the pursuit of power, exploitation of religion for political ends and recurring border conflicts and their impacts on the unity of the Sudan are really very important in Sudanese politics.

This is not because they are the source of the conflicts between the South and the North, but especially as threatening factors of unity of the whole country. The crisis over identity and ethnic discrimination have expanded to include other parts of the Sudan like Darfur, Nuba Mountains, Blue Nile, Eastern Sudan and the far North occupied by Nubians.

All these ethnic groups have stated their positions loudly on what was said to be domination of the Arabs' identity in the Sudan. The ethnic affiliation was applied by Sudanese elites as a mechanism for the pursuit of power whether by those already in power, trying to maintain it or by those who would like to get political power.

Hence, the idea of tribes as an element to defend and/or get into power has been instrumental. This step is dangerous to the unity of the country. Political processes should be based on political ideology and not ethnic affiliations.

The study also revealed the role of religion in a Sudanese political system as an element of getting political ends. Islam, as the religion of the majority, in the country, is considered by some Muslim leaders as inseparable from politics. Consequently, non-Muslim minorities suffer from political exclusion in the Sudan.

This left no option for the non-Muslims except to think of leaving the old Sudan and search for a country where people have equal rights and duties as citizens of one nation.

Nobody was expected to fight a religious war since the option of leaving the theocratic state in the North through self-government in 2011 was provided for by the CPA.

There were two conditions that could reignite the war with the North, as clearly put by many participants of this study: First, dishonoring the result of the referendum for the people of Southern Sudan by any political force in the country. Second, any attempt to re-draw South-North boundaries according to the wishes of the Government in Khartoum, thereby, cutting some areas from the South and adding them to the North. Any attempt at tampering with these two issues would immediately lead to war.

The last topic examined under this chapter is the recurring border conflict caused by the natural resources exploration in the area. The issue of oil in the South-North border is a problem which complicates the border demarcations. Similarly, the NCP refusal of the Abyei Boundary Commission (ABC) reports was connected to the oil fields in the area. There are complaints from the SPLM that the NCP retained some military garrisons in the South despite the Security Arrangements Protocol which indicates that all SAF are to withdraw north of the 1956 boundaries by the end of the second year of the CPA implementation.

In examining all these factors, one is made to believe that the chances of maintaining unity in the Sudan through a referendum in 2011 were few.

This brings us to the statement of Dr. John Garang de Mabior – the founder of revolution for marginalized people of Sudan – made in Rumbek town on May 15th 2005;

"I and those who joined me in the bush and fought for more than 20 years have brought to you the CPA on a golden plate. Our mission is accomplished. It is now your turn, especially those who did not have a chance to experience bush life. When time comes to vote at the referendum, it is your golden choice to determine your fate. Would you like to vote to be second class citizens in your own country? It is absolutely your choice."[107]

---

107    John Garang de Mabior, Rumbek, 2005.

# CHAPTER 7

**7. Applied Study of Dinka Malual And Riziegat**

This chapter constitutes an applied and analytical study of the impact of the ethnic politics on South-North Sudan relations: The case of the Dinka Malual and Riziegat tribes. These two tribes are living in Northern Bahr el Ghazal and Southern Darfur respectively.

The chapter is divided into three sections; the first section deals with a brief definition of the two communities as this was dealt with in Chapter One. The second section accounts for how the sample was taken from the population of the two communities. The last part of this chapter is an analysis of the results of the study in order to see how far the topic met the hypotheses of this study.

**7.1 Defining the Communities under the Study**

These two neighbouring communities share South-North Sudan borders and have been fighting over grazing lands. Sometimes, this conflict was politicized by the governments in Khartoum and the liberation movements in the South.

This politicization of local issues facilitates the shifting of the conflict from local to national level. The effects of war like slavery/abduction and human rights violations, invited the attention of the international community, under the pretext of maintaining the international values in the Sudan, and again the conflict took an international turn. Therefore, this is a study of conflicts that start as local but escalate and become international.

Another significant issue is that Dinka Malual of Northern Bahr el Ghazal is an African ethnic group and mostly Christians. Meanwhile, Riziegat tribe of Southern Darfur is of Arab origin and mostly Muslims. More details about the two communities are provided in Chapter One.

## 7.2 The Questionnaire and the Sample Population

The questionnaire that was used was meant for analytical purposes on the position of the two communities on ethnic politics and its impact on South-North relations. As socio-political studies, the research used non-probability sampling, especially what is known as quota sampling methods, that are associated with the selection of convenience sampling within groups of populations, This is due to the nature of the topic that needs to be addressed with wide representation of views from the targeted groups.

These groups are politicians, chiefs, armed forces, government employees, farmers, herders, traders, non-government organisations (NGOs) employees, students and those people not working either with a public sector or with private sector, (unemployed).

The sample taken from each group was five persons within Dinka Malual and five within Riziegat tribe. Questions were divided into two categories; the first category, was the personal background information to help in analyzing demographic and social conditions of the partic- ipants. This background information included names of participants, age, gender, residence, tribe, religion, and occupation.

The second category of the questions dealt with information which was vital in giving opinion about the topic such as reasons of the conflict in the area, chances for solving the conflict, the expected result of the 2011 referendum and whether that result will be respected or not by the parties to the agreement.

Gender was taken into account, among 100 people chosen to represent the population, 30 were females. The study considered geographical influences; for example, Khartoum as the political capital of Sudan was taken into account, in addition to Aweil; the capital of Northern Bahr el Ghazal and Nyala, the capital of Southern Darfur.

It can be noted that among the total participants six people did not give their responses. Among these people were Dinka Malual and Riziegat at ratio of 4:2 respectively.

## 7.3 Questionnaire Analysis

The illustration of the data in tables and figures is paramount in understanding the analysis, each sample is explained accordingly. The results of this study are illustrated in the tables and figures in this chapter, details of which are as follows:

1.  Distribution of samples in respect of those responded and not responded. Table (7.1) and Figures (7.1), (7-2), (7-3), (7-4) and (7-5).
2.  Participants according to residents Table (6.2) and Figures (7-6), (7-7), (7-8),
3.  Dinka Malual and Riziegat participants according to occupations Table( 7.3).
4.  Dinka Malual and Riziegat participants according to their ages, Table (7.4).
5.  Dinka Malual and Riziegat participants according to religion Table (7.5) and (Figure 7.9).
6.  Reasons of the conflict in the area according to the participants Table (7.6) and Figures (7-10), (7-11)and (7-12)
7.  Proposed solutions to the conflict according to the Participants, Table (7-7) and Figure (7-13).
8.  Expected results of 2011 Referendum South Sudan according to participants Table(7-8), and Figures (7- 14), (7-15),and (7-16)
9.  Opinion of the participants on whether the results of 2011 Referendum will be honored by the parties or not. Table (7-9) and Figures (7.17), (718) and (7-19).

*Table (7-1): Distribution of Sample in respect of those who responded and those who did not respond*

| No. | Tribe | Responded Males : Females | Not Responded Males : Females | Total |
|---|---|---|---|---|
| 1 | Dinka malual | 34 : 12 | 01 : 03 | **50** |
| 2 | Reziegat | 35 : 13 | -- : 02 | **50** |
| **Total** | | 69 : 25 | 01 : 05 | **100** |

*Source: Field Work Results*

Out of a 100 population sample, 94 persons responded. Dinka Malual participants were 46 and Riziegat were 48. Only six people received the questionnaire and failed to return it. Four were Dinka Malual participants and two were from Riziegat.

Among the 94 who responded to the questionnaire, 25 were female participants. 12 from Dinka Malual and 13 from Riziegat community.

*Figure (7-1): Distribution of sample in respect of those who responded and those who did not, male and female who responded to the Questionnaire*

| 1 | Responded |
|---|-----------|
| 2 | Not Responded |
| 3 | Male |
| 4 | Female |

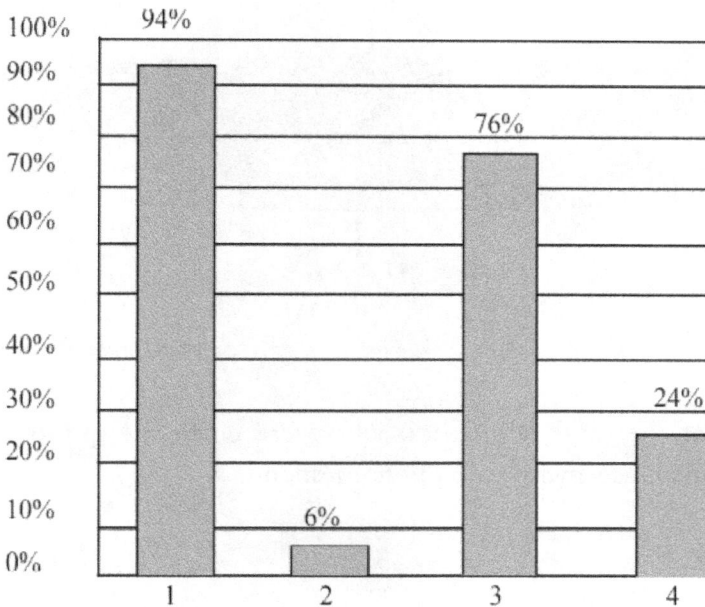

*Source: Field Work Results*

94% received questionnaires, responded and gave them back; 6% received questionnaires and did not turn up. 76% of the respondents were male participants, while 24% were female.

*Figure (7-2): Distribution of the Sample in respect of those
responded and those who did not*

| 1 | Responded |
| 2 | Not Responded |

6%

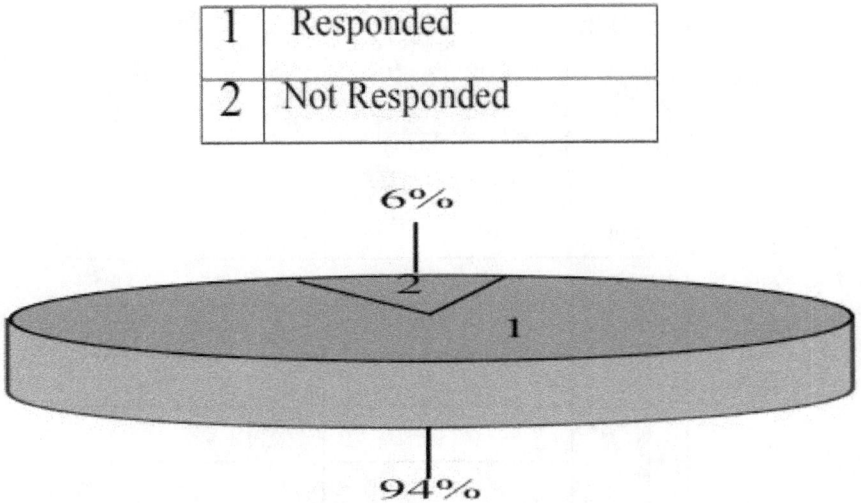

94%

*Source: Field Work Results*

94% of the total population who were given the questionnaire responded. Meanwhile 6% did not respond.

*Figure (7-3): Representation of the participants according to gender*

| 1 | Male responded |
|---|---|
| 2 | Female responded |

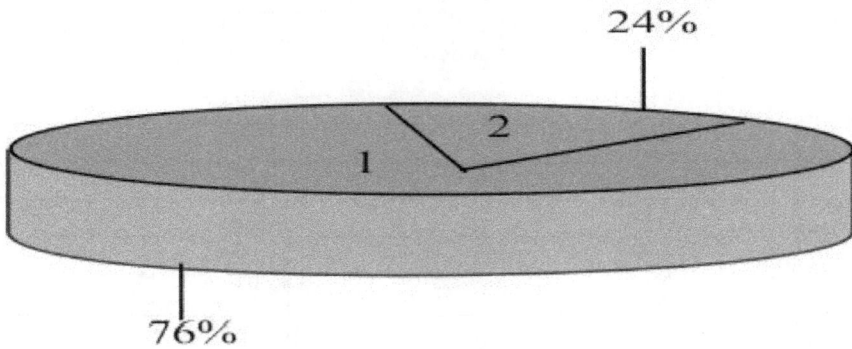

*Source: Field Work Results*

76% of participants were males, meanwhile 24% were female

*Figure (7-4): The Dinka Malual participants who responded and those who did not respond, plus male and female respondants to the questionnaire*

| 1 | Responded |
|---|---|
| 2 | Not Responded |
| 3 | Male Responded |
| 4 | Female Responded |

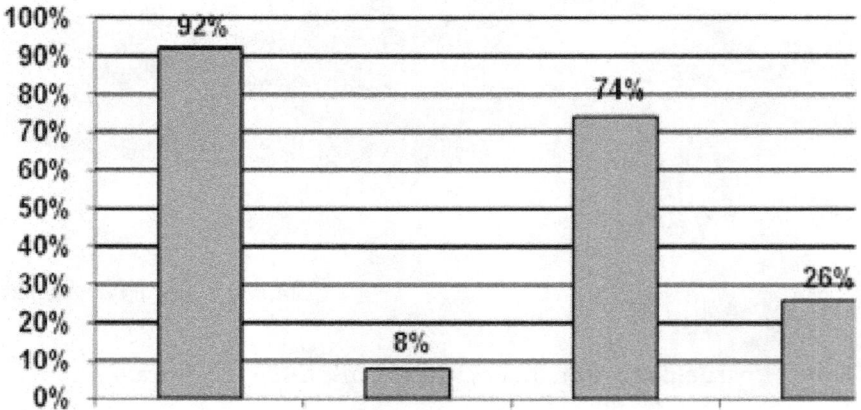

*Source: Field Work results*

92% of Dinka Malual participants responded to the questionnaire, meanwhile 8% failed. Those participants who responded to the questionnaire 74% were male and 26% were female.

*Figures (7-5): Those Riziegat who responded and those who did not respond plus male and female who responded*

| 1 | Responded |
|---|-----------|
| 2 | Not Responded |
| 3 | Male Responded |
| 4 | Female Responded |

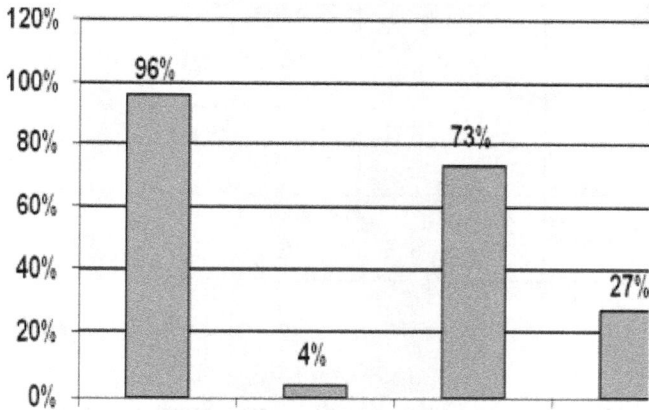

*Source: Field Work results*

96% of Riziegat responded to the questionnaire; meanwhile 4% failed. 73% of respondants were male and 27% were female.

## Table (7-2): Dinka Malual and Riziegat
### participants according to residence

| No. | Tribe | Khartoum | North Bahr El Ghazal | South Darfur |
|-----|-------|----------|----------------------|--------------|
| 1 | Dinka Malual | 14 | 32 | -- |
| 2 | Reziegat | 15 | -- | 33 |
| Total | | 29 | 32 | 33 |

*Source: Field Work results*

33 people who participated came from South Darfur State, whereas 32 people from North Bahr el Ghazal and 29 were those participants of Dinka Malual and Riziegat communities living in Khartoum.

*Figure (7-6): Dinka Malual-Riziegat*
*participants according to residence*

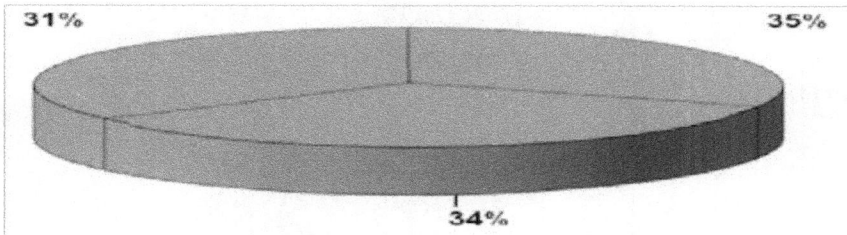

*Source: Field Work results*

34% of the participants were living in Northern Bahr el Ghazal and 35% were living in South Darfur; meanwhile 31% were both Dinka Malual and Riziegat who live in Khartoum .

*Figure (7-7): Dinka Malual participants according to residence*

| 1 | Northern Bahr el Ghazal |
|---|---|
| 2 | Khartoum |

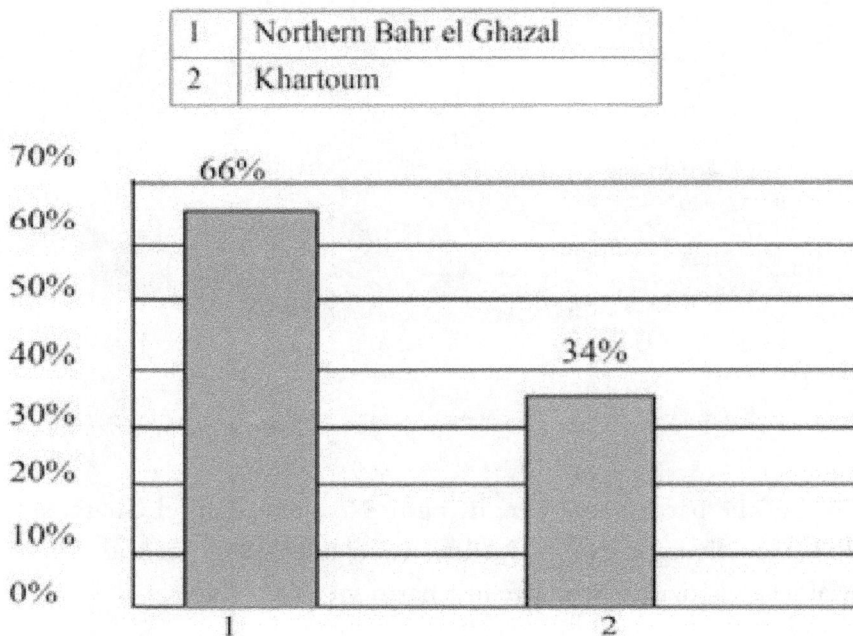

Source: Field Work results

Those Dinka Malual who participated in the study 34% were living in Khartoum, meanwhile 66% were from Northern Bahr el Ghazal

*Figure (7-8): Riziegat participants according to residence*

| 1 | Khartoum |
| 2 | Southern Darfur |

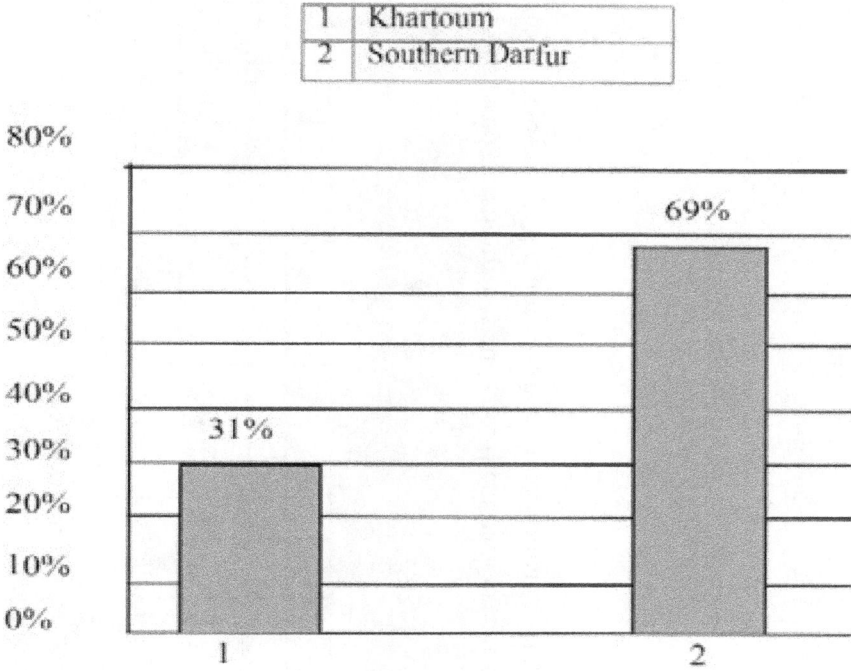

*Source: Field Work results*

Those Riziegat who participated in the study 31% were living in Khartoum, meanwhile 69% were from Southern Darfur State

### Table (7-3): Dinka Malual and Riziegat participants in regards to occupation

| No. | Tribe | Politicians | | Chiefs | | Farmers | | Traders | | Herders | | Gov. emp. | | NGOs | | Student | | Armed F. | | No work | | Total |
|---|---|---|---|---|---|---|---|---|---|---|---|---|---|---|---|---|---|---|---|---|---|---|
| | | R* | NR* | R | NR | R | NR | R | NR | R | NR | R | NR | R | NR | R | NR | R | NR | R | NR | Total |
| 1 | Dinka Malual | 5 | - | 5 | - | 5 | - | 4 | 1 | 4 | 1 | 4 | 1 | 5 | - | 4 | 1 | 5 | - | 5 | - | 50 |
| 2 | Rizeghat | 5 | - | 5 | - | 5 | - | 5 | - | 5 | - | 5 | - | 5 | - | 4 | 1 | 5 | - | 5 | - | 50 |
| Total | | 10 | - | 10 | - | 10 | - | 9 | 1 | 9 | 1 | 9 | 1 | 10 | - | 8 | 2 | 10 | - | 10 | - | 100 |

*Source: Field Work Results*

R* Responded
NR* Not responded

All groups received questionnaires and gave them back except traders, government employees and armed forces; each person from these groups did not return the questionnaire. Two students also failed to return their questionnaires.

## Table (7-4): Dinka Malual and Riziegat
## participants in regard to age

| S/No. | Tribe | 5-17 years | | 18-35 years | | 36-53 years | | Above | |
|---|---|---|---|---|---|---|---|---|---|
| | | Res. No. | | Res. No. | | Res. No. | | Res. No. | |
| 1 | Dinka Malual | 3 | 2 | 29 | 1 | 11 | - | 3 | 1 |
| 2 | Reziegat | 4 | 1 | 18 | - | 17 | | 9 | - |
| Total | | 7 | 3 | 47 | 1 | 28 | | 12 | 1 |

*Source: Field Work Results*

The study shows that half of those participants who responded to the questionnaire were between 18 to 35 years. The majority of those who failed to respond were young people aging from 5-17 years. It is assumed that the reason was their ignorance about the importance of the study.

*Res = Respondent*
*No = Non Respondent*

*Table (7-5): Dinka Malual and Riziegat*
*participants in regard to religion.*

| Serial No. | Tribe | Christians | Muslims | Total |
|---|---|---|---|---|
| 1 | Dinka Malual | 43 | 3 | 46 |
| 2 | Reziegat | -- | 48 | 48 |
| Total | | 43 | 51 | 94 |

*Source: Field Work Result*

51 persons were Muslims including 3 people from Dinka Malual; meanwhile 43 people were Christians. All these Christians were Dinka Malual.

*Figure (7-9): Dinka Malual and Riziegat*
*participants according to religion*

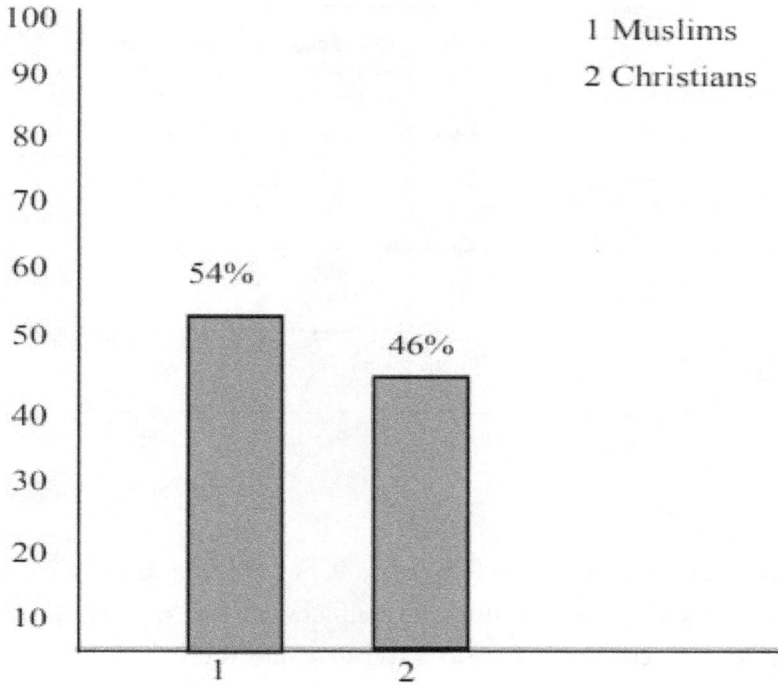

Source: *Field Work Result*

54% of the participants were Muslims, meanwhile 46% were Christians. Among Muslims, 3 people were from the Dinka Malual participants.

### Table (7-6): Reasons of the conflict in the area according to participants

| No. | Tribe | Competition Over grazing Resources | Ethnic and Religious Differences | Political and Territorial Encroachment | Other |
|------|-----------------|------|------|------|------|
| 1 | Dinka Malual | 11 | 08 | 22 | 5 |
| 2 | Reziegat | 23 | 09 | 13 | 3 |
| Total | | 34 | 17 | 35 | 8 |

*Source: Field Work Results*

35 people believe the reason for the conflict was a political and territorial encroachment. 34 people think the conflict was because of competition over grazing resources.17 people said that the conflict was because of ethnic and religious differences. Only 8 people think the conflict was because of other reasons and they declined to mention them.

### Figure (7-10): reasons of the conflict in the area according to participants

| 1 | Competition over Grazing Resources |
|---|---|
| 2 | Ethnic and Religious Differences. |
| 3 | Political and Territorial Encroachment |
| 4 | Other |

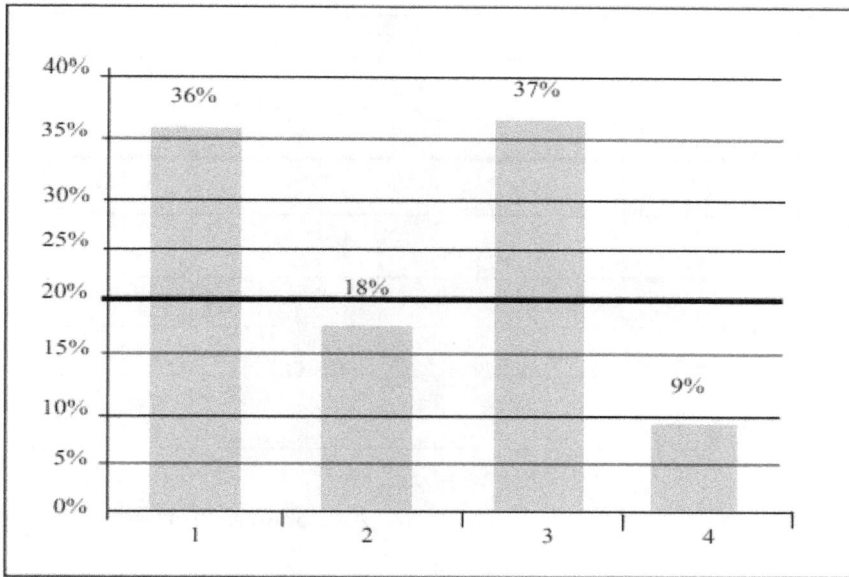

Source: Field Work Results

Those participants who think the reason for the conflict was political and territorial encroachment were 37%, and those who believe the conflict was because of competition over grazing resources were 36% Those who assume the conflict was because of ethnic and religious differences were 18%. Meanwhile 9% think the reason was because of other factors.

### Figure (7-11): The reasons for the
### conflict according to Dinka Malual

| 1 | Competition over grazing Resources |
|---|---|
| 2 | Ethnic and Religions differences |
| 3 | Political and Territorial Encroachment |
| 4 | Other |

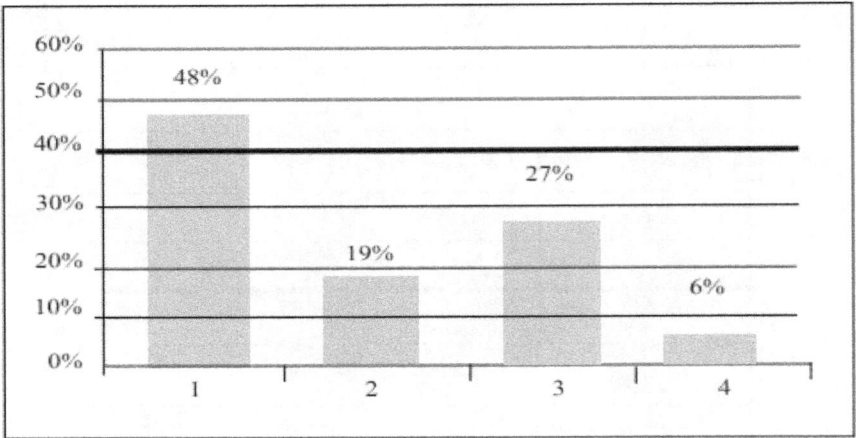

Source: Field Work Results

48% of Dinka Malual who participated believe the reason for the conflict was political and territorial encroachment. 24% think the reason was competition over grazing resources. 17% believe the reason was ethnic and religious differences. 11% think the reason was because of other factors.

### Figure (7-12): The reasons for the conflict according to Riziegat participants

| 1 | Competition over grazing Resources |
|---|---|
| 2 | Ethnic and Religions differences |
| 3 | Political and Territorial Encroachment |
| 4 | Other |

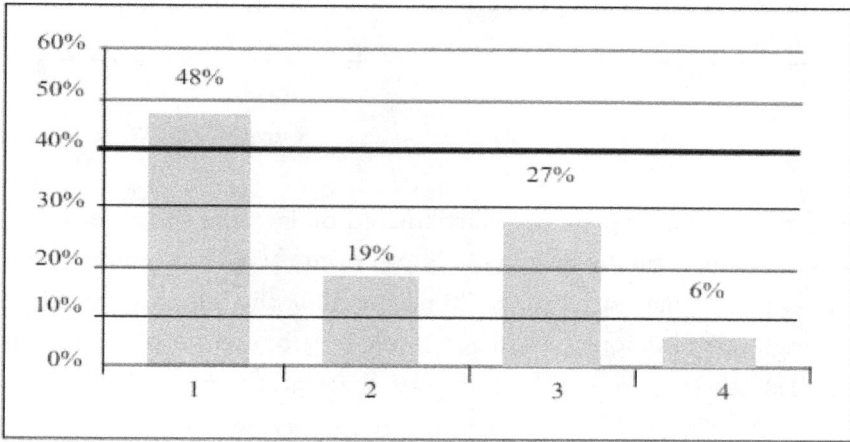

Source: Field Work Results

48% of Riziegat participants think the reason was competition over grazing resources, whereas 27% believe the reason to be political and territorial encroachment. 19% think the reason was ethnic and religious differences. 6% believe in other factors as causes for the conflict

## Table (7-7): Proposed solution to the conflict according to participants

| S/No. | Tribe | Socio-economic | Separation | Others | Total |
|-------|-------|----------------|------------|--------|-------|
| 1 | Dinka Malual | 4 | 39 | 3 | 46 |
| 2 | Reziegat | 22 | 18 | 8 | 48 |
| Total | | 26 | 57 | 11 | 94 |

*Source: Field Work Results*

57 persons from those who participated believe the solution of the conflict is through separating the South from the North. The majority was Dinka Malual participants. 26 people think the solution should be through introduction of socio-economic development programmes in the area. The majority of this group are Riziegat. Only 11 people think the solution should be different from those mentioned.

*Figure (7-13): proposed solution to the conflict according to participants.*

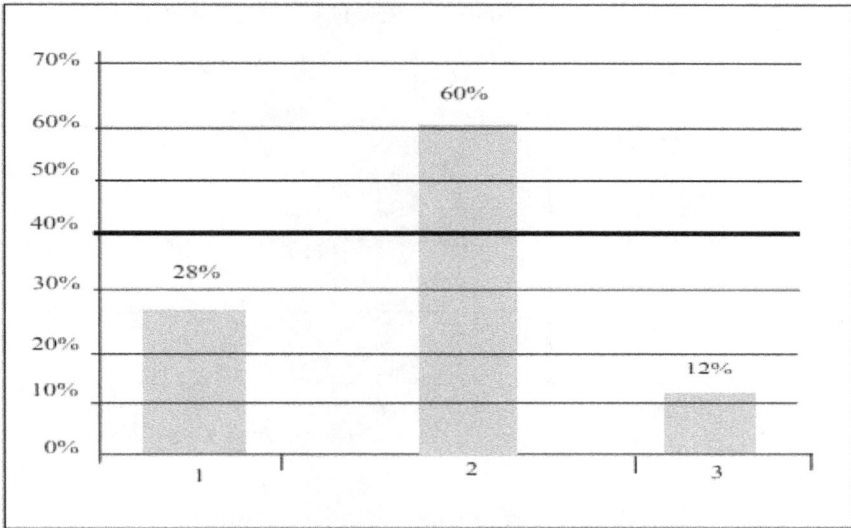

Source: Field Work Results

| 1 | Socio-Economic Development |
|---|---|
| 2 | Separation |
| 3 | Other |

60% of the participants think the solution for the conflict should be separation, the majority of which were from Dinka Malual. But 28% think that the conflict should be solved through socio-economic development, the majority came from Riziegat participants. 12% believe in other factors for the solution.

*Table (7-8): Expected result of the 2011 South Sudan referendum according to participants*

| S/No. | Tribe | Unity | Separation | Will not take place. |
|-------|-------|-------|------------|----------------------|
| 1 | Dinka Malual | 04 | 42 | -- |
| 2 | Reziegat | 38 | 07 | 03 |
| Total | | 42 | 49 | 03 |

*Source: Field Work Results*

49 people think that the result of the referendum in 2011 will be separation. The majority of this group are Dinka Malual .42 believe the result will be unity, the majority are Riziegat. Only three people think the referendum will not take place because of the South-South conflicts. These people are from Riziegat participants.

*Figure (7-14): expected results of the 2011 South Sudan referendum according to participants.*

| 1 | Unity |
|---|-------|
| 2 | Separation |
| 3 | Will not take place |

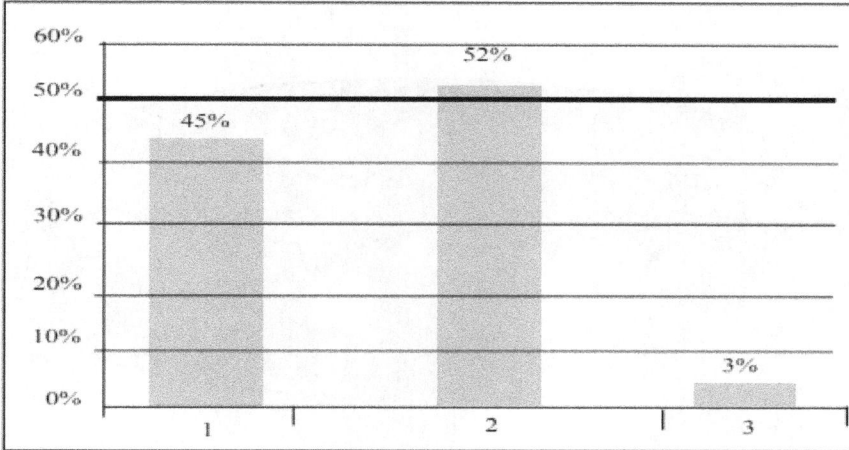

Source: Field Work Results

52% of participants think that the results of referendum for the south shall be separation. 45% think the result will be unity whilst 3% believe the referendum will not take place due to the South-South conflict.

*Figure (7-15): Dinka Malual participants'*
*expectations on the 2011 referendum results.*

| Unity | 1 |
|-------|---|
| Separation | 2 |

1

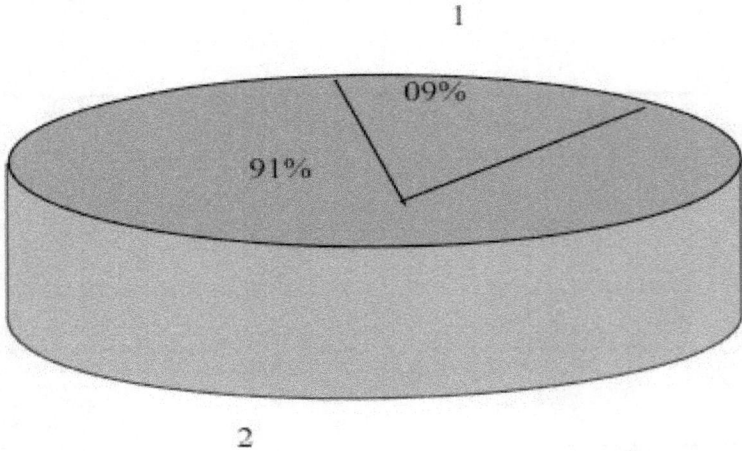

2

*Source: Field Work Results*

91% of Dinka Malual think the result of 2011 referendum is going to be separation, whereas 9% believe the result will be unity. It is worth mentioning that this 9% who believed in the unity 75% out of them were Muslims.

*Figure (7-16): Riziegat participants' expectations on the 2011 referendum results.*

| 1 | Unity |
|---|-------|
| 2 | Separation |
| 3 | Will not take place |

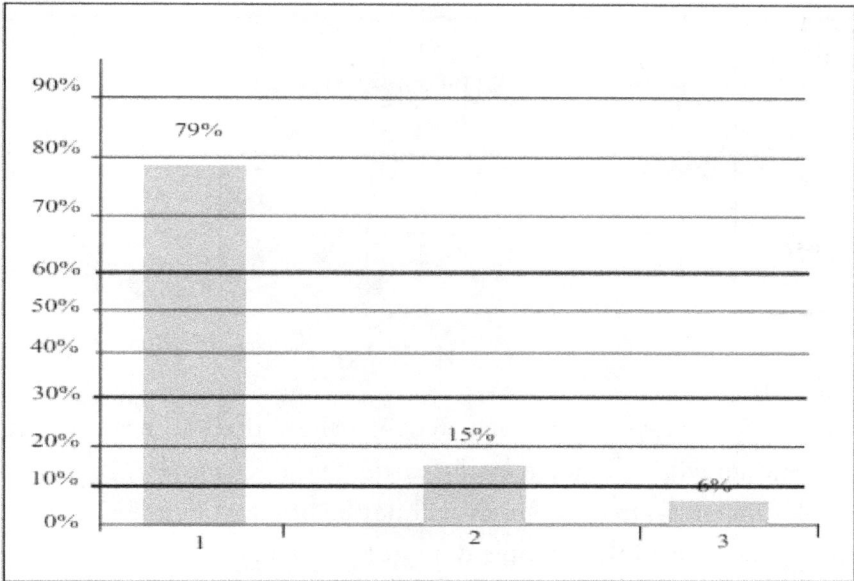

*Source: Field Work Results*

79% from Riziegat think that the result will be unity. 15% believe that the result will be separation, but 6% believe referendum will not take place due to the south-south conflict.

*Table (7-9): Opinion of the participants on whether the result of the 2011 referendum will be honored by the parties to the agreement or not*

| S/No. | Tribe | Honored | Dishonored | Do not know |
|-------|-------|---------|------------|-------------|
| 1 | D i n k a Malual | 37 | 09 | -- |
| 2 | Reziegat | 38 | 06 | 04 |
| Total | | 75 | 15 | 04 |

*Source: Field Work Results*

Among 94 people who participated 75 believe that the result of the referendum will be honored by the parties to the Agreement. 15 people think differently, that the result will not be honored by the parties to the Agreement .Only 4 people did not know what will take place.

*Figure (7-17): Opinion of the participants on whether the results of the 2011 referendum will be honored by the parties to the agreement or not*

| Honored | 1 |
|---|---|
| Dishonored | 2 |
| Don not know | 3 |

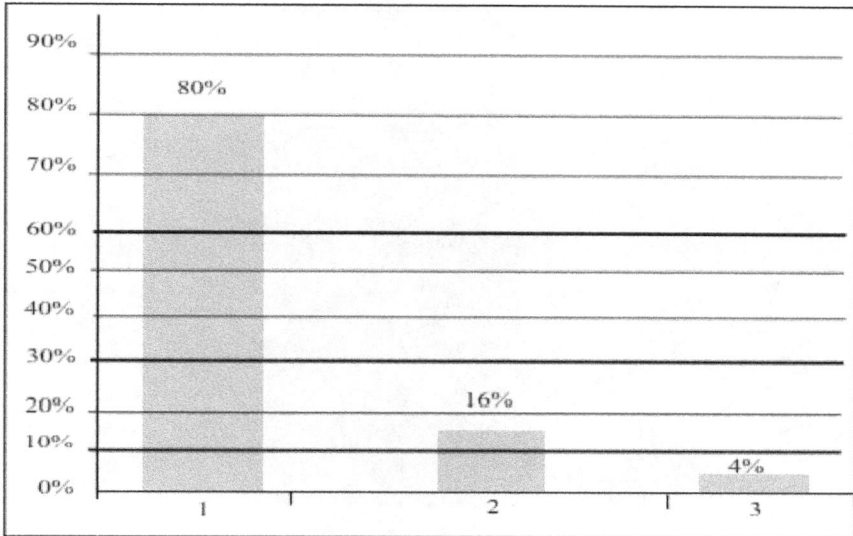

*Source: Field Work Results*

80% out of the population think that the result of the referendum will be honored by the parties to the Agreement. 16% think differently that the result will not be honored. Meanwhile 4% did not know anything about the issue.

*Figure (7-18): Dinka Malual opinion whether*
*the results of the 2011 referendum will be honored*
*by the parties to the agreement or not*

| Honored | 1 |
|---|---|
| Dishonored | 2 |

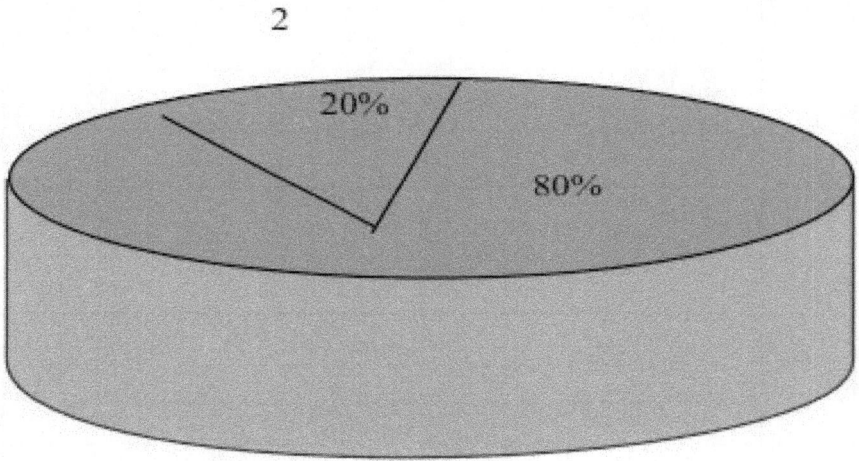

*Source: Field Work Results*

80% from Dinka Malual participants think that the results of the referendum will be honored by the parties to the Agreement, whilst 20%
believe that the result will be dishonored.

*Figure (7-19): Riziegat participants' opinion on whether the results of the 2011 referendum will be honored by the parties to the agreement or not*

| Honored | 1 |
| Dishonored | 2 |
| Do not know | 3 |

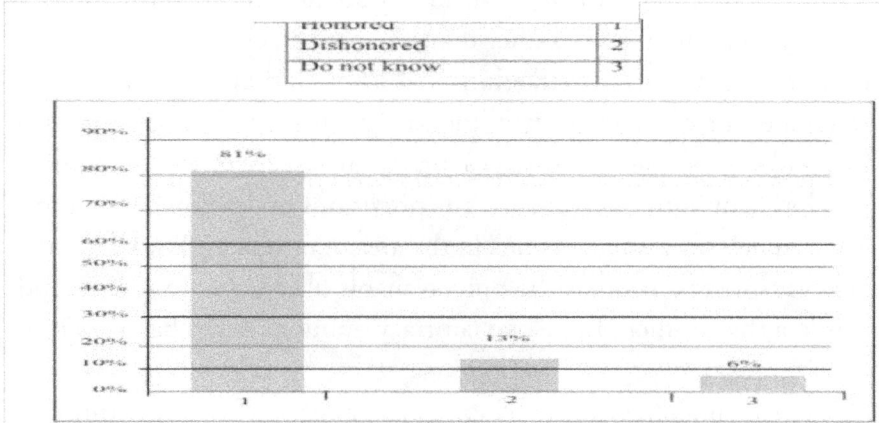

*Source: Field Work Results*

81% think that the results will be honored by the parties to the Agreement, whilst 13% believe that the results will not be honored. 6% of participants do not know whether the results will be honored or not.

## 7.4 Conclusion

This case of study of the Dinka Malual and Riziegat has accomplished its objectives. The issues assumed to be the causes of the conflict between Dinka Malual of Northern Bahr el Ghazal and Riziegat of Southern Darfur were addressed by the questionnaire and 94% out of selected participants gave their opinion clearly on these issues, despite their disagreements over some of these issues. However, the research asserted that the opinion of the majority must be taken into account. Whereas the views of participants considered being the minority should not be taken for granted. It is a responsibility of the concerned institutions to address the situation in its totality. The wide representation of participants considering gender, age, location, occupation, religion is appropriate in a social science study.

What was not in doubt as a leading factor for why Dinka Malual and Riziegat communities have been fighting all this time was the conviction that the political and territorial encroachments were a cause for this lengthy conflict. It is the dynamism of human behaviour which gives priority to current issues rather than the past. Issues like competition over grazing land and water, ethnic and religious differences were given less importance by a majority of the participants. The Riziegat community looks at the matter as being caused by an absence of socio-economic development in the area. Hence, the provisions of developmental projects can help in easing tensions in the area. Conversely, Dinka Malual believed in separation as the only available alternative to put an end this lengthy conflict. These two contrary opinions are to be taken into consideration.

Implementation of the developmental projects in the area within this short period would not be enough to arrest the situation. Nevertheless, the implementation of such programmes would help in minimizing the conflict and surely increase opportunities for sustainable peace, whether the country is united or divided. Meanwhile, the parties to the peace agreement had to start immediate preparations for the secession so that the event would not take people by surprise.

The majority of Dinka Malual participants thought that no chance was left for the unity of the country after what happened to the South. On the contrary, Riziegat participants believed in more chances to be given to Sudan to remain united. This could be done through the implementation of socio-economic development projects in the contested area of the South- North border. As a result of poverty in the area, separation would not create stability because of the nomadic life of those tribes living in the South-North border, but surely will create an international boundary where the state, rather than community, will be responsible for its supervision.

The danger of this change in roles is that any confrontation at the border would be a State vs. State instead of community vs. community, a situation that could lead to total war between the two entities.

Tranquility had a chance under one condition that the livelihood of these bordering tribes could dramatically change from a nomadic to sedentary life.

The attitude toward 2011's referendum was also tested and it was found that many people from both the Dinka Malual and Riziegat participants were convinced that the result of 2011 referendum would be respected by the parties to the Agreement.

Few participants from Riziegat thought that the referendum would not take place due to the South-South conflict which they believed would automatically prevent a successful conclusion of the interim period.

Some of these predictions were already under way like what happened in Malakal Town between SPLA forces and militias of Gabrial Tangyang, supported by SAF in January 2009, and tribal conflicts among southern Sudanese communities in many States.

# CHAPTER 8

**8. Manifestations of politics of Ethnic Discrimination as predicted**
This study for the purpose of earning a Ph.D. in Peace and Development Studies at the University of Juba. This research was conducted before the signing of the 2005 Comprehensive Peace Agreement (CPA) and published before the 2011 referendum in Southern Sudan.

In the first edition of the book publication of the thesis, the author made predictions which came to pass. Among these predictions were that more than 94% of South Sudanese would vote for secession, which was the case.

The second prediction was that there would be a border conflict between Sudan and the newly emerged South Sudan. This also happened in Abyei, Panthou/Heglig and Raja in 2012.

Lastly, the book predicted that there would be an internal ethnic conflict among South Sudanese and it happened in 2013.

The research provided recommendations to arrest the situation but were ignored by both Sudanese and South Sudanese policy and decision makers.

**8.1 Secession of South Sudan with 98.83%**
In the study, the author makes a call for stakeholders to work towards ensuring that the bloodshed is avoided in the process of separating the two Sudans. Recommendation number 14 of the study published in the

first edition states: "Finally, since the study reveals a strong possibility of separation of the South, then it is recommended that all measures be taken to ensure peaceful secession rather than chaotic separation."

The book further called for stakeholders to ensure that once the people have decided, their will be protected rather than try to force unity on them; "The two signatories to the CPA, regional and International Communities must work closely to implement this will of the majority of Southern Sudanese people. It is unwise to think that the remaining time of the interim period will help in making unity attractive."[108]

When the study that resulted in the publishing of this book was conducted in 2004, two years after the signing of the right of self-determination for the people of Southern Sudan in Machakos, July 2002. Participants predicted that the people of Southern Sudan would exercise their right for self-determination, entrenched by the CPA and the Sudan Constitution of 2005.

The results of the study were first published in 2009, two years before the referendum in 2011. Though the study predicted the results for the referendum to be 94% in favour of secession, the separation was attained by 98.83%[109] in January 2011 and six months later South Sudanese witnessed the declaration of independence on 9 July 2011.

### 8.1.1 Hurdles presented by the NCP

Had it not been for the wisdom of the SPLM leadership who led the people to secession, the NCP policies had made it difficult for peaceful separation. The policies were meant to sabotage the referendum. The use of Southern Sudanese armed groups allied to the NCP government to destabilize the process of the referendum was counteracted by President Salva Kiir. He initiated the South-South dialogue in Juba leading to the integration of these armed forces, including the forces of Paulino Matip

---

108    Wol, Dhieu M Diing, Politics of Ethnic Discrimination in Sudan: A Justification for the Secession of South Sudan, Netmedia, Kampala, 1st ed. 2009, pp.224.

109    Carter Center, Observing the 2011 Referendum on the Self-determination of Southern Sudan, Final Report, pp. 35.

Nhial, Gabriel Tinganang and Tom Al-Nuor into the SPLA in 2006.

Those who had remained with the government in Khartoum also crossed over in 2010, shortly before the referendum.

Another hindrance to the process of the referendum was the laxity of the NCP leadership in formulating a law that would guide the referendum process. Because the SPLM did not have a majority in parliament to pass such a law, they had to rely on the NCP's cooperation and support. Due to this reluctance, the Movement resorted to mobilizing the public to advocate for passing of the law, using such means as boycotting government and Parliament business and the use of popular demonstrations.[110] The third obstacle to the peace process was funding for the implementation of the CPA. The strategy adopted by the SPLM, to retain 50% of the oil revenues produced in Southern Sudan, helped the regional government in Juba to address the needs of peace and security including the implementation of the right of self-determination for the people of Southern Sudan through the referendum.

The oil proceeds were basically used to maintain the SPLA as guarantors for the implementation of the right of self-determination and execution of the referendum on January 9, 2011, rather than to implement developmental projects in the region. The only project that was worked on during that time was the Juba-Nimule highway which connects South Sudan with East Africa through Uganda. This project was financed by USAID.

The failure of the GoS to implement developmental projects for the southerners was enough motivation to vote for the secession. All these factors were a build up to that moment when H.E President Salva Kiir raised the flag of South Sudan in Juba as the youngest nation in the world on July 9, 2011.

### 8.1.2 Civil War in South Sudan

On December 16, 2013, President Salva Kiir announced a failed coup attempt against his government. He appeared before journalists in a combat

---

110     Termination of Southern Sudan, Final Report, pp. 35.

uniform announcing that "Riek Machar and his group planned and executed a coup but it was contained."[111]

He further declared that most of "the coup plotters were arrested but some were still at large, including their leader Riek Machar Teny." He revealed that Riek mobilized his tribesmen in the presidential guard to take power by force.[112]

This statement was misconceived by the paramilitary groups in Juba who started killing civilians at 107, Jabal and Gudele. Paul Malong, the former governor of Northern Bahr el Ghazal, was accused of commanding the forces.

The news that Dinka militia targeted Nuer in Juba[113] spread quickly in Greater Upper Nile, especially in Malakal, Bentinu, Ayod, Nasir and other counties. This in turn caused Nuer soldiers in the organized forces, and their militia the "White Army," to carry out revenge attacks in those towns, killing innocent Dinkas.

Many Nuer soldiers in Division Eight under Maj. Gen. Peter Gadet in Jonglei and Division Four commanded by Maj. Gen. James Koung in Unity State declared their allegiance to Riek Machar, who publicly embraced the resistance armed struggle against the government in Juba and declared a rebellion while addressing his supporters and tribesmen at Gatdiang in Jonglei.

He reiterated the same root causes of the conflict that the group highlighted during their press conference in the SPLM House on December 6, 2013. He said that the conflict started within the SPLM and it was triggered by lack of transparency in the party and the fighting was a result of an undemocratic attempt by President Salva Kiir to eliminate his political critics in the Party and Government.[114]

In the press conference the group identified the reasons why they believe the party had failed as follow:

---

111    SSTV 16/ 12/2013.

112    Ibid.

113    Rebeeca De Mabior on BBC English channel 17/12/2013.

114    Sudan Tribune, 18/12/2013.

### 8.2.1 Lack of internal democracy and dialogue within the SPLM

According to the group, the SPLM constitution and its organizational structures were abandoned by the party leadership. The only organ which used to meet occasionally was the Political Bureau (PB). In most cases the resolutions and decisions of PB were barely implemented because of the Chairman's suspicion about loyalty of the Secretary General (SG) and other cadres in the national secretariat.[115]

The group accused the Chairman of developing dictatorial tendencies that made it difficult for him to accept different opinions within the party. Because of this reason the Chairman decided to avoid meetings of the party organs and resorted to lobbying in the region, and ethnically, to manage the party affairs.

They believed that SPLM had become a ruling party that does not rule. The group made a lot of assertions that the appointments to higher positions and dismissals of leaders from government was never brought to the party for discussions and decisions.

The selection of candidates to represent the party in the 2010 elections was poorly conducted which led to many cadres contesting as independent candidates. Following the elections, the president appointed his cabinet based on regional and ethnic consultations. Individuals who lost elections were appointed to Parliament by presidential decree, thus giving key positions to individuals whose contributions were unclear to South Sudanese and the liberation struggle.

The Chairman repeated the same mistake by dissolving the government and appointing a cabinet majority of which were not SPLM members but his tribe-mates and friends the group insisted.

The committee on amendments of the constitution rendered its report and recommended some amendments in the constitution including mode of voting, election of leaders to various structures, composition and nominations to National Convention (NC). The group's members who were members of PB expressed their concern in the meeting and opted for voting by secret ballot, direct elections and

---

115     The Group Press Statement. SPLM House. 6/12/2013.

abolishing of the policy to have 5% appointees to the NC picked by the Chairman. However, their concerns were overlooked because they were a minority in the meeting.

Many political analysts believe the Chairman felt betrayed by this opposition and decided to fight back by conducting a reshuffle of cabinet in which he dropped those that had spoken against him, including the Vice President.

The group accused the Chairman of carrying out plans that undermined contributions of his comrades. They accused him of trying to relegate them from the party by implicating them in criminality.

They further asserted that the Chairman unilaterally declared dissolution of all structures of the party except his office in a move which surprised everyone in the SPLM.

The Chairman justified his decision by stating that he had dissolved all structures of the party except his office since the term of these offices had elapsed, contrary to laws and regulations of the party.

According to the party's constitution, rules and regulations, the agenda for the NLC meeting must be prepared by the PB or requested by 1/3 of its members. This had never happened in case of the last meeting of the NLC on December 14, 2013 that caused the fighting on December 15, 2013.

The Chairman relegated the PB and convened the NLC in spite of calls from peace lovers and religious leaders to postpone the meeting and heed to voices of reconciliation. The group claimed that they had cancelled their rally scheduled to take place on the same day of the NLC meeting.

They claimed that the Chairman took advantage of this and went ahead with his plans. When the group went to the meeting they expected dialogue hoping that he had learnt a thing or two about open governance from the Mandela Legacy celebration, but their expectations were in vain. The Chairman made it difficult for such wishes and hopes.

During the NLC meeting held on December 14, the group accused the Chairman of delivering a derogatory speech that left no room for dialogue. In his speech, the Chairman opened old wounds by requesting the meeting to approve his recommendation to remove the SG from the office and all party structures.

The group decided to boycott the meeting the following day, which agitated the Chairman further and he responded by implicating the group in a failed coup as an excuse to kill and arrest his opponents, the group alleged.

It is worth noting that all these differences within the party were addressed in Arusha, Tanzania and the various SPLM groups were supposed to reunite under the leadership of H.E. Salva Kiir Mayardit as Chairman and Riek Machar as First Deputy Chairman, James Wani as Deputy Chairman and Pagan Amum as Secretary General. However, to date nothing has happened and there is a possibility that Riek Machar and Pagan Amum (who is still in opposition) will form their own SPLM-IO and SPLM-Real, respectively.

## 8.2.2 Violations of the South Sudan Constitution 2011.

The group accused President Kiir of violating the Constitution for personal interests. They claimed that he removed the elected governors in Lakes and Unity States unconstitutionally.[116] The president suspected that Chol Tong Mayay and Taban Deng Gai were strong supporters of the Vice President Riek Machar.

The Constitutional articles used in the dismissal decrees were irrelevant to situations in both States, according to the group. The president quoted article 101/f which gives him powers to remove governors in case of serious insecurity that threatens national interest. The group believes that there were no such situations in both Lakes and Unity States.

The group stresses that this decree was applicable in Jonglei State which was under intense insecurity. Yet, Kuol Manyang, who was a strong supporter of the President was untouched, which shows how the constitution was manipulated to serve the president's interests.

The group holds a strong view that in democratic countries, the

---

116    The Group Press Statement. SPLM House. 6/12/2013.

running mate is part of electoral programme and constitutes an integral component of votes of an elected president; as such the running mate should not be dismissed before the end of the electoral term. However, the president chose to remove the VP without clear reasons. However, it is alleged his dismissal stemmed from his expression of interest in running for the presidency in the following elections. His dismissal had not been discussed in the party or in the Parliament contrary to the constitution.

The group went ahead to say that the Constitution stipulated that the Speaker of the National Assembly (NA) is elected by the majority of its members in an open session. The President violated this article by appointing Manasah Magok Rundail as Speaker of NA and threatened members that dared oppose his choice.

The group claimed that the Judiciary under President Salva Kiir is part of his executive. The president compromised independence of this important government arm and frequently interfered in many cases by summoning and ordering the Chief Justice to compromise justice. According to the group, the case of preventing Pagan Amum from travelling, without citing any law, was an example of a weakened judicial system.

The group further claimed that Chief Justice Chan Reec Madut paralyzed the Judiciary and brought it to its knees, dismissing competent judges on grounds that they advocated for independence of the institution.

### 8.2.3 Federalism

Federalism has been a demand and quest of Southerners since the time of the Juba conference in 1947. Unfortunately it was dismissed in the Transitional constitution of the Republic of South Sudan 2011, following the independence of the country.

It is worth mentioning that the Interim Constitution of 2005, which was derived from the CPA was advanced in decentralization. The Government of Southern Sudan (GoSS) instead of capitalizing on the CPA model, decided to drawback by centralizing some powers in the Transitional Constitution of 2011. The state judiciary, legal system and all law enforcement institutions were centralized.

Powers were concentrated in the hands of President, Chief Justice and the Minister of Justice. The President was empowered to dismiss elected leaders and appoint governors and members of parliament as he saw fit. John Luk Jok the former Minister of Justice and Chair of the Constitutional Review Committee before the independence was accused as masterminded for the constitutional crises in the country.

The people and governments of Greater Equatoria region consistently asked for federal arrangements as a good system of governance in South Sudan. The resolutions of the first, second and third conferences of Greater Equatoria region indicate this fact. The delegation representing the region arrived at the peace talks' venue in Addis Ababa early May 2014 to convey a message that the region was demanding federalism to be immediately adopted as a system of governance during the interim period.

The delegation was led by Clement Wani Konga, the Governor of Central Equatoria, Louis Lobong Lojore the Governor of Eastern Equatoria and Joseph Bangazi Bakosoro the Governor of Western Equatoria.

The Church leaders in their document presented to the IGAD Mediation Team, in the presence of the warring parties, envoys and observers in a plenary meeting in Addis Ababa recommended federalism as a preferred system of governance that could resolve the current conflict in the country.

The SPLM/A-IO in a consultative conference held at Nasir County, Upper Nile State between April 15 and 18, 2014, and attended by representatives of different forces including members of political parties, Civil Society Organizations, Faith-Based Organizations, Youth and Woman associations, Disabled and voluntary fighters (The White Army), all resolved that federalism is the best system of governance in the Republic of South Sudan and should be implemented immediately if the government wanted to address the current conflict in the country. Such a system can address fundamental issues and restore peace, justice, equality and prosperity.[117]

---

117    SPLM/A-IO First Conference in Nasir April 2014, Nasir, South Sudan.

Unfortunately, the Chairman of the SPLM/A-IO, instead of adopting federalism based on resolutions and recommendations of the first and second conferences in Nasir and Pagak, opted for the colonial districts' local government model, and worse still, he distorted the boundaries by creating Adar and Latjor States as a way of assimilating the Dinkas in Renk, Maluoth and Paluoch to Nuers of Nasir, Maiwut and Pagak.

The headquarters of the two states were situated in Nasir and Pagak despite the fact that Renk was a separate province during the colonial rule. This attempt was meant to create an ethnic domination of the Eastern bank of the Nile River.

The distortion of colonial boundaries by the SPLM-IO leadership is a clear indication that the leaders in South Sudan claim things but they don't necessarily commit themselves to their execution when get a chance to rule

## 8.2.4 Marginalization and Political Exclusion

Marginalization and political exclusion were among the fundamental reasons why Southern Sudan took arms against the North in 1955 and 1983 respectively. It is considered as part of the colonialist policy.

The 1983 the SPLM/A Manifesto articulates factors and forms of colonialism and believes that colonial attitude does not have a colour or border. Someone may marginalize a kinsman or countryman.

The government institutions and the private sector in South Sudan are alleged to be dominated by a few tribes and this can't bring peace and stability to the country. Despite its bitterness, the current peace agreement represents a unique opportunity for South Sudan to correct all mistakes created during the implementation of the CPA and beyond.

The liberation was fought by all tribes in South Sudan. Those who fed soldiers to prosecute war against the oppressors are as well liberators. The independence of the country which started as an armed struggle and ended with ballot boxes was not the making of one tribe. It came as a result of sacrifices of all tribes in South Sudan since the time of Anya Nya, Anya Nya Two and the SPLM/A. It is imperative that the contribution of tribes fighting war against the successive regimes in

Sudan be considered proportional and relatively different from one tribe to another and from one region to another region.

The degree of contribution also differs from one individual to another. There were those who sacrificed their lives in frontlines (heroes and heroines), those who were injured (wounded heroes and heroines) and those brave men and women of the gallant forces of the SPLA who fought liberation wars at the frontlines without fear. Also there were those who contributed food and logistics to feed combatants and those who fought intelligence and intellectual wars by providing information and articulating the position of the Movement respectively.

All these categories contributed to the liberation and the leaders of the SPLM/A recognize all these contributions in their public speeches. The Diasporas' front basically includes those who were in foreign countries and South Sudanese in the government-controlled areas inside Sudan. It is therefore, irrelevant to completely dismiss the role of others and claim that the war was fought by a few tribes or individuals.

The attribution of the entire struggle and liberation of the country to a few tribes in South Sudan is a historical mistake and can undermine the efforts of the people of South Sudan in the nation building processes.

This serious claim attributed to individuals should be completely dismissed and considered dishonorable. Institutions should be established far away from tribal affiliations or ethnicity.

## 8.2.5 Human Rights Violations

Human rights violations were among the reasons of rebellion against the successive regimes in the Sudan in 1983. The former president of the Sudan Jaafar Nimeiry imposed Sharia Law on Southern Sudanese and many people had their hands cut off in North Sudan because of alleged thefts. To escape the oppression, many ran away and joined the rebellion. After its independence, South Sudan continuously, takes a leading position in the list of human rights violations according to international human rights organizations.[118]

---

118     United Nations Human Rights Council Commission, 20 February, 2019.

When the war erupted in 2013, IGAD and the AU made two significant steps; one was the formation of the IGAD-led mediation committee and the other was the AU Commission of Enquiry, led by the former President of Nigeria, Olusegun Obasango. The two processes were to be complementary to each other. Meanwhile, the first was perceived to provide solutions, the second considered to dig out the root causes of the conflict. Whether the two committees succeeded in fulfilling their tasks or failing in them is not the purpose of this publication.

What is of the essence is that the Mediation Committee faced difficulties in performing their responsibility. The mediation processes came to surface as a result of the visit of some of the IGAD Ministers of Foreign Affairs to Juba, following the fighting between the Presidential Guards, and rampage of killings in Juba and other towns in Greater Upper Nile.

The IGAD Council of Ministers proposed a mediation process and planned for an IGAD Summit in Nairobi. On December 27, 2013 the Summit was convened and it resolved to address issues of conflict in South Sudan including calling for immediate ceasefire, mediation process and humanitarian access to victims of the conflict.

Seyoum Mesfin of Ethiopia was named to lead the mediation together with Lazarus Sumbieywo from Kenya and Mohamed Ahmed Mustafa Al-Dabi from Sudan. One of the problems with this group of mediators was that there was no harmony in their work.

The IGAD countries had already taken sides supporting the warring parties in South Sudan. Kenya and Uganda supported the government in Juba, while Ethiopia and Sudan sympathized with the rebels. This condition impacted negatively on the mediation process, and the mediators, instead of working closely to fill the gap between the negotiating parties, they widened the gap by creating unnecessary conditions that derailed the processes.

Sometimes the negotiating parties came to the rescue of mediators to resolve differences on the procedural issues in the negotiations. For example, Mesfin was pushing for participation of the civil societies in the SPLM-IO controlled areas but Sumbieywo objected to that idea, insisting that the selection of representatives of CSOs should be done in Juba. The mediators were also divided on the concept of African solutions for African problems.

Meanwhile, Ethiopia supported involvement of actors outside the continent Sudan was resistant to participation of the international community in the peace process. This situation couldn't allow the mediators put together a document to address the root causes of the conflict hence the agreement collapsed three months after the formation of the Transitional National Unity Government and Machar returned to the rebellion.

In Banjul, The Gambia, on December 30, 2013, the African Union Peace and Security Committee (AU/PSC) requested an investigation into human rights violations and other abuses committed during the armed conflict in South Sudan and to make recommendations on the best ways and means to ensure accountability, reconciliation and healing among all South Sudanese communities.[119]

On March 7 2014 a commission was formed with a three month mandate to perform its task. The commission was headed by former President of Nigeria, Olusegun Obasango. It comprised of Justice Sophia A.B. Akuffo, the president of the African Court on Human and Peoples' Rights and a Ghana Supreme Justice; Professor Mahmood Mamdani, the Executive Director, Makerere Institute of Social Research, Makerere University in Kampala, Uganda and lecturer at Columbia University in the United States; Bineta Diop, AU Chair's Special Envoy on Women, Peace and Development; and Professor Pacifique Manirakiza, Member of the African Commission on Human and Peoples' Rights and a criminal law specialist.[120]

In its findings, the commission identified individuals who were allegedly responsible for killing civilians in Juba and recommended the establishment of a legal mechanism under the African Union with support of the international community to bring those individuals to court.[121]

---

119    Final report of the African Union Commission of Inquiry on South Sudan, 27 Oct 2015.

120    Ibid.

121    Ibid.

The members of the commission differed on approach and decided to submit two different reports. While the rest of the Commission members believed that the violence in South Sudan is criminal,

Professor Mamdani believed it was political and each of these concepts has its own justice and accountability ingredients. He decided to publish his own report which was later named the "Minority Report."

Despite the work of African Union Commission of Inquiry on South Sudan (AUCISS), human rights organizations at international level were engaged in South Sudan. Their concern was that the commission would not release the report on time or even shelve it.[122]

As such some groups started publishing their own reports. For example, the United Nations, Amnesty International and The Rule of Law Initiative all published their reports on human rights violations in South Sudan.

The AUCISS final report found evidence of wide spread human rights violations committed by both government and rebels and recommended that those who had committed the crimes be brought to court. They suggested the implementation of an African ad-hoc legal mechanism to deal with accusations.[123]

On a separate note, as part of its report the ARCSS demanded formation of a hybrid court to be established by South Sudan and the AU. This provision was a key issue that the international human rights organizations wanted to be implemented. They urged the parties to the conflict to re-instate the same provision during the negotiation of R-ARCSS in Addis Ababa in 2018.

As part of United Nations Mission in South Sudan (UNMISS), the Human Rights Department (HRD) was created in South Sudan in 2011 with its headquarters in Juba and branches in Aweil, Bentiu, Bor, Kuajok, Malakal, Rumbek, Torit, Wau, and Yambio.[124] Its mandate

---

122     Ibid.

123     Ibid.

124     United Nations Human Rights, Office of the High Commissioner, UN Human Rights in South Sudan, June 2020.

was to monitor the situation of human rights in the country. As an example of communal conflicts, in Greater Jonglei, many people were killed and wounded, women and children were abducted and women were raped.[125]

Cattle rustling and theft in the in Murle, Lou Nuer and Dinka Bor areas of Unity, Lakes and Warrap States, known as the "death triangle," increased drastically in the previous two years.

The human rights organizations criticized the restrictions on freedoms of expression, association and movement by the government and the rebel groups. Arbitrary arrests, extra-judicial killings, abduction, rape, roadblocks and ambushes were carried out by the rebels and the government. Many security experts believe the situation would improve with unification and deployment of the forces that were still in training centers. Also the negotiations are going on in Rome and Nairobi to convince hold-out groups to join the peace process in the country. All these will significantly improve conditions of human rights in South Sudan.

### 8.2.6 Corruption and Nepotism

Corruption and nepotism are encouraged by weak institutions of governance in the country and the public service is politicized. Before and during the CPA, the recruitment was done on a kinship basis. Ministers appoint staff from their tribes and not on merit. There is the "godfather syndrome" in all recruitments and qualified or experienced candidates who have no uncles are relegated in the process.

An anti-corruption commission was established but has not been allowed to operate freely. The group claimed that many cases fail to reach courts because of weak institutions, and an absence of strong political will to fight corruption and continuous interferences.

### 8.2.7 Foreign Policy

South Sudan foreign policy after the independence needs to be given

---

125    UN NEWS Reader, United Nations, Human Rights, 15 March 2021.

special attention. The SPLM as a movement managed to maintain strong ties with many countries which facilitated the liberation struggle and later helped in the process of recognising South Sudan as an independent state. Unfortunately, the Republic of South Sudan has not managed the liberation politics well and many former friends have turned enemies.

Recruitment to foreign missions was based on nepotism and tribalism, meritocracy wasn't considered. One ethnicity dominates the Foreign Service. People complain that the majority of Ambassadors deployed and accredited in foreign missions are from only two tribes.

## 8.2.8 Exploitation of Natural Resources and wealth distribution and management

South Sudan is blessed with natural resources many of which are yet to be exploited. Apart from oil, there is no clear plan or strategy to exploit these resources. Therefore, the country depends on the oil revenues, about 90% of its budget The distribution of oil revenues has not been fair between states, on one hand, and between the government ministries and institutions, on the other hand.

For example, the National Government takes 90% of oil money, leaving the States and Administrative Areas to distribute 10%. Institutions like the Ministry of Defense and Ministry of Finance and Planning take the lion's share of the national budget. Some institutions have resisted electronic payrolls and auditing so that they can continue looting by using the ghost names.

Recently a group called Peoples' Coalition for Civil Action came up and called for demonstrations across the country to overthrow the Revitalized Government of National Unity (R-GONU) led by Salva Kiir. However, many political analysts believe that President Salva is the only unifying figure for the people of South Sudan and any change that can't take into account democratic transformation will never succeed. President Kiir must be part of the political processes in order to achieve a peaceful transfer of power and democratic transformation.

## 8.3 SPLM-IO and the Politics of Ethnic Discrimination

The SPLM/A-IO, is an institution perceived to be a national liberation movement. and could be a political platform that advocates for change and brings together all people of South Sudan from different walks of life. However, is also plagued by the same mistake of appearing as a tribal political organization. It came into existence for the first time, when the IGAD Mediation Committee met with the delegation of the opposition led by Taban Deng Gai, January 4, 2014.

In the first sitting the delegation was requested to identify and tell the meeting about themselves and how the conflict started in Juba. It was on that ground that the name SPLM/A-IO came into existence.

Initially, when the IGAD Mediation Committee visited Riek Machar at Gatdiang on December 27, 2013, he gave the Committee a list of his negotiating team headed by Pagan Amum, and listed as members, all the individuals who were in detention in the Blue House[126] and Taban Deng. The author, Hussein Mar and Stephen Par Kual were part of Machar's delegation but were in East Africa. Riek asked the three individuals to join Taban Deng in Addis Ababa to negotiate the release of the rest of their colleagues.

It was several weeks before the first group was released from the Blue House detention and the chair of the negotiating team was not among the first seven men who were released on January 29, 2014. On February 12, 2014 the first group led by Deng Alor Kuol arrived at the venue of negotiations.

The group was warmly welcomed by the SPLM-IO delegation and held a joint briefing. Unfortunately, the SPLM-IO was surprised by the group asking to hide their identity as a way of protecting the lives of their comrades who were still in the Blue House. Their argument was that if they joined the SPLM-IO, they would be confirming that those in detention were part of the rebellion and since the SPLM-IO declared a rebellion against the government, it would be dangerous for those still in the detention and impact any court case they were planning to bring.

---

126    Blue House is a name given to the headquarters of National Security in Juba.

During that time, Riek Machar was still in Jonglei and his access to communication was difficult. He requested the team to visit him in Gatdiang but they refused. The group first named themselves G7 before Pagan joined them and later changed to their name to Former Political Detainees (FPDs). They were allowed to join negotiations and given space to present their grievances within the overall negotiation platform.

Pagan Amum and the rest of his comrades were released and sent to Nairobi where they were given political asylum on April 25, 2014, few days before Riek Machar arrived in Addis Ababa for their first meeting with President Kiir on May 9, 2014. Pagan joined his colleagues in Addis Ababa to participate in the negotiations and the name G7 was dropped and replaced with the Sudan People's Liberation Movement Leaders and Former Political Detainees (SPLM-LFPD) but because the abbreviation was long and tedious it was shortened to SPLM-FDs. (Former Detainees).

The first meeting that brought together SPLM-IO leadership with SPLMFDs, led by Pagan Amum, was confrontational with the SPLM-FDs accusing SPLM-IO of being a Nuer movement. They criticized the formation of the leadership structure with the institutions dominated by the Nuer ethnic group.

Pagan challenged the relevancy of the author in a Movement where 90% of the fighters were from one ethnic group, saying both Dinka and Nuer people would consider the author a stooge. He advised the author to go back to President Kiir or stay at home. Unfortunately Pagan did not recall those days when he was leading non-Chollo troops in the SPLA/M.

He aggressively questioned the appointment of Alfred Lado Gore as Deputy Chairman of the SPLM-IO, stressing that Lado was not a member of the SPLM/PB and that he must relinquish that seat. The SPLM-IO leadership retaliated by accusing FDs of instigating war in Juba and trying to distance themselves, saying that President Kiir and Riek Machar's hands were stained with the blood of innocent civilians and that the war was their making as a way of relegating both President Kiir and Riek Machar from power.

Lado Gore defended his position and accused Pagan of being ignorant, arrogant and delusional, which led to the death of the SPLM vision. He compared his tenure as SPLM/A ideolque in the 1980s with that of Pagan. He believed Pagan lacked expertise and the popularity to make him such a senior person in the SPLM.

The young officers who attended the meeting attacked the FDs, accusing them of being the forces behind the collision between President Kiir and Machar in order to take over power, and vowed that they would not allow it to happen on their watch.

The meeting which was meant to foster reconciliation instead widened the rift and ended with Pagan walking out, having reached no other resolution except the formation of his SPLM-FDs. The exit of Pagan Amum and his FDs, majority of whom were non-Nuer SPLM leaders, created vacuums for an ethnic balance in the leadership of the SPLM-IO. Beside a few leaders from different parts of South Sudan, like Alfred Gore and Aggry, Idri Martin Abucha from Equatoria, Dhieu Mathok, Mabior Garang and Ayii Ayii Akol from Dinka ethnic group, the rest were all Nuers.

The organization was dominated by Nuer sections (Bentiu, Nasir, Pangak and Akobo) known as BNPA. The representation of each of these sections in the Movement's structures was the same as the entire region of Bahr el Ghazal or Equatoria. All Dinkas of Bahr el Ghazal were represented by one ministerial portfolio meanwhile, a section of BNPA has to be represented in the cabinet.

This segregation didn't stop in the rebellion but also continued in Juba after Machar quit the government. It worsened when Taban Deng assumed the position of the First Vice President of the Republic of South Sudan, with Ezekiel Lol Gatkuoth as close adviser. In the 2016 cabinet, Lou Nuer alone was represented by four ministers because SPLM-IO nominated two ministers, SPLM- IG nominated one minister and so did the SPLM-FDs. The same thing happened with the Nuers of the Greater Nasir, where the SPLM- IO appointed three ministers.

As an attempt to create regional balance in its leadership, the SPLM- IO elected Machar as Chairman of the Party, Alfred Lado Gore as Deputy

Chairman and the author, as Secretary-General of the Movement. The position of Secretary-General is elected by the National Liberation Council, a body with 80% of its membership coming from one tribe which poses challenges to contestants from different tribes. However, the author was elected to the position because of his history in the Movement, as the first Dinka from Bahr el Ghazal to join Machar in the bush. With the support of Machar himself and his wife Angelina Teny he was elected. Also the position was marked for Bahr el Ghazal as a way of creating balance within the leadership of the Party.

Above all the author enjoyed a cordial relationship with most of the Nuer leaders whom he believed were nationalists and assets to the country.

The author arrived in Addis Ababa on January 2, 2014 to join the negotiating team and on January 23' he went to Gatdaing and met with Machar who had relocated when he departed from Juba. There was a debate within the SPLM-IO whether the author should accompany the IGAD mediation team to Gatdaing or not. People expressed their concerns that the author may be killed by the White Army because of their grievances against the Dinkas. The author insisted accompanying the IGAD delegation. Machar also insisted on going to Gatdiang with the IGAD mediators. Machar tried very much to argue that the war was not between the Dinka and Nuer but the White Army refused to accept his argument. Whether Machar was right or not, for them it was still about the Dinka.

One of the Dinka instructors in Pagak training center escaped death because he was preaching that the war was not between Dinka and Nuer but it was about differences within the SPLM.

During the first SPLM/A-IO conference in Nasir, in April 2014, the author and Mabior Garang, both from the Dinka ethnic group, also gave examples of Nuer leaders fighting alongside President Kiir including Chief-of-General Staff James Hoth Mai and others, to convince the audience that the war was not between Dinka and Nuer.

However, for the White Army these were not Nuers but stooges of the Dinkas. This was the same way Dinka individuals who joined the SPLM/A-IO were perceived. In this case Pagan was right to assert that the war was tribal and those who were in opposite sides would be victimised. It was an impossible mission to convince people, particularly the White Army, that the war was not tribal. It was not Pagan alone, the author faced a lot of challenges at the hands of some of his colleagues who believed that he should not represent the SPLM-IO as Secretary-General or Secretary for Foreign Affairs.

One of his responsibilities was to sell the vision of the Movement and convince the world that the SPLM-IO was fighting for democratic transformation, nation-building and equality. It was not an easy task because many friends globally believed that the SPLM-IO was worse than that of SPLM-In Government (IG) in terms of participation of other ethnicities, destruction of towns that were captured from the enemy, keeping POWs alive and human rights violations.

Any town captured by the SPLM/A-IO was turned into a ghost city because of looting and destruction. Malakal was completely destroyed because changed hands between the White Army and the SPLA three times. China reversed its long-standing foreign policy principle of not receiving non-state actors. The author was received in Beijing by the Chinese Minister of Foreign Affairs and International Cooperation as the first rebel leader invited and received by the government in its history.

The Chinese government was worried about their personnel and facilities in the oilfields in Upper Nile and Unity States. They invited SPLM/A-IO to Beijing for dialogue and assurances that their properties would not be destroyed in those areas.

The SPLM/A-IO has no history of keeping Prisoners of War (POW) especially from the Dinka ethnic group. The POW who were captured including civilians in Nasir, Akoba, Ayod, Bentiu and Bor were all killed. Mathiang Anyoor[127] soldiers who withdrew from the battlefield in Upper Nile couldn't reach home despite the fact that Machar tried to create a safe exit for them by wiring messages to different units.

---

127    Mathiang Anyoor was a name given to the government militia that fought the 2013 war in South Sudan. It literally means buffalo.

In 2016, when fighting erupted in the Presidential Palace, known as J1, and Machar fled to Congo, there were officers nominated by the SPLM/A-IO Headquarters to join the Joint Military Ceasefire Committee in Juba. They were assembled in Kaldak before being transported to Juba for training. Unfortunately, the war erupted in J1 and those officers were allegedly killed by their colleagues under the command of Johnson Olney in Upper Nile.

In Pagak, in December 2014, during the second SPLM-IO convention one of the Generals who came from Pangak area heard the name of the author being called in the conference and he approached him. The General told him that he had managed to save the lives of many innocent Dinka citizens with his statements on Radio Tamazuj. The General had been told that this war was between Dinka and Nuer but the author's speeches on radio indicated that the war had nothing to do with the Dinka tribe and his statements had saved many lives.

In that convention, a committee was constituted to draw-up policies, strategies and political discourse on how war should be fought in South Sudan. Unfortunately, the committee produced a policy that cements tribal incitements by concentrating on the Dinka of Northern Bahr el Ghazal, Warrap and Lakes States as enemies of the Movement and all affiliates of other tribes to not be enemies to the SPLM/A-IO.

The author questioned this policy and where he and other non-Dinkas in President Kiir's camp stood on this proposal. The policy document was criticised by Riek Machar and Madam Angelina Teny as well. The Committee was left with nothing but to withdraw the proposal for good. It is believed that policy document even if publically denounced by the leadership of the SPLM-IO, is still in operation used by some individuals who have tribal agenda in the Movement.

When the author was elected as SG of the party, some colleagues and close friends were livid that the SPLM-IO was committing such a serious mistake of bringing a Dinka to its leadership.

They were worried that Machar may rule the country for two terms and retire while Alfred Gore was an old man who may not be fit for leadership of the party after 10 years. Bringing the author in so close to the top would automatically qualify him to assume leadership of the SPLM-IO and consequently a Dinka would ascend to leadership of the country again.

During the SPLM-IO leadership visit to the USA, Ezekiel Lol Gatkuoth in his speeches, claimed that the Juba government was Dinka dominated and the Dinkas were plundering the country. He pointed out all seats occupied by Dinkas including D/Gs and concluded that their turn, as Nuer, to plunder the country was coming. He continuously referenced Michela Wrong book *"It's Our Turn to Eat: The Story of a Kenyan Whistle-Blower,"* referring to the statement of a Kenyan friend John Gthongo. IN 2016 Taban Deng nominated Lol to lead the Ministry of Petroleum and Ezekiel started implementing this policy with a few friends and he left out the entire Nuer tribe.

In President Kiir's camp there are people who believe that Nuer shouldn't be allowed to rule the country regardless of their contributions in the liberation of South Sudan. Supporting a leader who is Nuer by tribe is a crime that warrants death. The author was arrested in Juba in 2016 by a group of Dinka who hated Riek Machar and the Nuer tribe, but was rescued shortly after. He opened a case against these criminals but realized that these young men were victims and the attempt to assassinate him was engineered by certain circles. He also realized that a continuation of the case would punish innocent young men so, he decided to pardon them as a way to foster peace, stability and reconciliation.

The issue of ethnic discrimination in South Sudan is being exercised by all political parties. Thomas Cirillo Swaka from Bari in Equatoria is reported to have refused to admit Paul Malong into his opposition alliance (SSOMA) because the former SPLA Chief-of-General Staff, who parted ways with President Kiir and rebelled, is a Dinka and doesn't want the Dinkas in SSOMA. In Equatoria Dinkas were named MTN by the affiliated of Thomas Cirillo and many innocent civilians lost their lives, especially women and children in Equatoria. His SSOMA is a tribal organization dominated by Bari-speaking groups.

Sometimes the acts of the opposition groups make people to believe that President Kiir is being targeted not because of mistakes he has made but because of his tribe. This type of categorization is destroying our beloved country and must stop.

In Khartoum, it was difficult for the SPLM-IO to sign the peace deal without pressure from former President Omer al-Bashir. Going back to the Dinka government in Juba was a red line to many commanders of the SPLM/A-IO. Many leaders of the SPLM/A-IO tendered their resignations to the Chairman of the Movement complaining of mismanagement in the party. Riek Macahr was accused of turning the SPLM-IO into a family organization by appointing relatives and friends to senior positions in the government. Some of these leaders, who resigned from SPLM/A- IO, accused Machar of being a tribalist and sectionalist, and that hatred against the Dinkas was a visa to many individuals who made their way to senior positions in the government. The more you hate Dinkas the more you get a senior position. There is no evidence for these serious allegations.

In 2015, a close relative to Machar, Youhanis Musa Puok wrote a book claiming that Machar was controlled by his immediate family referring to Angelina Teny and Taban Deng as Telareen[128] (Two-Telar).

He was referring to the Telar Deng Ring who was accused of manipulating and controlling decisions of President Kiir in 2012. Comparatively, this means if President Kiir let one Telar corrupt his leadership then Riek Machar was worse by having two Telars; Angelina and Taban. Musa Puok was inaccurate in his judgment otherwise, we would not have witnessed war in 2016. When Taban Deng was denied to lead the Ministry of Petroleum, the angry GitKwang group, led by Simon Gatwech and Johnson Onley, was another example that explains the organization called SPLM-IO.

In conclusion, the journey towards a nation that all South Sudanese could proudly say, "this is our country," is still far-fetched and requires that people move as one person, leave aside the leadership struggles and build the nation because democracy is about the institutions of governance. Otherwise we will loose it all.

---

128  موقع القصر الجمهوري ، يوهانس موسى فوك الخرطوم2015.

People do not need to be members of one ethnic group or one tribe or even one region to build a nation, they can do it collectively because the most beautiful nations are those with diversities.

## 8.4 South Sudan and Sudan border conflict

The war of borders and territorial claims between South Sudan and Sudan was predicted by this study in 2004 before the signing of the CPA and it was published in 2009 before the independence of South Sudan. Apart from Abyei, there were many disputed territories including Kafia Kingi, 14 Mile, Egelig /Panthou, Kaka and the area around it, Bebnis, Jebel Megeinis and Jordah border area.[129] There was a confrontation in Kafi Akingi but no detailed account has been made here.

### 8.4.1 Abyei conflict

This area, belonging to the Dinka Ngok, was transferred to Kordofan Province in 1905 because it was difficult for British colonial administration to manage Abyei from Wau. During peace negotiations in Naivasha, Kenya, the SPLM argued that the area should be transferred to Bahr el Ghazal by administrative order as it was done in 1905 but the government refused the proposal and insisted that the area remain part of Kordofan. The two parties couldn't reach an agreement and resorted to a compromise that a referendum be conducted in the area to seek the opinion of the Dinka Ngok whether they wanted to be part of Bahr el Ghazal or remain in Kordofan. The conduct of the Abyei's referendum was mandatory and stipulated in the CPA.

In examining the Abyei Protocol, inked by the Sudan government in 2005, and considering the determination that the Ngok Dinka have, a lay person in the discipline of law can easily reach a conclusion that Abyei would have been part of Bahr el Ghazal if its referendum was carried out simultaneously with the Southern Sudan referendum on the 9' January 2011.

Analyzing the CPA, the Interim National Constitution of Sudan

---

129    Craze, Joshua, Contested Borders: Continuing Tensions 0ver the Sudan-South Sudan Border, 2014.

(INCS), Interim Constitution of Southern Sudan (ICSS) and Permanent Court of Arbitration, Abyei Tribunal Award (PCA/ATA) a person could begin to a believe what Abel Alier wrote in his book "*Too Many Agreements Dishonoured.*"

The focus here is not on how the area was transferred to Kordofan but on challenges that faced the implementation of the Abyei Protocol.

In Naivasha the NCP totally refused to discuss issues beyond 1/1/1956 South-North Sudan borders, saying they were not provided for by Mashokos[130] basic principles document. Meanwhile, the SPLM was advocating for re-transfer of Abyei to Bahr el Ghazal through an administrative order from the Presidency, while the GoS was insisting that Abyei must remain in Kordofan. The SPLM believes that since the area was transferred from Bahr el Ghazal to Kordofan by the colonial regime, administratively the government in Khartoum must revise that decision by issuing another administrative order. The mediators of the process, headed by the US proposed a middle position which compromised both positions of the SPLM and GoS, arguing for referendum in Abyei as a win-win position.

It is worth mentioning that, the silence of the Machakos Agreement, the guiding document on the peace process, about the status of the three regions of Abyei, Nuba Mountains and Blue Nile, cemented the position of the government of Sudan and gave their delegation in the peace talks legitimacy to maneuver around issues of the three areas.

After the SPLM delegation accepted the position paper of the mediators presented by US, the government delegation requested further consultation before presenting their final opinion to the Mediation. The delegation traveled to Khartoum and conducted a lengthy discussion in the Party's Leadership Office and accepted the American proposal.

The placing of Abyei under the presidency with dual citizenship from both the Bahr el Ghazal and Kordofan regions in the interim period

---

130    The Machakos Protocol was a framework agreement between North-South parties, signed in Machakos, Kenya on July 12, 2002. It provided the right of self-determination for the people of Southern Sudan to be exercised through a referendum after an interim period of six and half years.

was a way of harmonizing different positions until its referendum was carried out. Notwithstanding, the Abyei Protocol is the document most affected by many violations and negligence in terms of implementation.

After signing the agreement, the formation of administration that governs the area took three years to be constituted. The area has been denied its 2% ratio of its oil revenues. The GoS militias and Sudan Armed Forces (SAF) elements frequently attacked Abyei and murdered innocent civilians. Roads leading to the area were continuously blocked to obstruct the repatriation process to Abyei.

The storm caused by former President Omer al-Bashir's speech in South Kordofan when he said, they would not recognize independence of South Sudan if its constitution included Abyei, was considered as a statement that was driven by election fever but also could be a declaration of war in the region because the referendum process was a red line to many South Sudanese.

As it was mentioned before, the CPA provisions, especially that pertaining to the Abyei Protocol, articulated clearly that the referendum in Abyei should be carried out concurrently with Southern Sudan referendum to ascertain opinions of the Nine Chiefdoms of Ngok Dinka and non-Ngok Dinka residing in Abyei and whether they wanted to remain in Kordofan or rejoin Bahr el Ghazal. During the negotiations in Naivasha, the critical question on table was what is the territorial entity that was transferred from Bahr el Ghazal to Kordofan by the colonial administration in 1905. In an attempt to answer this question, the Abyei Boundary Commission (ABC) was formed and given the task of identifying Abyei territory that was transferred to Kordofan.

The Terms of Reference (TOR) of the ABC were made for its smooth functioning and its membership including the Government of Sudan, SPLM, and experts from the mediating countries, with each party represented by five members. The most important article in the TOR was that the findings and reports of ABC are compulsory and final.

When the Commission submitted its reports to the leadership of the two parties, the government refused the reports on the grounds that the ABC violated its mandate in identifying the territory of Abyei area by stating in its reports that the Commission had not found the exact area which was transferred from Bahr el Ghazal to Kordofan in 1905. The government argued that ABC should have seized the reports, which violated its mandate since it failed to identify the contested area. In their opinion, it was a total breach of the TOR.

The issue of eligibility for the voting became a central problem was a serious matter during the negotiations, so the question of who would or would not vote in the referendum was not given much attention and even escaped schedules and matrices of the implementation modalities.

The overwhelming opinion within negotiating groups was that the problem of Abyei was much associated with boundaries rather than voting eligibility, hence the matter was geared towards solving that particular problem and subsequently taken to The Hague for arbitration as a consequence of continuous failure of the parties to reach a solution after a long engagement.

In The Hague, the Court identified clearly, the boundary of the Ngok Dinka Nine Chiefdoms, regarding northern borders with Kordofan as requested by the parties when presenting their position papers to the Court. Each party assured the tribunal and audience of their compliance with the Court ruling, whatever the result.

The government accepted the ruling of PCA in the first place with ululations and acclamations, by shouting "God is Great," "God is Great," indicating that they had won the case because 10 kilometers were recovered from ABC and annexed to Kordofan by the Court decision. There were celebrations in Khartoum, Fulla, Mujeld and Miaram.

They publicly praised the God of Mohammed, the messenger of Allah who had not let them down, by proving them right against the position of the ABC. To the disappointment of those interested in solving the problem, the government rejected the ruling the same way they had approached the ABC report after their assurances of respecting the outcomes and their readiness to honour the ABC reports which were later declined. The government was selective in implementing the Hague ruling by insisting that Panthou/Egegil was given to them by the court ruling.

Within a few months and after careful studies, the government found that the ruling of the Court was not up to their expectations and the area which was annexed to Kordofan by the decision of the Court has only one significant oilfield. The remaining part has a bulk quantity of oil, which made the government renege from their commitment to honour the ruling of the court and started creating different strategies to avoid implementation of the Abyei Protocol. The Missieryia nomads were involved in these newly designed strategies and scenarios to spoil the implementation of the protocol.

It was clear that the problem had nothing to do with grazing areas for the Missieryia tribes, because the PCA gave the nomads the grazing rights in Abyei and beyond.

In addition, all regions bordering Sudan, like Bahr el Ghazal, Unity, Upper Nile and Warrap welcomed the decision of the leadership of South Sudan and expressed readiness to receive pastoralists from Arab nomads in South Kordofan, South Darfur, White Nile and Blue Nile, to use their grazing lands. This negated the government allegations that the problem was connected with communal grazing rights.

There was confusion on the direction chosen by the government. The matter also had nothing to do with Messiria nomads, but rather believed to be connected with the oil in the area.

It was reported by an undisclosed source that in one of the meetings of the technical committee, a senior official from the government delegation proposed that South Sudan should allocate a percentage of the oil produced in South Sudan for Sudan to allow Abyei to join South Sudan. A representative from the SPLM asked the government delegation to submit a written position on the proposal to be discussed in the next agenda when the meeting reconvened. However, to the surprise of the SPLM delegation, the Sudan government representatives declined their proposal and reiterated their previous position which made it difficult to attain peace in the area.

In the legal framework of the Abyei protocol, the parties to the peace agreement, agreed that Abyei should be governed by the presidency with dual citizenship in Sudan and South Sudan, prior to its referendum.

For this status to become an obligation it needed to be necessitated by constitutional provisions both in Sudan and South Sudan to be regulated by law in the two countries. This is exactly what happened in South Sudan after independence in 2011.

The Abyei Administrative Area appeared in article 183 of the Interim National Constitution of Sudan (INCS) and article 176 of Interim Constitution of Southern Sudan (ICSS). The two versions were an identical photocopy of one another.

The independence of South Sudan necessitates reviewing of constitutions in both countries to comply with emerging situations. Khartoum proceeded in amending its constitution without bringing the issue into the joint political committee forum to recommend on how sections, articles and provisions connected to the Abyei Administrative Area, were to be handled since the Presidency would not exist after independence of South Sudan on the 9th July 2011.

Furthermore, the US Presidential Envoy Scott Gration and African Wise Men Committee Chairperson, Thabo Mbeki the former President of South Africa, failed to bring the matter to the attention of the Presidency in their last meeting before July 9th 2011, and the Sudan government decided to keep Abyei in its constitution on the same condition that the area would be administered under the Presidency.

The inclusion of Abyei in the constitution of Sudan without consulting the South Sudan leadership or the joint political committee of peace partners, saw the government of South Sudan do the same thing by also including it in their constitution.

The South Sudan and Sudan Peace Talks processes, coordinated by African Union High Implementation Panel (AUHIP) and chaired by President Thabo Mbeki, put in place structures and mechanisms to address post-independence issues. Beside the two heads of state mechanism; President al-Bashir-President Salva Mechanism (PBPSM), there were other structures including High Political Level (HPL), which was chaired by Pagan Amum representing South Sudan, and Abdel Rahim Hussein from Sudan government.

There were established technical committees on different issues; the

Committee on Economics Affairs, the Committee on Citizenships and Immigration, the Committee on Security Matters, the Committee on Border Demarcation and the Committee on Abyei. Each committee was either chaired by a senior member of the ruling party or a cabinet minister from the each state. The committees were authorized to conclude or defer issues of deadlock to HPL & PBPSM, but all the efforts failed.

The PBPSM delivered efficiently and managed to open up a window of opportunity after the troops from the two armies dragged their boots into the territory of each other's country in 2011.

The PBPSM resolved different outstanding issues including military confrontations, establishment of demilitarized border zones, oil transportation, establishment of corridors for movement of people and goods, grants for freedoms and transitional financial assistance to Sudan.

However, on November 14, 2013, the PBPSM couldn't resolve the commencement of the referendum in Abyei. When the AUHIP released its proposal on final status of Abyei in September 2012, the AUPSC endorsed it with conditions that the two countries must reach consensus on the proposal within six weeks, despite the fact that the Council was aware that there would be no consensus between the two parties.

Records justify this claim since the time of the post-referendum negotiations. It was in this state of no-consensus that the Abyei referendum reached the AUHIP. Otherwise it would have been concurrently carried out with the Southern Sudan Referendum on January 9th 2011.

The AUPSC missed the point in December 2012 when it referred the Abyei issue to the PBPSM which met several times on the same occasion without progress. Instead of endorsing the proposal as final and binding, and seeking endorsement from UNSC to enforce its implementation, it again sought the PBPSM consensus.

President Kiir declared on many occasions that he had reached a deadlock with president al-Bashir on Abyei and urged the regional and international organizations to look for other possible alternatives. Unfortunately, the AUPSC continuously demanded the PBPSM meeting on Abyei should reach consensus. It was clear that the parties had serious disagreement on voter eligibility. South Sudan didn't understand the logic behind allowing nomads from Kordofan to take part in the referendum, meanwhile Sudan insisted that Messiria must vote in the referendum.

The issue of the nomads taking part in the referendum was resolved amicably by the agreements on Abyei and the proposal on the final status itself put it clearly that historically, nomads had no right to vote in similar referenda.

The AUHIP identified October 2013 as a day of commencement of the referendum in Abyei but it was dishonored by the parties to the conflict specially the Government of Sudan. Upon realizing that things were not going well in the area and nobody was listening to their advice, the AUPSC warned the parties against any unilateral decisions on Abyei, and requested the two presidents to meet for a consensus on Abyei but this didn't happen.

However, the citizens of Abyei insisted and carried out their historic referendum and it was successful in favour of joining South Sudan but this was not recognized. The lesson from East Timor in 1999 when the UN, under Kofi Annan, carried out a referendum successfully without influence of Indonesia could be drawn. These successful stories from other nations that brought peace and stability need to be studied by the recently formed committee by President Kiir in June 2021 to address the Abyei final status as per the CPA. The Committee appointed by President Kiir led by Tut Gatluak Manime and deputized by Deng Alor Kuol is supposed to meet with their Sudanese counterpart from the Sudan and resolve the matter. However, until the publication of this book they have not meet.

## 8.4.2 Panthou/Heglig

The Heglig village locally known as Panthou of Panarou Dinka of Ruweng Administrative Area has not been a part of Western Kordofan as alleged by the regime of the former president Omer al-Bashir in Khartoum.

The processes of annexing the area to Kordofan started during the regime of The National Salvation. It came to surface for the first time in 1997 when President Omer al-Bashir paid a visit to Panthou/Heglig for inauguration of the oil production. The state government led by Abdelrahaman Mukhtar ordered the Commissioner of Peace for the province that includes Abyei, al Miaram and Muglid to transport Ngok Dinka citizens residing at Abyei and surrounding areas to the venue of the ceremony at Panthou/Heglig. The purpose was to welcome the President and participate in the occasion under the belief that the area is a part of Abyei and owned by Ngok Dinka.

This strategy was not known to the then state government in Unity state. Micheal Mayiel Chuol who was the Wali (Governor) was not aware of this conspiracy. When the Governor of Unity State arrived at the venue for the ceremony with his cabinet members, he found the place and the occasion hijacked by the Western Kordofan government officials and the populace from Abyei. They were welcomed as guests from the neighboring state. He was denied a speech in the ceremony, and Abdelrahaman Mukhtar was accorded welcoming remarks as the host state and asked to welcome the President to deliver his speech and officially launch the project.

Upon receiving a copy of the programme, Micheal Mayiel immediately objected to it.. The two governors exchanged insults in the presence of the President who was supposed to give the speech on the occasion and who owned the area. The President intervened and asked the two governors to give their speeches saying the area belongs to all the Sudanese. However, the oilfields were officially inaugurated on the assumption that the area was part of Western Kordofan not Unity State.

In 1999, when the first oil was shipped to international market through Port Sudan, again the chance was given to the oil producing states; the two governors of the Western Kordofan and Unity State were asked to give speeches.

Subsequently in 2004, the conspiracy of annexing Panthou/Heglig to Sudan became a reality during the annual presentation of the state government reports to the National Council of Ministers. In one of its meetings, the Council of Ministers chaired by President al-Bashir witnessed a heated debate between cabinet members from the North and South when the governor of Unity presented his reports about the situation in Panthou/Heglig. He was asked by a certain Abdelhamid Musa Kasha to immediately delete Panthou/Heglig from his map arguing that the area was not part of Unity state. The cabinet members from Southern Sudan, who were attending the meeting, including the author, stood their ground and supported Governor Joseph Monytuil and succeeded in maintaining Panthou/Heglig on the map as part of Southern Sudan. Subsequently, after the meeting Nafi Ali Nafi who was in charge of the Federal Affairs portfolio in the Cabinet wrote to Joseph Monytuil to drop Heglig/Panthou from the map of the Unity State. However, Joseph ignored the request and didn't respond to Nafi.

The situation became complicated when the CPA was signed, and the Abyei Boundary Commission (ABC) was formed, mandated to draw Abyei boundaries. The experts made a mistake by including Panthou/Heglig and other areas in Western Abyei. Maybe the assumption was that since there was confusion surrounding the status of Panthou/Heglig it could be best solved within the ABC mechanism.

It was on this assumption that the court of arbitration in The Hague came out and dismissed the claim that Panthou/Heglig was not part of Abyei. The judges indicated what was supposed to be the Abyei boundaries and left out what they believed was not geographically part of that area and not necessarily part of Kordofan. This is how Panthou/Heglig became a disputed area between South Sudan and Sudan.

The GoS intentionally misinterpreted the ruling, exploited it and claimed that the court ruling had confirmed their claim over Panthou/Heglig, since the ruling carved it out from the Abyei territory without knowing that it was purposely left out, as it has nothing to do with the ABC report and the Abyei boundaries. It was very surprising to know that the GoS rejected part of the ruling and accepted part of the same verdict. By embracing Panthou as their area and refused to recognize Abyei as South Sudan

The information that the area was claimed as part of Western Kordofan and not South Kordofan is very significant to the readers to see the degree of confusion and weak position on the side of the government of Sudan on Panthou/Heglig. This is important because it will enable us to relate geopolitics of the area to the historical events, because South Kordofan, which borders Panaru Dinka was supposed to be the one claiming the ownership of Panthou/Heglig and not Western Kordofan. Conflicts over ownership too, were expected to be between Micheal Mayiel Chuol the governor of Unity State by then and the late MagizubYusuf Babaker the then governor of South Kordofan and not between Micheal and Mukhtar. However, because the conspiracy was designed to make the area a part of the disputed Abyei, the scenario went on in that way.

On April 10, 2012 the SPLA captured Panthou/Heglig but was widely condemned by the international community who urged South Sudan to withdraw from the area.

The Sudanese mobilized themselves to recapture Panthou/Heglig but couldn't take it by force. In response to the international and regional plea, President Kiir ordered the forces to withdraw from the area and started withdrawing before the Sudanese army claimed it back.

This was another mistake because withdrawing from a disputed territory without conditions is unusual. The GoSS should have made a trade-off since there were unresolved post-independence issues. The international pressure is a normal practice because nobody can support claiming territories by force.

The first mistake was when the ABC, which was meant for Abyei boundaries, included Panthou/Heglig as part of Abyei territory in the Hague and failed to defend the claim in the court.

The author was invited by a High Panel of Experts of African Union High Implementation to make a presentation on 14 Mile in Northern Bahr el Ghazal which was reported as a disputed area between South Sudan and Sudan in the Cooperation Agreements. After his presentation he was given an opportunity to ask questions of the panel. He asked about the status of Heglig/Panthou because the panel had been silent about it as a disputed area. The panel said a mistake had been made in taking Panthou/Heglig to The Hague as part of the Abyei area and to rectify the mistake they advised South Sudan to go back to the court with a new argument and evidence to justify that the area was not part of Abyei. Precisely, Panthou/ Heglig would have not been part of the Abyei territory that went to Hague for arbitration.

### 8.4.3 14 Mile Dispute

The 14 Mile area, though historically marked as grazing area for Riziegat, has never been included in any peace agreement between Northern Sudan and Southern Sudan on the boundary separating Northern Bahr el Ghazal and Southern Darfur. It was not part of the Addis Ababa Accord and also not included in the CPA. It only appeared in the Cooperation Agreements as a disputed territory between South Sudan and Sudan in September 2012.

This issue surprised many South Sudanese specially citizens of Northern Bahr el Ghazal who did not know the area was a grass corridor for the Riziegat tribe of Southern Darfur.

A brief history on developments of this disputed area in the colonial era; on February 21, 1922, British troops from Wau, under the command of Bimbashi Middleton, clashed with a force loyal to Araithdit and defeated them in Akuoya (Alok) at Pongo River.[131] The assault went ahead to Wundiing, the headquarters of the resistance, and destroyed the base, but the leader escaped to Mareng village near Aweil Town.

On March 7, 1922, Araithdit surrendered to the colonial authority at Mareng, without causalities. He was arrested and sent to Wau for imprisonment and from there he was transferred to Omdurman and finally to el-Damer where he spent 14 years before he was released in 1936.[132]

Bol Yel, a young man of the PAraith sub-clan from Wundiing Abiem West disappeared from the local population 1915 and returned home after two years with a strange stick and divine name Araithdit. He

---

131     Majak, D.D. The Northern Bahr el Ghazal People, Alien Encroachment and Rule 1856-1956, Unpublished Dissertation for PhD, University of California, 1989.

132     Ibid.

claimed that he was summoned by God for divinity and had returned to take Dinkas to a happy land where there were no governments. He performed several miracles in Abiem, Twic, and Ngok areas, which convinced the local population that he was a real prophet.

In 1918, a group of people who were angered by the presence of the government at Nymalell, and the way the taxes were being collected, attacked for the first time the station established there since 1911. The situation at Nymalell had been calm before Araithdit announced his resistance against the authorities. This led to the perception that the group was influenced and mobilized by him.

Messages of his teaching reached other neighboring communities in Tonj, Rumbek, Raja and Wau. The colonial administration feared that if the situation continued, it would undermine its authority in Bahr el Ghazal. So, it was decided to dispatch troops to arrest him after he refused government initiatives for peaceful settlement.

The declaration of the resistance against the colonial administration in Bahr el Ghazal, headed by Araithdit, came shortly after the downfall of the Ali Dinar Sultanate in 1916.

Riziegat and Meisseriyia, as Arab origin tribes, played a big role in the downfall of the Fur kingdom, in Darfur. They were very cooperative with the British authorities to bring down the kingdom. It was as such that the Savile Burges-Watson agreement of 1918 on the grazing rights to the Arab nomads emerged as a reward to these allies.

The Savile-Watson agreement could be interpreted in two ways; as a reward to Riziegat for their role in fighting along with British troops against Ali Dinar or that Dinkas were hostile to the colonial administration and the danger of the rebellion spreading all over the Dinka territories, especially in the northern part of the area could be reduced by allowing Arab nomads to herd their cattle up to 40 miles south of the Kiir, an area which covers most of Pajouk land.

During that time, the Dinka Malual territory was divided into two sections; Pajouk covers the area extended north of the Kiir River up to Lol River and Paliupeny which extends from south Lol River up to the border with Western Bahr el Ghazal.

Chief Autiak Majak (Chak Chak) was the prominent leader of Paliupeny based at Nymalell where colonial authorities established their base in 1911 through a forced invasion of the area from Western Bahr el Ghazal.

It was reported that Chak Chak was the first chief of the Dinka Malual, who sent an emissary with a letter of support to the colonial authorities in Wau 1902 (Stefand, 1977).

The second area was Pajouk, ruled by Wal Doorjok as overall chief plus other chiefs. After he died his son Yor Wal took over, and he was not in good relations with the administration because of his previous malignity to Turko-Egyptian rule, who imprisoned him in Wau. A certain trader called Dirar Ali who spoke Dinka fluently left for Wau and reported to the authorities that Yor Wal was the one behind Araithdit's rejection of peaceful settlement (Dut, 1984). This is why the Pajouk area was badly targeted by allotting part of their land to Arab nomads.

After the resistance was suppressed, and its leader was arrested, the government moved its headquarters from Nymalell to Aweil in 1922, and Mr. B. Owen made a District Commissioner of Northern Bahr el Ghazal. The issue of the borders with Riziegat was brought to the attention of the District Commissioner by the chiefs as an urgent matter.

He took initiative and wrote to the governor proposing a meeting that should bring together the authorities and the local leaders instead of conducting official meetings alone to discuss communal affairs, which had been the case since he assumed office.

His request was considered, and the meeting scheduled to take place in April 1924, at the time when the leaders of the two communities were at the Kiir River.

On April 22nd 1924 the meeting convened at Adiem ( Safaha), and the following people were presence; Mr. M.J. Wheatley, Governor of Bhar el Ghazal province, Mr. P. Munuro, Governor of Darfur Province, Mr. B. Owen, District Commissioner of Northern Bahr el Ghazal, E.S. Fiddes, District Commissioner of Southern Darfur and Mr. R.T. Johnston Assistant District Commissioner of Baggara, (Wol, 2009).

The Riziegat tribes were represented by eleven delegates headed by Nazir Ibrahim Musa Madibo and the delegation includes his brother Yahia Musa, Amir el Momin, Dawod Abu Khelik, Abdullahi Abul Ghasim, Fadhalla Bombome, Mohamed el Nur Wad Hamid, Bashir Abdullhi, Younis Damass, Mohamed Dom Fellati and Kheir el Nur. Meanwhile, the Dinka delegation composed of eight chiefs namely; Autiak Akot, Lual Dau Marac, Anyuon Aturjong, Diing Wol, Nyang Amash, Tong Bek, Gout Tong and Lual Habishe.

The meeting made a resolution by reviewing Savile Burges-Watson Agreement of 1918 and reduced the distance to 14 miles instead of 40 miles. The discussion went on positively and in the end of the meeting, the Dinka delegates were misinformed that the Savile- Watson agreement had been cancelled. Other issues, including child abduction, fishing, hunting and trading were discussed, and the meeting was announced closed. The new agreement was named after the two governors; Wheatley-Munuro.

In the following year the situation did not change on ground. Arab nomads were still crossing the Kiir River. They went as far as demanding permission from the Dinka chiefs to go to the river. Again, the meeting was requested by the Dinka chiefs but convened at the time of the new governor of Bahr el Ghazal, Mr. Ingleson, in 1935.

Riziegat tribes on their part started re-naming the Dinka wouts situated at the Kiir River and the nearby areas.

For example, Maijot was changed to Dar el Harr, Piany Thou became Dar el Heglig, Kang-a Bar renamed el Bagheili, Kang-a Gok, Adiem Ajowak of Chief Anyuon Aturjong changed to Agar, Safaha and el Seleimi respectively. Bour Pieny of the Chief Ngang Jonkor was changed to el Dumug el Telieh, Kang a-Bek and Wair Liad of the Chief Diing Wol were named as Jabaya, and Abu Guma respectively. Doup of the Chief Nyuol Deng was changed to Ardieba, Kang-a Diat of the Chief Acien Yor was named as el Hamara, ans Pieny Gaut of the Chief Diing Majok was changed to el Grief.

When the Dinka chiefs learnt that their lands were demarcated as grazing corridors to Riziegat nomads and the new occupants renamed all their areas, they sent a delegation to Aweil to meet with the new District Commissioner Capt. J.M Stubbs, who took over from Mr. Owen.

The new District Commissioner took the matter seriously and convinced the Governor of Bhar el Ghazal Mr. P. Ingleson to convene a meeting as a way of trying to bring tensions down. The meeting was convened and attended by Mr. C.G. Dupuis, Governor of Darfur and the Riziegat tribal leaders in 1935.

The resolutions of the Wheatley-Munuro agreement were read out for the first time to the Dinka delegation in 1935, and Chief Anyuon Aturjong protested and marched out of the meeting.

The expectation of the Dinka was not met hence they wrote again to the Governor of Equatoria, who was also governing Bhar el Ghazal when the two provinces were merged to be administered as one unit.

On November 25th, 1938, the governor wrote to the Civil Secretary in Khartoum urging for immediate abrogation of Wheatley- Munuro Agreement. The appeal says,"There is a sense of injustice felt by the Dinka at the present application of the Munuro-Wheatley agreement, and it should be cancelled" (Governor Notes, 1938).

However, the Civil Secretary sent the Equatoria Governor's message to the Acting District Commissioner of Southern Darfur Mr. E.H. Nightingle: "If the changes advocated by the Governor of Equatoria were effected, the Riziegat would feel a sense of injustice at least as great." From that point the civil secretary turned down the issue and did not write back to the governor.

Let us go back to the conditions said above as reasons why the colonial rulers gave away 14 miles of Dinka land as grazing corridors to Riziegat nomads, and agree that those reasons were irrelevant and the real intention was for peaceful coexistence between the two communities across the borders and so the cattle of the Arabs did not die.

If we take this latter assumption as a real reason we will find that there was no records of the Dinkas denying their neighbors the grazing rights in history. Sometimes it is the Riziegat political leaders who were/ are submissive to Khartoum trying to confuse peaceful coexistence between the two communities.

The grazing right is not a problem between Dinka Malual and Riziegat. However, if Khartoum continues to instigate the neighboring tribes as means of implementing its own agenda, then the nomadic communities in the borders with South Sudan will suffer a lot.

Riziegat tribal leaders should continue pushing for peaceful coexistence with their counterpart at South Sudan-Sudan borders and should not listen to politicians in Khartoum whose aims have no relation to what is happening on the surface, but have hidden agendas. As long as they stand by peace nothing could prevent their animals to come to Kiir river.

### 8.4.3.1 The September 2012 Cooperation Agreements and conflict escalation in the14-Mile

There is a lot of evidence to show that the colonial administration created the 14-Mile to ease access to pastures for the Arab nomads. The area was designated as a grazing corridor at an annual peace conference, which were organised to address pastoralists' issues that had been emerging for more than nine decades. Both the Addis Ababa Peace Accord of 1972 – which created a regional government in Juba with the territory of 1/1/1956 boundaries – and the CPA signed in Nairobi in 2005 did not mention the 14-Mile area as a boundary. It was therefore surprising for the people of Northern Bahr el Ghazal that the area was claimed by the Government of Sudan as its territory during the negotiation of the Cooperation Agreements in Addis Ababa on 27 September 2012. The Cooperation Agreements signed by the two governments addressed security arrangements, which necessitated the immediate operationalisation of the SDBZ, with special emphasis on the 14- Mile area in North Bahr el Ghazal. This SDBZ was one of the post- independence issues agreed upon by the two countries to prevent insecurity at the borders after the independence of South Sudan. The Cooperation Agreements also addressed the agreement on border issues, especially border demarcation, which was agreed upon by the JBC and JDC. The leaders also signed other protocols in the fields of economic cooperation including trade, banking, oil, and river and rail transport.

The inclusion of the issue of the designating a grazing territory of the 14-Mile in an expanded demilitarised buffer zone between the two countries as a boundary has raised a wave of criticism (Affa'a-Mindzie, 2012). South Sudan citizens in the capital city, Juba and Aweil town – the headquarters of NBGS – staged demonstrations condemning the inclusion of the 14-Mile in the Cooperation Agreements. The Aweil community in Juba subsequently formed a committee, chaired by the late Chief Pio Tem Kuac Ngor, who was also a Member of Parliament (MP) representing Aweil East, to investigate the issue and engage with the government on how to resolve the matter peacefully. The committee visited the area and drew up a report identifying the Dinka Malual villages that were affected by the demilitarisation policy at the border between South Sudan and Sudan. The committee also registered villages located north of the Kiir/Bahr Arab.

In the National Legislative Assembly in Juba, the majority of MPs representing the area voted against the Cooperation Agreements, despite all consultative meetings conducted by their party, the SPLM aimed at persuading members to vote in favour of the agreements. The Bellario Ahoy Ngong, an MP representing Aweil South, seized the opportunity and said: "I find it difficult to swallow the deal, especially the part connected to the 14-Mile area. Therefore, I decided to vote against the Cooperation Agreements." During the demonstrations in Aweil and Juba, citizens mobilised themselves to take the frontline, should the security agreement signed on September 27, 2012 between South Sudan and Sudan in Addis Ababa be implemented and the SPLA was withdrawn from the 14-Mile area. Kawac Makuei Mayar, an Anya Nya veteran who also fought the war of liberation with the SPLM/A and was Chairperson of the Aweil community in Juba, declared in a public rally organised by the community in Juba that they would not resist pressures to secede the 14-Mile to Sudan. Rather, they would ask the Government of the Republic of South Sudan to show them their southern boundary with the new nation, such that they could join Sudan. The rally ended with threats to the two governments in Juba and Khartoum not to think of the 14-Mile as a boundary.

The Aweil community in the diaspora mobilised and donated medicines to the soldiers at the frontlines in Majak Woi, War Guet and Kiir Adem, in preparation for war should the 14-Mile be conceded. The deal was described as bloody, because it would never bring peace between the communities but would rather create new and severe conflicts that had never existed previously, according to the interview with Yel Ngang Gum. The State Legislative Assembly (SLA) in Aweil followed suit, holding an emergency session – which ruled out the acceptance of the Cooperation Agreements, particularly the part connected to the 14-Mile. The state government in Aweil warned against attempts to cede the area to Sudan. It warned that the act would cause major unrest, and demanded that the Riziegat tribe should come out clearly on whether they needed land or pastures and water, especially with the dry season round the corner.

Following the conclusion of the Cooperation Agreements on 27 September 2012, the South Sudan negotiating team sent to Addis Ababa was welcomed home with demonstrations, because the agreement it had negotiated authorised the demilitarisation of the 14-Mile area. Some members of the negotiating team released statements such as those issued by the British administrators during the colonial era. They stated that the Dinka Malual community misunderstood the agreements, such as in the statement released by the Hon. Makuei Lueth on the "Wake Up Juba" radio show and in the forum organised by the al-Masier Arabic newspaper. In a meeting with President Kiir in May 2013, Aweil community representatives in Juba raised this issue with bitterness. The president condemned the issue and apologised for the statement released by the politicians who had participated in the Addis Ababa talks. Contrary to what was believed to be a fair deal, the Dinka Malual were proven right, and the implementation of the policy demilitarising the 14-Mile – as suggested by the SDBZ document and signed by the two governments – faced difficulties in South Sudan. The UNSC established the UNISFA through its Resolution 1990, on 27 June 2011, which was issued 10 days before the declaration of independence of South Sudan. The force was given the mandate of peacekeeping in the disputed area of Abyei, and was granted leeway to use force to protect civilians and humanitarian workers. Despite its strong mandate under Chapter Seven of the UNSC, the UNISFA failed to adequately exercise its mandate. Abyei Paramount Chief Kuol Deng Kuol (Kuol-Adol) was killed in cold blood by Messiria militia in front of the UNISFA soldiers. On 16 November 2012, the UNSC adopted Resolution 2075, establishing the SDBZ as a result of continuous confrontations at the border areas. In the Cooperation Agreements, the parties had agreed to establish a zero line, with the army of each country withdrawing 10 kilometres farther back. The establishment of this zero line, in a situation where the boundaries are not clearly delineated, posed a challenge. The Sudanese government demanded that South Sudan withdrew from the 14-Mile before the setting of the zero line, which went deep inside the Dinka Malual headquarters of Gok Machar in Aweil North. The UNISFA, as mandated by the UNSC, attempted to draw a buffer zone beyond the 14-Mile – which became a problem to the village populations living within the buffer zone. This led to demonstrations by civilians in Aweil North, who demanded that the UNISFA leave the area immediately. The Dinka Malual then levelled accusations against the UNISFA, that it had infiltrated their ancestral land as part of Sudan and, as such, demanded that they leave the area immediately. The claim that the 14 Mile was part of the Riziegat territory was difficult to be apprehended by the Dinka Malual. They believed their boundary with the Riziegat is 38 miles north of the Kiir/Bahr Arab.

## 8.5 Conclusion

As stated in the introduction, the purpose of this research was to earn a Doctorate of Philosophy in Peace and Development Studies concentrating on ethnicity and politics particularity role of ethnic politics in the separation of South Sudan from Sudan. Many issues which were predicted during the study became real in the  years that followed as explained in this Chapter and this was the reason why the author reviewed the book and reissued an updated edition.

It was unfortunate that policy and decision-makers in both South Sudan and Sudan couldn't pay attention to the study hence no precautions were made to arrest the situation especially the internal conflict in South Sudan in 2013 though the study was published and discussed in many forums including a presentation of findings organized by "Kwato"[133] a cultural group in Khartoum.

As advice to the governments in Africa, research and scientific studies must take a central role in their planning and management. As has been seen in the West, evidence-based decision making will lead to a smooth road forward.

---

133    Kwato was a cultural group formed in Khartoum to promote African cultures and support the independence of South Sudan.

# GENERAL CONCLUSIONS

During the study many issues emerged pertaining to communal relations between Dinka Malual and Riziegat tribes. What was considered to be a communal dispute over pastures and water in the area was exploited by politicians in Sudan. This communal dispute was transformed to a national conflict to resist marginalization and exclusion that was engineered by successive regimes in Khartoum toward South Sudanese. The outcome of this coercive resistance was the independence of Republic of South Sudan.

It is regrettable that the same issues of state and nation-building in the young country that was emerging from protracted wars were not handled with consensus and harmony and were instead met with violence. The following issues were significant in the understanding of the standoff between the North and South Sudan but also with understanding that the same issues contributed to the internal conflict in South Sudan as it was discussed in Chapter Eight:

## 1. Source of the conflict between Dinka Malual and Riziegat

The conflict in the area started as a competition over grazing resources between two communities. This was eventually exploited by politicians after the independence of the country for political ends. Furthermore, the escalation of the conflict from competition over grazing resources into a politically-oriented tension invited foreign actors to become involved under the slogans of protection of human rights values such as slavery/ abduction and so forth. This is also what happened in Darfur where senior government personnel including, President al-Bashir were accused of war crimes against the population in the Darfur region. UN and AU forces were deployed to protect civilians and Sudan came under the view of the international community.

## 2. The role of religion in the conflict

In the past, religion was not part of the conflict between Dinka Malual and Riziegat. It became part and parcel of the conflict after the Sudan obtained independence in 1956, the time the national governments took over political power in the country. However, many people in Dinka Malual areas believed that the role of Islam has contributed greatly to the deterioration of North-South relations, especially during the era of National Salvation government in Khartoum. They (Dinka Malual) believed that the South had been pushed towards secession by Islamic fundamentalists in Northern Sudan. Consequences of this assumption were realized in the 2011 referendum.

## 3. The role of ethnicity in the conflict

The use of ethnic affiliations for political gain has acquired a significant position in Sudanese politics. It can be realized through different war fronts taking place between those ethnic minorities controlling the power in the centre and those ethnic groups on the peripheries of the State, who are fighting for fair power sharing and equitable distribution of the wealth of the country. These conflicts were considered by many people as wars between Arabs and non-Arabs in Sudan as a result of ethnic exploitation by the Northern elites. The use of politics of ethnic discrimination justifies secession of Southern Sudan.

## 4. The problem of the territories' encroachment

Although it was an old phenomenon in Sudan, tension over this issue are very recent. They started during the first rebellion of the South as an issue, especially in the Addis Ababa Peace Accord between the Anya

Nya Movement and the May regime in 1972. Subsequently, the issue became more important after the exploration of oil in the South in the 1970s. Currently, the ongoing South-North borders demarcation acquires its importance over the assumption that the oil has been found in big quantities in the areas between the South and the North border. The North wants to retain these oil fields as part of its territory which the South deems as an aggression that should not be ignored.

## Recommendations

Despite the findings about the general issues discussed in this study, its evaluation is best left to the readers. As social study findings, two things are to be considered. First, there is no concrete certainty of the outcomes; secondly, sociological matters are subject to change according to prevailing circumstances.

In the past many people believed that the reason for the conflict was competition over grazing resources. Later, the majority of participants, particularly from Dinka Malual, believe the conflict was caused by political differences between the South and the North, and territorial encroachment of every party on the other territory.

In addition, the use of ethnicity for political ends has affected unity of the country. These changing attitudes can be seen as attributed to the variable political environment in the Sudan after signing the CPA in 2005. The expectations of the South rose as a result of obtaining self-determination from the North.

There are some issues which have acquired a permanent position and work as guidelines in an attempt to draw conclusions. These issues include, but are not restricted to, geographical setting of the area (grazing difficulties), nature of people inhabiting the area (cultural diversities and habits), a degree of severity of war related problems (slavery/ abduction of women and children), and influences of the diverse ethnic identity, (ethnicity and politics) political and religious differences (Islamic State in Sudan), and territorial encroachments (Oil fields claim).

All these issues proved to have a permanent position in any suggested solution and recommendations. It's important to mention that some of these recommendations found their way to implementation and become sources of peace and tranquility at the border between Dinka Malual and Riziegat communities especially recommendation No. 6. Since 2008 the joint annual peace conferences continue to be organized by the two communities without failure which has contributed effectively to the peace and harmony in the area. Other recommendations need to be effectively implemented because they are still relevant despite the independent South Sudan and they are as follow;

1. Grazing difficulties can be solved through the introduction of measures like a formulation of rules and laws governing the herders and farmers. The introduction of development projects in livestock and agricultural sectors are needed as well.

2. The issue of cultural diversities can be reconciled by strengthening those cultural aspects which are common between the two communities and making them a unifying factor between the two tribes. The non-identical culture trends and norms should be respected by the members of both communities of Dinka Malual and Riziegat. Politicization of these socio-cultural issues has complicated the situation.

3. The issue of slavery/abduction can be best solved through mutual understanding. That mutual understanding necessitates that Riziegat and Misseriya confess and apologize to the Dinka and other tribes in Southern Sudan for what they have done in the field of slavery/abduction, and then try to return those children and women still in bondage in Darfur and Kordofan. This action requires Dinka Malual and other affected communities in Southern Sudan to forgive Riziegat and Misseriya, and start a new era where human values, identity, and other cultures are respected.

4. The Government of National Unity (GONU) and Government of Southern Sudan (GOSS) must invite the international community to work in collaboration with CEAWC to eradicate the practice of slavery/abduction and reinstate women and children abducted during war time.

5. The Government of National Unity (GONU) and the Government

of Southern Sudan (GOSS) must take necessary action in addressing political matters including the human rights situation in Khartoum and Juba. This is the only way foreign intervention could be stopped from intervening into internal affairs otherwise people will be frequently complaining for external intervention.

6. Revival of traditional peace conference forums, which proved to be effective mechanism of traditional conflict resolution.

7. Necessity of formation of joint chiefs' courts between the two tribes on the border to deal with these mutual crimes committed in the area. This was proposed as a temporary arrangement until the time of secession of South Sudan.

8. Strengthening of Native Administration by giving it more powers in the areas of security and the judiciary to solve local crimes until modern institutions of law enforcement agencies are founded.

9. Creation of joint civil society organisations forum to work collaboratively to pursue development and fostering of sustainable peace in the area.

10. Engagement of these two tribes on the border trade activities to culminate at peace dividends to those citizens sharing the borders.

11. Collection of small illegal arms from the hands of citizens, and stoppage of unauthorized trade of arms in the area.

12. There is a need to negotiate, demarcate, and distinguish grazing routes from agricultural areas. This can facilitate harmony between herders and farmers.

13. There was need to disseminate awareness of the CPA in the area, so that those issues concerning border demarcations, and self-determination for the people of Southern Sudan were made clearer to the citizens.

14. Finally, since the study revealed a strong possibility of separation of the South, then it was recommended to take all measures that ensure peaceful secession rather than chaotic separation. It was recommended that the two signatories to the CPA, as well as regional and international communities work closely to implement the will of the majority of Southern Sudanese people. The author advised that

it was unwise to think that the remaining time of the interim period would help in making unity attractive. Two stable and peaceful countries are far better than two chaotic failed states.

# BIBLIOGRAPHY

*English Language Sources*

**Books:**

Ahmed, Abdel Ghaffar Mohamed (1989) (Ed.), Management of Crises in the Sudan, Khartoum University Press, Khartoum 1989.

Akol, Lam (2001) SPLM/SPLA: Inside An African Revolution, Khartoum University Press, Khartoum, Sudan.

Ali, Taiser M., and Robert O. Mathews (Eds.) (1999) Civil War in Africa, McGill Queen's University Press, London.

Arop, Madut Atop (2006) Sudan Painful Road to Peace, Book Durge, ILC, London.

Bakheit, G.M.A (1985), Native Administration in the Sudan and its Significance to Africa, in Hassan, Y.F. (ed), Sudan in Africa, 2nd ed., Khartoum, Khartoum University Press,1985.

Baldo, Suliman Ali and Ushari Ahmed Mahmoud (1987), Human Rights Violations in the Sudan, 1987: The Daien Massacre: Slavery in the Sudan, 1987, (Scheduled for translation from Arabic).

Beshir, Mohamed Omer (1968), The Southern Sudan: Background to Conflict, C. Hurst, London.

Bashir, Mohamed Omer (1975) The Southern Sudan from Conflict to Peace, C. Hurst and Company, London.

Bashir, Mohamed Omer (1984) Regionalism and Religion: Selected Essays, (Graduate College Publication No. 10), University of Khartoum, Khartoum.

Binsberger, Wim Van (1981) Religious Change in Zambia: Exploratory Studies, Kegan Paul Int, London.

Blaxter, Loraine (1966) How to Research, Philadelphia, Open University Press, Buckingham.

Deng, Francis Mading (1972) The Dinka of the Sudan, Reinehart and Winston, Holt, New York.

Deng, France Mading (1982) Recollection of Babo Nimir, Ithaca Press, London.

Hoile, David (Ed.) (2002) The Search for Peace in the Sudan: A chronology of the Sudanese Peace Process, 1989- 2001, The European-Sudanese public Affairs council, 1 Northumberland Avenue, London, 2002.

Force Majeure: The Clinton Administration's Sudan Policy 1993-2002, The European-Sudanese Public Affairs Council, London, 2002.

Craze, Joshua, Contested Borders: Continuing Tensions Over the Sudan-South Sudan Border, 2014.

Johnson, Douglas H. (2002) The Root Causes of Sudan's Civil Wars, The International African Institute in Association with James Currey, Indiana University Press, Oxford, Blomington.

Jok, Jok Madut (2001), War and Slavery in Sudan, University of Pennsylvania Press, Philadelpha, Pennsylvania.

Lemke, Douglas (2002), Regions of War and Peace, Cambridge University Press, Cambridge.

Machakos Framework Agreement between GoS and SPLM signed in Machakos, Kenya on July 12, 2002.

Majak, Domasio Dut (1990) The Northern Bahr el Ghazal:People Alien Encroachment and rule 1856-1956 Unpublished Doctoral Thesis, University of California.

Sudan Constitution, 1998.

Woodhouse, Tom (et.al) (2002) Peace Keeping and Conflict Resolution, Frank Cass, London.

Wol, Dhieu Mathok Diing (2009), Politcs of Ethnic Discrimination in Sudan: A Justification for the Secession of South Sudan, Uganda, Kampala, Netmedia Publishers.

Wol, Dhieu Mathok Diing (2003), Dinka Malual-Riziegat Relations: The Role of Third Party (Unpublished M. A. Thesis) University of Juba – Khartoum.

## Periodicals and Reports:

Abdin, Hassan, (Under Secretary for Foreign Affairs/ Sudan, Comments on the Issue of Slavery in Sudan African Union Commission of Inquiry on South Sudan, Final report, 27 Oct 2015.

Assistant District Commissioner, Baggara, Report to Governor of Darfur, 1926 & 1941, Khartoum Central Records Office, Khartoum.

BBC English channel, Rebeeca De Mabior, 17/12/2013.

Carter Center, Observing the 2011 Referendum on the Self-determination of Southern Sudan, Final Report.

Civil Secretary Files 1924 & 1925, Khartoum Central Records Office, Khartoum.

DMR, Report on Grassroots Peace Conference in Addis Ababa, Ethiopia February 2004.

Dottridge, Mike, "Statement by Mike Dotridge, Director General of ASI on Sudan", Washington Post, March 3, 1999.

John Garang De Mabior, Public Statement, Rumbek, 2005.

Mukhtar, Albagir report on the Fringes of Northern identity: What's missing in the Darfur peace process, institute of peace. Washington, Dc. July 2006.

Nye, Joseph, S., (Jr.), Understanding International Conflicts, Longman, New York , 2002.

Independent on Sunday, (The), "Scam in Sudan: An Elaborate Hoax Involving Take African Slaves and less than Honest Interpreters in duping concerning Westerners", 24 February, 2002.

International Eminent Group, Report on Abduction, Slavery and Servitude in the Sudan, Khartoum, 2002.

Irish Times (The) "The Great Slave Scam." The Irish Times, 23/2/2002.

McNair, (Lord), Report on Slavery in Sudan, London , 4-11 October 1997.

El-Mufti, Ahmed, The Experience of (CEAWC) Sudan Gathering Information Training and Reunification of Persons Abducted during Armed Conflicts, Khartoum, January, 2003.

SPLM Manifesto 1983, Amended 2008.

SPLM Leaders Press Conference in the SPLM House 6/12/2013.

SPLM/A-IO First Conference in Nasir, South Sudan, April 2014.

Stubb, J.M., (Captain), Notes on MALUAL Section, Central Records Office, Khartoum, 1930.

Sudan Tribune Report, Rebeeca Nyendeng De Mabior, 18/12/2013

UNICEF, UNDP and MOHE, Conflict Surveys and Mapping Analysis, Khartoum, August, 2002.

United Nations Human Rights Council, Commission , Final report of the African Union Commission Nairobi/ Geneva, 20 February 2019.

UN NEWS Reader, United Nations, Human Rights, 15 March 2021.

Washington Office on Africa, Briefing Paper Issue on Slavery, War and Peace in Sudan, Washington, 25/2/1999.

Washington Post ,Vick, "Ripping off the Redeemers" Tuesday, February 26, 2002.

**Internet Sources**

Bush, George (U.SA. President), News MAX.Com UUIRUS, American News Pages, Saturday 5th. 2003.

Klare, Michael, War, Weapon , and Sustainability in Post- Cold War Era. 1996,.pawss.hampshire.edu/

Ottaway,Marina, Challenge of Democracy in Africa,2003, www. carnegieendowment.org

Rawlinson, Alexis , The Political Manipulation of Ethnicity in Africa, 2003 www.insolens.org

**Interviews:**

A/Bagi Akol Agany, (Dinka chief), Northern Bahr El Ghazal, (April, 2004).

Ahmed El Mufti, Chaiman of CEAWC and Director General o Khartoum Center for Human Right, (May, 2004).

Albino Akol Akol, (Major General), Former Anyanmya One officer, Ex-Governor of Bahr el Ghazal and current Minister in GOSS (June, 2004).

James Aguer Alic, Chairperson of Dinka Committee working with CEAWC in field of Slavery/Abduction, (March, 2004).

Mohammed Issa, Chairperson, Riziegat Consultative Council, Khartoum, (May,2004).

Other people, including students, youth, women and intellectuals in both area (different dates during 2004).

## 3. مراجع باللغة العربية :

أحمد إبراهيم أبو شوك ، *الإدارة الأهلية ، النشأة والتطور* ، الخرطوم ، دار الوثائق المركزية ، 1993م

ـــــــــــــــــ ، *الإدارة الأهلية بين الإلغاء والإبقاء* ، الخرطوم ، دار الوثائق المركزية ، 1993م.

أحمد عبدالله آدم ، *قبائل السودان : نموذج التمازج والتعايش* ، الخرطوم ، شركة مطابع السودان للعملة المحدودة ، 1990م.

آدم الزين محمد ، *رؤى حول النزاعات القبلية في السودان* ، معهد الدراسات الأفريقية والآسيوية ، جامعة الخرطوم ، 1988ن.

التجاني مصطفى محمد صالح ، *الصراع القبلي في دارفور : أسبابه وتداعياته وعلاجه،* الخرطوم ، شركة مطابع السودان للعملة المحدودة ، 1999م.

جون وول ماكينج ، *القانون العرفي للدينكا في السودان* ، ترجمة هنري رياض وعمر محمد الطاهر ، بيروت ، لبنان ، دار الجيل ، 1991م.

حامد البشير إبراهيم ، *محاولة لفهم العلاقات القبلية وديناميات الحرب والسلام في جبال النوبة* ، ترجمة عائشة برعي (بلا ناشر) ، (بلا مكان) ، 2002م.

حسن علي حسن الساعوري ، *التأصيل والمشاركة السياسية* ، دار جامعة أفريقيا العالمية للطباعة والنشر ، الخرطوم ، 1999م.

الصديق عمر الأمام ، *التطورات التاريخية لمشكلة جنوب السودان (1821-1989م)* ، أم درمان ، مركز محمد عمر بشير للدراسات السودانية ، 1998م.

عبدالغفار محمد أحمد وشريف عبدالله حرير ، *المجتمع الريفي السوداني : عنصر حركته واتجاهاتها* ، مركز الدراسات والبحوث الأثمانية ، جامعة الخرطوم ، 1981م.

عبدالله محمد آدم حامد ، *الأبعاد الفكرية والسياسية والتنظيمية للحركة الشعبية والجيش الشعبي لتحرير السودان* ، الخرطوم ، جامعة أفريقيا العالمية ، مركز البحوث والدراسات الأفريقية ( إصدارة رقم 44) ، 2001م.

عزام أبو بكر علي ، *معوقات الوحدة بين الشمال والجنوب السوداني* ، الخرطوم ، شركة مطبعة النيلين ، 1999م.

علي عيسى عبدالرحمن ، *الحركة الإسلامية السودانية من التنظيم الى الدولة 1949-2000م* ، مطبعة التسير ، الخرطوم ، 2006م.

مادينق ، فرانسيس دينج ، *الدينكا في السودان* ، ترجمة شمس الدين الأمين ضو البيت ، الخرطوم ، مركز الدراسات السودانية ، 2001م.

محمد إبراهيم نقد ، *علاقات الرق في المجتمع السوداني* ، الخرطوم ، عزة للنشر والتوزيع ، 2003م.

محمد سلمان محمد ، *السودان حروب الموارد والهوية* ، دار كمبردج للنشر ، كمبردج ، المملكة المتحدة ، الطبعة الأولى ، 2000م.

محمد هارون كافي ، *نزاع السودان* ، مطبعة ارو ، الخرطوم ، 1999م.

مصطفى عثمان أسماعيل ، *النظام العالمي الجديد : قوة القانون أم قانون القوة* ، دار الأصالة للصحافة والنشر والأنتاج الأعلامي ، 2003م.

*ملف السكرتير الأداري في عهد الحكومة البريطانية المصرية 1899-1900م* ، الخرطوم ، دار الوثائق المركزية.

النذير صالح الخليفة ، *الحقوق الدستورية للأقليات الدينية في الدولة الإسلامية بالتركيز على السودان* ، (بلا مكان ، بلا ناشر أو تاريخ).

الواثق كمير ، *جون قرنق رؤيته للسودان الجديد وأعادة بناء الدولة السودانية* ، ماسئر للطباعة ، سبتمبر ، 2005م.

**يوهانس موسي فوك، موقعة القصر الجمهوري: قصة التي زلزلت جنوب السودان، الخرطوم 2015**

# APPENDIX 1

*University of Juba*
*Center for Peace and Development PhD Programme*
*Research Questionnaire*
*Impact of Ethnic Politics on South-North Relations:*
*The Case of Dinka Malual and Riziegat*

Dear Mr/Mrs _____

The significance of this questionnaire lies on the fact that the subject matter of the research is sensitive and vitally important for coexistence of the Nation and stability of the Country, particularly South – North Sudan borders. The questionnaire imposes questions that enable the study to find the causes for the conflict and possible solutions. Also it predicts the type of relationship between the South and the North after the referendum for the people of Southern Sudan in 2011 to choose either unity or separation. With this research, it is hoped to arrive at the best ways and means to recover trust and confidence between Dinka Malual and Riziegat, hence the future of South-North relations is predicted and work for its better hence forth onwards.

With best regards,
*Dhieu Mathok Diing Wol February 2005*

Name: _____

Tick ( √ ) or check the box

What is your age?
◊   7-17
◊   18 – 35
◊   36 – 53
◊   Above 53

Are you
◊   Male
◊   Female

What is your tribe?
◊   Dinka Malual
◊   Riziegat
◊   Other

What is your religion?
◊   Christian
◊   Muslim
◊   Other

Where are you living?
◊   Northern Bhar el Ghazal
◊   South Darfur
◊   Others

What is you academic qualification
Basic education (primary)
◊   Secondary
◊   University
◊   Postgraduate

Where are you working?

With Sudan govt.

◊   NGOs

◊   Self employee

◊   Not working

What do you think as the reason(s) of Dinka Malual and Riziegat conflict?

◊   Competition over grazing resources and water

◊   Ethnic and Religious differences

◊   Political and territorial encroachments

◊   Others

How can this conflict best be addressed?

◊   Socio-economic Development

◊   Separating the South from the North

◊   Through other means

What do you expect as a result of 2011 south Sudan referendum, if your answer is (iii) explain.

◊   Unity

◊   Separation

◊   Will not take place: _____

What do you think about the 2011 referendum?

◊   Honoured by the parties to the CPA

◊   Dishonoured by the parties to CPA

◊   Do not know

God bless you.

# APPENDIX 2

*Table 7-1: Recorded Boundary*
*Changes, 1905-1960*

| Date | Change | Source |
|------|--------|--------|
| 1905 | Transfer of Ngok & Twic Dinka from BGP to KP | SIR 128 AR 1905 |
| c. 1912 | Transfer of Twic Dinka from KP to BGP | KRWWN |
| 1912 | Adjustment between UNP & KP around Kaka | AR 1912 |
| 1913 | Separation of NMP from KP | SGG 227 AR 1913 |
| 1917 | Adjustment of UNP — WNP boundary | SGG 337 |
| 1918 | Adjustment of UNP – WNP Nile boundary | SGG 337 |
| 1920 | Adjustment of UNP—WNP boundary | SGG 363 |
| 1921 | Adjustment between UNP & NMP | SGG 386 |
| 1923 | Transfer of Kaka from UNP & NMP | SSG 414 |

| 1925 | Transfer of Daga from Fung [ to UNP | AR 1925 |
|---|---|---|
| 1926 | Transfer of Tonga & Morada from UNP to NMP | SSG 480 |
| 1927 | Transfer of Nuer & Dinka from NMP to BGP | SSG 489 SMIR 399 |
| c.1927 | Transfer of Kaka from KP to UNP | M R S 1927 |
| 1928 | Amalgamation of NMP and KP | SGG 511 AR 1928 |
| 1928 | Transfer of Tonga & Morada from NMP to UNP | SGG 511 |
| 1931 | Transfer of Rueweg Dinka from KP to UNP | SGG 546 |
| 1938 | Transfer of Koma, Meban & Uduk from BNP to UNP | SGG 660 |
| 1953 | Transfer of Koma & Uduk from UNP to BNP | SGG 858 |
| 1956 | Adjustment between UNP & BNP boundary | SGG 896 |

| 1960 | Transfer of Hofrat en-Nahas from BGP to DP | SGG |
|------|---------------------------------------------|-----|
| AR | Annual Report (Report on the Finances, Administration and Condition of the Sudan) | |
| BGP | Bahr el-Ghazal Province | |
| BNP | Blue Nile Province | |
| DP | Darfur Province | |
| KP | Kordofan Province | |
| KRWWN | Kordofan and the Region West of the White Nile, 1912 | |
| M R S 1927 | The Anglo-Egyptian Sudan (Tribal)' map printed by the Ordnance Survey Office, Southampton, 1928, accompanying General Staff; War Office, Military Report on the Sudan, 1927, London: HMSO, 1928 [ in UNP 1931, pp. 450  1) | |
| NMP | Nuba Mountains Province | |
| SGG | Sudan Government Gazette | |

| | |
|---|---|
| SIR | Sudan Intelligence Report |
| SMIR | Sudan Monthly Intelligence Report |
| UNP | Upper Nile Province |
| U  N  P 1931 | Willis, C.A., The Upper Nile Province Handbook: A Report on Peoples and Government in the Southern Sudan, 1931, Douglas H. Johnson (ed.), Oxford: Oxford University Press for the British Academy, 1995 |
| WNP | White Nile Province |

*Source: Report of Douglas Johnson to GOSS on issues of Borders Demarcation between the South and the North, submitted on August 2007.*

# APPENDIX 3

Documents Signed during the peace making process The Munroe-Wheatley Agreement

RIZIEGAT-DINKA (Malual)

The following arrangement was made at the meeting of Safaha on the 22nd April 1924.

Present:
- The governors of Bahr el Ghazal and Darfur provinces District Commissioner Northern District
- District Commissioner Western District
- District Commissioner Bahr el Ghazal province) District commissioner Baggara, Darfur District Nazir Ibrahim Musa
- Omda Amir el Muminin Omda Jawad Abu Kheilik Omda Abdullahi Abul Gasim
- W/omda Mohd. El Nur Wad Hamid Sheikh Beshir Abdullahi
- Sheikh Younis Damass Sheikh mohd Dom Fellati Sheikh Kheir El Nur Sultan Akoli Chuk Chak Sultan Lewel Dow Maraj Chief Nuan Atogon Chief deng wol
- Chief Nyung Amash Chief Tong Bek Chief Gott Tong Chief lewel habishe

1. The Bahr El Arab and the country south of the river to an approximate distance of about 14 miles is recognized at (Dar) of the Riziegat.
2. Not withstanding No. 1 general permission is given the Dinkas(Malual) by the Nazir of the Riziegat to continue to water their cattle on the southern bank of the Bahr al Arab, and to fish in te river. This permission cannot be withdrawn without the approval of the Governor of the Bahr el Gazal before action is taken.

No Arabs are to enter the "Dar" of the Malual Dinkas for hunting or other purposes.

In exception to this paragraph there is no objection to any Arabs visiting Nyamlell, Meding, Aweil or other towns in the Bahr El Ghazal for the purposes of selling cattle, horses and sheep or of carrying of any legimitate trade provided they keep to the Government roads.

1. All slave and other cases erasing between the two tribes will be heard at an annual meeting in the Bahr el Arab between the district commissioner Baggara and the District commissioner, Northern District, Bahr El Ghazal province.
2. The Arabs have general permission to enter the western District Bahr El Ghazal province to water and graze their cattle, between the river SOPO on te East and the river SHELEKA on the west and the North of a line approximately twenty miles south of the river UMBELACHA.
3. The Arabs have permission to enter the western District Bahr El Ghazal to hunt, provided they keep to the west of a line drawn fron sahal on the Bahr El Arab to the junction of the rivers SOPO and BORO and are in possession of a permit in English from the Nasir of their tribe.
4. They must also obtain permission from the local chief in whose country they wish to hunt.

(Sgd) M.J Wheatley Mir,
Governor,
Bahr El Ghazal Province (Sgd) P. Munro

**RESOLUTIONS, DINKA MALUAL AND MESSIRIYA GRASSROOTS PEACE CONFERENCE, AWIEL TOWN, NORTHERN BAHR EL GHAZAL STATE, NOVEMBER 11 – 14, 2008**

SECTION I

RECOMMENDATIONS ON EQUITABLE SHARING OF GRAZING LAND AND WATER POINTS

1. The conference recommends the Dinka Malual to allow the Messiriya pastoralists or nomads to enter Northern Bahr El Ghazal without carrying firearms.

2. The conference recommends the creation of a native administration from the two tribes which should be facilitated (empowered) so that it is able to do the following:
   a) Maintain security and rule of law and inculcation of the spirit of fraternity and mutual respect between the two communities.
   b) Maintain social texture and rejuvenation of the traditional alliances and nourish the spirit of natural love and respect.

3. Formation/establishment of joint native courts with wide powers to look into common customary laws and prevent stealing of livestock and properties.

4. Regarding the routes for the nomads, the conference recommends the following:
   a) Demarcation of movement routes every year as early as possible, before the beginning of the migration season to entering Dinka grazing land; and the two communities may establish suitable mechanisms for the implementation of these recommendations.
   b) Determining the date and the period for entrance into and exit from Dinka grazing areas.
   c) Establishment of mobile veterinary clinics to accompany the pastoralist or nomads throughout their movements within Dinka Malual areas.
   d) Protect pastures from fires and enact laws to prevent this.
   e) Harmonize livestock tax throughout the states.

5. Dredging of the channel of the River Kiir (El jerf) to restore normal flow of the water; and establish hafirs, dams and water pumps in this area.

6. The conference recommends the holding of annual conferences, exchange visits for the following reasons:
   a) Invigorate the agreements of peaceful coexistence between the two tribes.
   b) Activate the role of youth from the two parties and encourage cultural activities for the youth to deepen the culture of peace among them.
   c) Ensure participation of women in all community affairs.

7. Open roads to and from joint markets to ease the flow of commerce between the two states.

8. The two tribes understand (agree) that the entrance of the Messiriya with their animals into Northern Bahr El Ghazal State is for grazing only; and have no rights to own land in Dinka land and, likewise, the Dinka have no right to own land in Messiriya land, except grazing.

RECOMMENDATIONS ON ABDUCTION OF CHILDREN AND WOMEN

1. The two sides agree that abduction is a condemnable action by all religions, customs and human conscience and undermines the long standing relationship between the two sides. This practice impacts negatively on the abductees and their families; and also constitutes a big obstacle which must be removed in order to support peaceful co-existence between the two tribes.

2. Both the Dinka and Messiriya commit themselves to full cooperation with CEAWC so that it can fulfill its work and programs.

3. The conference affirms that this problem is as a result of the war in the Sudan and appreciates the role of the national institutions, especially CEAWC, to control this practice.

4. The conference appreciates the role of the GONU, GOSS and the state governments of Northern Bahr El Ghazal and Southern Kordofan in their efforts to put an end to this practice.

5. The conference recommends granting funds to CEAWC, so that it can return the abductees to their families and close this chapter as soon as possible.

6. The responsible body should cooperate with the native administration in Messiriya area, in order to secure the ways for the voluntary return of displaced persons and refugees returning to Northern Bahr El Ghazal State; and also to remove all the impediments to investment, and to encourage investment from sons (daughters) of the two states.

SECTION III

RECOMMENDATIONS ON SHARED DEVELOPMENT

1. Regarding education, the conference recommended the following:
   a) Improve school infrastructures in both the Dinka and Messiriya areas.
   b) Recognizing the importance to the education of nomads' children from both tribes.
   c) Recognizing the significance of education to adults.
   d) Recognizing the importance of education for women.
   e) Construction of primary and secondary schools to absorb school dropouts.
   f) Implementation of free education policy at the level of the basic schools.
   g) Recognizing the significance of technical and vocational education.

2. Regarding health, the conference recommended the following:
   a) Establish and improve hospitals and health centers in the area.
   b) Avail trained qualified medical cadres.
   c) Establish new specialized hospitals in larger towns in Southern Kordofan, like Meiram and in Northern Bahr El Ghazal like Awell.
   d) Increase health awareness campaigns to fight epidemic diseases.
   e) Implementation of free medical treatment for mothers and children.

# Joint Communiqué

Dinka Malual and Messiriya Grassroots Peace Conference
November 11 to 14, 2008 Aweil Town, Northern Bahr el Ghazal
State, South Sudan

November 14, 2008

**Joint Final Communiqué
Dinka Malual and Messiriya
Grassroot Peace Conference
Aweil Town,
November 11 to 14, 2008**

1. **Conscious** of the present and of the future expectations and desire, by the Dinka Malual and Messiriya Communities, for common and shared development projects and efforts to the attainment of the Millennium Development Goals (MDGs) and unhindered access to right of our people to their portions of national wealth as stipulated under the Protocol on Wealth Sharing Agreement of CPA;

2. **Recalling** the long history of peaceful coexistence between Dinka Malual and Messiriya sombreness and compassion, respect of lives, fraternity that augment and brace us as two communities with interest in socio-economic development and good neighbourliness;

3. **Recalling** the long history of suffering as a result of the just ended North/South war that destroyed lives and loving youth from our communities and looting of livestock that has further caused profound grievances to our convictions and continued to by the cause of mischief to our mutual trust;

4. **Cognizant** of the significance of mutual recognition of each other's cultures, values, beliefs and respect of each other's right and of unhindered access to natural resources inside the lands of Dinka Malual and Messiriya;

5. **Mindful** of our shared desire to return of the innocent abducted children and women as documented by Committee for Eradication of Abduction of Women and Children (CEAWC);

6. **Recognizant, respect and committed** to full and timely implementation of Comprehensive Peace Agreement (CPA);

7. **Recalling** that this conference shall signal lasting end of long history of marginalization and exploitation of our natural resources and neglect to our local interest and needs;

8. **Inspired and encouraged** by wisdom and good leadership of H.E Paul Malong Awan, Governor of Northern Bahr el Ghazal and H.E. Omer Suleiman Adam, Governor of Southern Kordofan and his personal representative H.E. Mohamed Doriek Bakhat and wisdom and leadership of the Presidency, H.E President Omar El Bashir, First Vice President General Salva Kiir Mayardit and Vice President Ali Osman Taha; and **appreciative** of diligence by members and leadership of the Joint Committee, led by Mr Aldo Ajou Deng and Hon Alkhair Al Fahiem El Makki, Lt Gen. (RT) Abdel Rahman and Dr. Dhieu Mathok Diing for their excellent planning and supervision of this historical Conference; grateful to the funding from USAID, PADCO/AEM, Government of NBGS and Southern Kordofan State, supported by Sudan Peoples' Liberation Movement (SPLM) with flights; and the facilitation by Policy Advocacy & Strategic Studies (PASS); and we **urge the** United State Agency for International Development (USAID), European Union (EU), United Nations (UN), International/Local NGOs and both GONU and GOSS to timely response to our needs to empowerment of our traditional authority, local government and priorities of our local development and support to our desire to live as good neighbourliness and people of common destiny;

9. **We the conferees** deplore war and we are committed to end the instability and mutual destruction to our resources and resulting unjustified impediment of development and therefore the two parties on the following recommendations that emerged from our conference as per attached to be immediately implemented upon the date of signature;

10. **Thankful** to the outstanding hospitality extended to this historic Conference for peace organised by the Dinka Malual, the administration and people of Aweil Town;

11. **We renew** our confidence and urge the current leadership and membership of Joint Technical Committee (JTC) and Joint Steering Committee (JSC) to form a gender balanced institution; which should also involve youths, faith and the religious institutions that includes Dinka and Messiriya communities inside and outside the Sudan to advocate for peace and development in the area;

12. **We the delegates,** the representatives of Dinka Malual and Messiriya Al Humur of Al Fiyareen and Awlad Kamil, have deliberated and reached consensus and passed the following resolutions:

Name: Chief Acien Acien Yor

Signature:

Date:

Name: Chief Makuac Makuac Kuol

Signature:

Date: 14/11/2008

Name: Amir Harika Osman

Signature:

Date:

Name: Amir Ismail M. Yousif

Signature:

Date:

**Witnesses**

Name: H.E. Maj. Gen. Paul Malong Awan
      (Governor NBGS)

Signature:

Date: 14/11/08

Name: Mr Aldo Ajou Deng (Chair DMMPC)

Signature:

Date:

Name: Mr Marko Ujomo (Adviser WBGS)

Signature:

Date:

Name: Hon El Taher El Rigig El Haj

Signature:

Date:

**Witnesse**

Name: Mr Omer Sulieman Adam
      (Governor SKS)

Signature:

Date: 14-11-008

Name: Mr Alkhair A. El Makki
      (D/Chair DMMPC)

Signature:

Date: 14-11-2008

Name: John Marks (USAID)

Signature:

Date: 14-11-2008

Name: Hon Garang Jal Akuer

Signature:

Date: 14/11/2008

*Source: Author 2009*

# ABOUT THE AUTHOR

In 2013, Dhieu Mathok parted ways with the sitting government of South Sudan, having served as the chairperson of the Employee Justice Commission. He joined a splinter political party and rebel group, the SPLM - In Opposition (SPLM-IO), led by former Vice President Dr Riek Machar.

Political tensions between President Salva Kiir and Dr. Riek Machar occurred over leadership of the SPLM. The tensions grew between forces loyal to President Kiir and Dr. Machar in the Presidential Guards known as "Tiger Division" and South Sudan plunged into civil war.

In the first edition of this book, published in 2009 both in hard copy and on Amazon.com, the author predicted this civil war when he stated that while a majority of South Sudanese would vote for secession from Sudan in the 2011 referendum, there was need for authorities to ensure that the situation after separation would not escalate into ethnic discrimination that may lead to tribal conflict in the new nation. Also the study predicted border conflict between South Sudan and Sudan because of natural resources in border areas that were not delineated.

Indeed both predictions came to pass despite the countless interpretations of what has happened in South Sudan ever since the formation of the government. This book puts them into better perspective because the author's narrative is not just from hearsay but from his personal experience and partcipation in the events as they unfolded. The book takes the form of an authoritative narrative of events since before, and after, secession.

Dr Dhieu Mathok Diing Wol previously served as Associate Professor in the Center for Peace and Development Studies, University of Juba.

He is currently working as Minister of Investment and at the same time a Secretary of the South Sudan Mediation Committee on the Sudanese armed conflicts.

Dr Wol was awarded a peace prize and named as Peace Ambassador by Universal Peace Federation for his role in mediating peace negotiations in Sudan, 2020.

# INDEX

Paleupiny 66
Paliet 3
Paliupeny 186-187
Paliuping 3
Paliupiny 3
Paluoch 159
Panarang 2
Panarou 181
Panaru 184
Pangak 168, 171
Panthou 181, 183
Pariak 44
PAraith 55, 185
Pasha 11, 25, 29-30
Paul 65, 153, 172, 202
Paulino 151
Pawac 4
Pennsylvania 202
Peter xvi, 153
Peterson 52
Petroleum 172-173
Philadelpha 202
Philadelphia 202
Piany 188
Pibor 60
Pieny 188
Pio 191
Pochalla 60
Politcs 203
Politicization 198
Presidency 46, 71, 175, 179
Prof xxx
Puok 173
Qazi 78

Quez 8
Rachel xv
Ragab 8
Ragaba 8
Rahan 13, 20
Rahim 179
Rahman xxi, 7
Raja 3, 12, 40, 66, 150, 186
Rapporteur 46, 75
Rapporteurs 45
Rawlinson lv, 101, 204
Rebeeca 153, 203-4
Redemption 83
Reec lii, 13, 65, 157
Reech xvi
Rehabilitation 83
Reinehart 202
Reinstatement 40
Reizegat 10
Relatedly lii
Renk 2, 159
Reunification 46, 204
Revitalized xxv, 165
Rezeigat xvi, xix, xx, xxi, xxv, xxx, xlv, 19, 25-6, 38-9, 51, 68, 72, 84, 92
Rezgiegat 52
Riziegat xxi, xxi, xxi, xxv, xxv, xxx, xxx, xxx, xxx, xli, xli, xli, xlv, xlv, xli, li, lii, lii, liv, lvi, 1, 5-17, 19, 21-30, 32, 36-8, 42-5, 49-50, 52, 54-8, 62-9, 74, 76, 93, 105, 111, 113, 117-120, 125-7, 129-133, 137-140, 143, 147-9, 185, 195-6,